THE
MATACHINES DANCE

Frontispiece. *Matachine Dancers at the Mission of San Lorenzo (Picuris Pueblo).*
Painting by Gerald Nailor. Reproduced courtesy of the Indian Pueblo Cultural Center.
Photograph by Miguel Gandert.

THE
MATACHINES DANCE

A Ritual Dance of the Indian Pueblos
and Mexicano/Hispano Communities

by

Sylvia Rodríguez

with a
New Foreword
by the
Author

SOUTHWEST HERITAGE SERIES

SUNSTONE
PRESS

SANTA FE

Sunstone books may be purchased for educational, business, or sales promotional use.
For information please write: Special Markets Department, Sunstone Press,
P.O. Box 2321, Santa Fe, New Mexico 87504-2321.

Library of Congress Cataloging-in-Publication Data

Rodríguez, Sylvia, 1947-
  The Matachines dance : a ritual dance of the indian pueblos and Mexicano/Hispano communities
/ by Sylvia Rodríguez.
     p. cm. -- (Southwest heritage series)
  Includes bibliographical references and index.
  ISBN 978-0-86534-634-5 (softcover : alk. paper)
  1. Matachines (Dance) 2. Pueblo dance--New Mexico. 3. New Mexico--Ethnic relations.
I. Title.
  GV1796.M35R638 2009
  793.3'19789--dc22
                              2009010130

WWW.SUNSTONEPRESS.COM
SUNSTONE PRESS / POST OFFICE BOX 2321 / SANTA FE, NM 87504-2321 /USA
(505) 988-4418 / ORDERS ONLY (800) 243-5644 / FAX (505) 988-1025

The Southwest Heritage Series is dedicated to Jody Ellis and Marcia Muth Miller, the founders of Sunstone Press, whose original purpose and vision continues to inspire and motivate our publications.

CONTENTS

SOUTHWEST HERITAGE SERIES

I

THE SOUTHWEST HERITAGE SERIES

"The past is not dead. In fact, it's not even past."
—William Faulkner, *Requiem for a Nun*

The history of the United States is written in hundreds of regional histories and literary works. Those letters, essays, memoirs, biographies and even collections of fiction are often first-hand accounts by people who wanted to memorialize an event, a person or simply record for posterity the concerns and issues of the times. Many of these accounts have been lost, destroyed or overlooked. Some are in private or public collections but deemed to be in too fragile condition to permit handling by contemporary readers and researchers.

However, now with the application of twenty-first century technology, nineteenth and twentieth century material can be reprinted and made accessible to the general public. These early writings are the DNA of our history and culture and are essential to understanding the present in terms of the past.

The Southwest Heritage Series is a form of literary preservation. Heritage by definition implies legacy and these early works are our legacy from those who have gone before us. To properly present and preserve that legacy, no changes in style or contents have been made. The material reprinted stands on its own as it first appeared. The point of view is that of the author and the era in which he or she lived. We would not expect photographs of people from the past to be re-imaged with modern clothes, hair styles and backgrounds. We should not, therefore, expect their ideas and personal philosophies to reflect our modern concepts.

Remember, reading their words and sharing their thoughts is a passport back into understanding how the past was shaped and how it influenced today's world.

Our hope is that new access to these older books will provide readers with a challenging and exciting experience.

II

FOREWORD TO THIS EDITION

When I first saw the Matachines dance in the early 1980s after a long lapse since childhood, its poignant, enigmatic beauty compelled me to try to understand its history and meaning. My inquiry started at Taos Pueblo, New Mexico, and worked its way slowly down the river to Las Cruces, New Mexico. For over a dozen years I watched and puzzled over performances at the Indian Pueblos of Taos, Picurís, San Juan, and Jemez, and the Hispano-Mexicano communities of Arroyo Seco, Alcalde, El Rancho, San Antonio, San Antonito, Bernalillo, and Tortugas. My effort resulted in the original publication of this book in 1996. The book won the 1997 Chicago Folklore Prize and the 1997 Border Regional Library Association Southwest Book Award. Gradually the edition sold out and the book went into university press limbo until happily, Sunstone Press decided to publish a new edition.

Now, more than ten years later, the Matachines tradition in the Upper Rio Grande Valley appears as vital—and unfathomable—as ever. Returning to venues once scrutinized, I see subtle changes in surface details while the basic format remains the same. The power and fascination of the dance lies in how its basic plot gets played out with astonishing local and situational variation.

The Matachines is the one ritual drama both Pueblo Indian and Hispano communities perform in the Upper Rio Grande Valley. Some dance it in midwinter, others in summer. Style and detail vary widely from place to place, but common elements define a distinctive regional complex that stretches between Taos in the north and Tortugas in the south. There, a symbolic battle of transformation is enacted in several musical and choreographic sets by a king and a young girl, a bull, usually two clowns, and two lines of eight or ten *danzantes* or soldiers. Many will tell you the dance portrays the triumph of good over evil, the holy virgin's conversion of the pagan king. Others allude to a spiritual marriage. Another reading finds a hidden transcript of reconquest and resistance against foreign invaders. The intricacy of each movement, the ritual precision of every gesture, paradoxically engender the dance's ambiguous, elusive message.

Encounter, struggle, and transformation between light and dark forces is a story for all times and places, whether medieval Spain, sixteenth century Mexico, or New Mexico today. I wonder if the old theme of Christian-Moorish struggle will assume fresh significance in the military aftermath of 9/11 and the many changes in the American political climate. The Matachines remains a vibrant and cherished tradition in New Mexico because it resonates on so many levels at once: personal, spiritual, aesthetic, interethnic, collective, historic, geopolitical. One can watch or dance it five hundred times and never arrive at a fixed, authoritative account of what it means. Familiar though it be, every time people perform the dance something new happens.

—Sylvia Rodríguez
January 2009

III

THE MATACHINES DANCE

CONTENTS

ILLUSTRATIONS

PREFACE

Everyone comes to know the Matachines dance via the particular version she or he first sees. This version becomes the prototype and model, the measure by which all others are gauged. It is therefore not uncommon for devotees of the dance to consider their particular community's version to be the original and best. Although performances of the Matachines dance throughout New Mexico are characterized by the same distinct cluster of elements, every community does the dance in its own manner and style, adding its own idiosyncratic embellishments. My entrée into the dance was affected by the version I first saw, at Taos Pueblo. From the beginning, it drew my attention to the clowns.

At first, like many spectators, I didn't really watch the dance very carefully and took its execution pretty much for granted. But I was impressed by its brilliant colors, poignant music, complicated choreography, and, above all, its odd combination of solemn religiosity and ribald clowning. At some point this obscure but startling spectacle began to rivet me. It intensified in memory and gradually pushed me into an attempt to understand or decipher what the dance means to those who do it. Today, roughly a decade after I first began to reflect on the dance and some eight years and nine more versions after undertaking to study it, I make no claim to have unveiled or discovered that meaning. Rather, I have arrived at an ethnographic construct that posits what ten individual versions of the dance are about and what the regional complex as a whole symbolizes.

Originally my intention was to analyze just the Taos Pueblo version, which seemed comprehensible in light of its immediate social and ecological-political contexts. But chance and Taos's lapsed performance schedule soon forced me to look beyond it to two neighboring versions, those of Arroyo Seco and Picurís Pueblo. Picurís's performance, similar to yet different from Taos's, aroused my curiosity about other Pueblo versions. Arroyo Seco's 1985–86 revival raised questions about how the dance might differ between Pueblo and Hispano/Mexicano villages.

I pursued comparison by observing the dance at San Juan Pueblo and its Mexicano neighbor, Alcalde, as well as the dual Indian/Spanish-Mexican version performed at Jémez Pueblo. I next observed performances in four additional Mexicano communities: El Rancho, two Albuquerque area complexes—Bernalillo and San Antonio—and the border community of Tortugas. In embarking on this comparative journey down the Río Grande, I reasoned that a systematic look at a variety of versions might reveal the basic commonalities of the dance as a regional complex, as well as specific information about each individual performance community. In all, ten versions of the upper Río Grande Matachines dance were observed and considered with reference to both their universal or generic and their local, idiosyncratic features. Thus my inquiry began at the northern end of the Río Grande corridor and concluded at the Mexican border.

Two factors affected my initial approach to the Matachines. First, I was already engaged in research on interethnic relations in the greater Taos area when I began fieldwork on the dance. The subject matter and social constituency of the dance posed an ideal opportunity to observe the sometimes elusive public interface between Indians and Mexicanos in Taos. I therefore approached the dance conceptually and methodologically less as a simple dance ethnography and more as a study of ethnic relations. Ultimately, of course, the project represents a fusion of both perspectives.

The second factor is that I am a native of Don Fernando de Taos, the same community that was the central focus of the original, larger research project of which the Matachines study became an offshoot. I am a bi-ethnic (Mexicano-Anglo, or *coyote*) town daughter who grew up Catholic and middle class, not far from Taos Pueblo, went away to school, became a professor, maintained active familial and other personal attachments in New Mexico, and eventually returned to study my hometown as an anthropologist. My attraction to the Matachines stems in part, I believe, from my coyote affinity for symbolic themes of ethnic intermediacy, *mestizaje*, liminality, boundary crossing, and reversal.

Because the second factor was a motive for the first and directly affected the conditions under which my research in Taos was carried out, I must address some reflexive aspects of this study. The question of reflexivity looms large in modern anthropology and seems especially inescapable in the case of the native ethnographer. But regardless of whether an anthropologist is a native or a stranger, the intrinsic ethnographic stance is that of an outsider who seeks to know what an insider knows. Not unlike the conventional non-native ethnographer, the native ethnographer is by definition as much outsider as insider to the culture under study, although she arrives at that ambiguous, liminal position by a different, somewhat more convoluted route.

The native ethnographer may enjoy epistemological privilege with respect to basic cultural knowledge and understanding, as well as a degree of automatic social entrée into the community under study. At the same time, native familiarity and standing can pose problems and liabilities, such as unconscious blind spots because too much is taken for granted, or susceptibility to the social affinities, restrictions, alliances, and enmities that membership in a community invariably entails. Whether the ethnographer is native or stranger, objectivity remains perennially problematical in sociocultural and, particularly, interpretive anthropology. My purpose here is not to take on the issue of whether true objectivity is possible in anthropology and for whom, but merely to acknowledge that a necessary step toward its realization requires, among other things, a frank and minimal account of the salient conditions under which any given piece of research is conducted. Reflexivity is thus important to all three of the primary case studies on which this book is based.

That I was local and from a family known to people at Taos Pueblo, along with my personal familiarity with the setting and some of the performers, made my research on the dance easier than it probably would have been otherwise. My genealogical and social connections proved particularly felicitous in 1992, when, by remarkable coincidence, the man chosen to play the role of La Perejundia happened to be my third cousin. But whereas my familiarity facilitated entrée in the case of Taos Pueblo, at Arroyo Seco it proved a mixed blessing. This was because as a local I had become identified as an open sympathizer in a political cause unpopular with the extended family that organized the Matachines revival there (see Rodríguez 1987:n 119). My personal association with grassroots community protesters against resort development prejudiced potential key informants against me. Although this attitude was not shared by all participants in the revival, it did affect my access to certain sources of information. It became the only instance in which I was not hospitably or at least tolerantly received as someone seeking to learn about the dance. Ultimately I found the courage to submit my completed case study to the organizer, who had rejected my earlier efforts to inquire about the dance, and received important and insightful feedback that was incorporated into the final version. My access to and interpretation of the Arroyo Seco revival, like that of the Taos Pueblo performance, was thus affected by my own position within the larger setting in which the dances occurred. These circumstances served to highlight the perspective I brought to bear on how and why the Arroyo Seco revival occurred and what it "meant."

In the case of Picurís Pueblo, my general acquaintance with the county proved helpful, but I entered the project as a stranger, albeit it one from a semidistant neighboring town and with extended family, I was surprised to learn, known to locals. As at Taos Pueblo, I worked closely with a few key informants who were interviewed and given early versions of the (Picurís) manuscript for critical assessment.

I entered each of the secondary case studies as a stranger with no prior ethnographic knowledge or personal ties. They are examined much more superficially than the first three, in order to place the Taos County materials in comparative perspective. These secondary cases were selected for reasons of interest and opportunity. Each embodies a distinct perspective on the regional complex.

As critics point out, complete ethnographic knowledge is impossible, for a variety of reasons. Fieldworkers typically observe only a small sample of ritual events at discrete points in time, and they may easily mistake the ephemeral features of those events as constant. Although local versions differ among themselves and vary through time, occasional observers tend to focus more on what persists than on this fluid changeability itself. The anthropologist cannot escape incompleteness and inaccuracy, even in simple, direct recording. From the point of view of what a native knows, the ethnographer is intrinsically ignorant and usually a step or two behind what is really going on from day to day in any community. Yet the deliberate and systematic nature of ethnographic inquiry eventually illuminates patterns that otherwise remain invisible.

The Matachines dance both stays the same and changes in minor but nonetheless significant ways from year to year, whereas my accounts specifically refer to performances that occurred between the mid-1980s and the early 1990s. One difficulty in bringing closure to this project is the ever-observable fact that each version of the dance is changing constantly. Unavoidably incomplete, outdated, and doubtless containing errors, my accounts nevertheless provide the most contextualized and thorough ethnographic descriptions of the Río Grande Matachines dance to date. At best, these descriptions are approximations of what natives might consider true about what they did or do, and why.

Thus I am less troubled by how other anthropologists will regard this ethnography than by what those who perform and participate in the Matachines will think of it, especially when it comes to their own particular version. To the people of Taos Pueblo, Arroyo Seco, Picurís Pueblo, Alcalde, San Juan Pueblo, Jémez Pueblo, El Rancho, Bernalillo, San Antonio, San Antonito and the Holy Child parish, and Tortugas, I express my deep gratitude and offer my apologies for whatever inaccuracies mar my description of their fiesta. I hope they will find some truth in what I have presumed to say, and that where my account strays too far from what should stand, they will be moved to set the record straight. This book is dedicated to them.

ACKNOWLEDGMENTS

The work that went into this book was made possible by several funding sources and was assisted by many individuals. Support for the first years of fieldwork and data analysis was provided by the Institute of American Cultures, awarded through the UCLA Chicano Studies Research Center and the American Indian Research Center. Funding for later phases of the project came from the Research Allocation Committee, the Southwest Hispanic Research Institute, and the Center for Regional Studies, all at the University of New Mexico.

Among those who graciously gave me hospitality, interviews, insights, suggestions, critical feedback, or other assistance, I wish to thank Benito García, Edwin Concha, Bobby Lujan, Tony Reyna, Ann Rainer, Dave Cordoba, Julian Lucero, Samuel Lucero, Danny Jaramillo, Guillermo Rosete, Juanita Jaramillo, Eduardo Lavadie, José Damian Archuleta, Larry Torres, Gregorita García, Gerald Nailor, Kim Nailor, Richard Mermejo, Margie Mermejo, Corina Durán, Clarence Fernández, Randy Sahd, Rafael Lobato, Frances Martínez, Albert Vigil, Vicente Martínez, Cliff Mills, Melitón Medina, Rudy Herrera, Robert García, John Phillips, and Aleta Lawrence.

I am grateful also to the following colleagues who provided valuable criticism, advice, references, ideas, encouragement, and intellectual companionship at various stages of the project: Marta Weigle, Ramon Gutiérrez, Herb Dick, Frances Leon Quintana, Enrique Lamadrid, Brenda Romero, Keith Basso, Deidre Sklar, Alfonso Ortiz, Phil Bock, and Juliette Cunico. Anonymous reviewers for *American Ethnologist* and *Journal of American Folklore* provided helpful feedback on earlier versions of the Taos Pueblo and Arroyo Seco chapters, respectively. These versions were published as "The Taos Pueblo Matachines: Ritual Symbolism and Interethnic

Relations," *American Ethnologist* 18, no. 2 (1991): 234–67, and "Defended Boundaries, Precarious Elites: The Arroyo Seco Matachines Dance," *Journal of American Folklore* 107, no. 424 (1994): 248–67. Finally, I wish to acknowledge the careful readings and useful suggestions provided by Jill Sweet, Dana Everts, and Jane Kepp.

1 · INTRODUCTION
The Beautiful Dance of Subjugation

When it comes to the colonial documents of Mesoamerica, for example, we have tended to use them as clues to the reconstruction of Prehispanic culture and society. . . .

From a dialogical point of view, such documents as these are interesting not in spite of the fact that some European got there first but precisely because of it. They show, from both sides and with moments of thunderbolt clarity, the dialogical frontier between European and Mesoamerican cultures during the colonial period.
—Dennis Tedlock, *The Spoken Word and the Work of Interpretation*

Montezuma serves not only as a mediating symbol to communicate between the two religious traditions but also as a temporal marker for the intrusion of the notion of history in the Pueblos. . . .

The change in world view, stimulated by the Spanish conquest and motivated by the intensity of the Roman Catholic missionary effort, was a threat to the Pueblo conception of the universe. Through the Montezuma legends, the Indians understood this threat. . . .

Montezuma, finally, is the signpost for the Pueblos' encounter with historical consciousness.
—Richard J. Parmentier, "The Pueblo Mythological Triangle"

The Matachines dance is a ritual drama performed on certain saint's days in Pueblo Indian and Mexicano/Hispano communities along the upper Río Grande valley and elsewhere in the greater Southwest.[1] The dance is characterized by two rows of masked male dancers wearing mitrelike hats with long, multicolored ribbons down the back. In the upper Río Grande valley of New Mexico, these ten or twelve masked figures are accompanied by a young girl in white, who is paired with an adult male dancer wearing a floral corona. They are joined by another man or boy dressed as a bull and by two clowns. The crowned man dressed like the other dancers is known as Montezuma, or El Monarca, while his female child partner is called La Malinche. The dance is made up of several sets or movements accompanied by different tunes, usually played on a violin and guitar. The performance, not counting the procession and recession that typically bracket it, takes roughly forty-five minutes.

Most scholars agree that the Matachines dance derives from a genre of medieval European folk dramas symbolizing conflict between Christians and Moors, brought to the New World by the Spaniards as a vehicle for Christianizing the Indians. Iberian elements merged with aboriginal forms in central Mexico, and the syncretic complex was transmitted to Indians farther north, including the Río Grande Pueblos, probably via Mexican Indians who accompanied the Spanish colonizers (Dozier 1970:187). As performed today in the greater Southwest, the Matachines dance symbolically telescopes centuries of Iberian-American ethnic relations and provides a shared framework upon which individual Indian and Hispanic communities have embroidered their own particular thematic variations.

The Matachines dance exhibits a distinctive choreographic and dramatic pattern in the upper Río Grande valley and is generally considered to be identical among Indians and Mexicanos or Hispanos. Nevertheless, the ways in which these two major ethnic groupings perform and regard the dance differ significantly. Both agree it is Christian rather than pagan or aboriginal, but most Pueblos claim the dance was brought to them from Mexico by Montezuma, who is portrayed in the dance by the figure of El Monarca. Hispanic villagers, on the other hand, attribute its introduction to colonizer don Juan de Oñate, reconquest leader don Diego de Vargas, or Cortés himself, because the drama portrays the advent of Christianity among the Indians by referring to the expulsion or conversion of the Moors, a paradigm the Spanish colonizers instantly projected onto their conquest of the New World. The dance thus has historical but differential meaning for Indian and Hispano groups because the advent of Christianity in the region does not have the same meaning for those who brought it as for those it subjugated. The differences between Pueblo and Mexicano perspectives may be mapped through close comparative examination of local Matachines performances within and across traditions. The dance both joins and divides the ethnic groups.

THE RÍO GRANDE COMPLEX

The upper Río Grande valley as referred to here consists of the length of the river that bisects the state of New Mexico from north to south, distinguishable from the lower Río Grande valley, which runs along the Texas-Mexico border from El Paso to Brownsville. New Mexico became New Spain's far northern frontier during the sixteenth century, when conquistadors and colonists followed the river to Taos, northernmost of the eastern pueblos, and began to establish missions and settlements along this corridor. The frontier colonial society that developed during the next three hundred years involved miscegenation as well as segregation of Hispanic and Indian populations and persistence of the social and territorial boundaries between them. Despite massive demographic reductions and shifts, nineteen of the more than one hundred pueblos existing at the time of contact survived into the late twentieth century (Dozier 1970; Schroeder 1979:254). Most of the Río Grande pueblos are surrounded by clusters of colonial and subsequent Mexicano settlements that coalesced upon the New Mexican landscape during four centuries of mutual opposition, growing interdependence, and, finally, separate enclavement within the U.S. nation-state.

Although the New Mexico Matachines dance shares a number of choreographic, dramatic, and symbolic elements with the dance elsewhere in the greater Southwest and Mexico, it nevertheless exhibits its own characteristic configuration. Thus it is possible and appropriate to speak of a distinctive upper Río Grande Matachines dance complex. The most basic or universal dramatic elements of the Río Grande Matachines performance involve several dance sets by the characters El Monarca and La Malinche, an exchange of trident (*palma*) and rattle (*guaje*) between them, a variable combination of choreographic interweavings, crossovers, and reversals between the two columns of dancers, a movement involving El Toro—the bull—and his ultimate demise, and processional and recessional *marchas* at the beginning and end. The clowns, known as Los Abuelos (the grandfathers), function as conductors and provide comic relief throughout the proceedings.

The Matachines dancers, also referred to as *matachines* or *danzantes,* are distinctively costumed. Their mitrelike headdresses, or *cupiles,* with ribbons streaming down the back and fringe in the front, are their signature symbol. The mask consists of the band of fringe (*fleco*) over the eyes and a folded kerchief over the lower face. Each danzante carries the palma in his left hand and the guaje in his right. Large colorful scarves hang like capes from the backs of their shoulders. They move in two parallel rows of five or six dancers each.

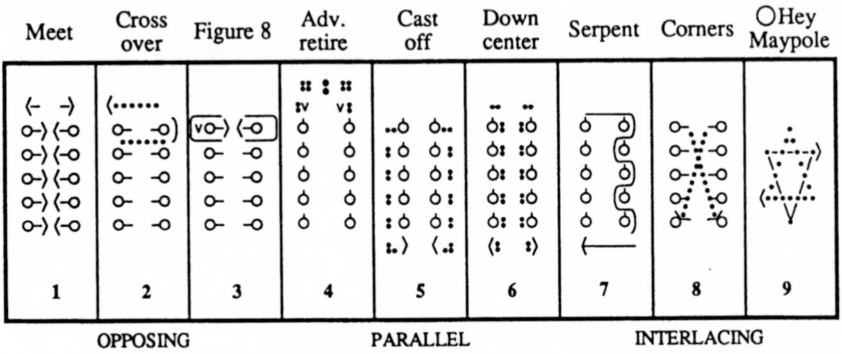

Meet	Cross over	Figure 8	Adv. retire	Cast off	Down center	Serpent	Corners	⃝Hey Maypole
1	2	3	4	5	6	7	8	9

| OPPOSING | PARALLEL | INTERLACING |

Figure 1. The basic choreographic patterns diagrammed by Gertrude Kurath (1949) for the dance form known as the morisca, to which Matachines dance patterns in the upper Río Grande generally correspond. Reproduced by permission of the American Folklore Society.

El Monarca dresses like the danzantes but wears a floral corona instead of a cupil, and often white lace leggings (*fundas*) over his pants from the knees down. He is paired with La Malinche, a preadolescent girl in a First Holy Communion dress. El Toro is a male animal-dancer with horns and forestick(s), played in some villages by a grown man, in others by a young boy. These three characters and the danzantes are accompanied by the Abuelos, usually two masked figures who move about freely, joke or clown, interact with and keep back the audience, and generally direct the proceedings. The number and personality of the Abuelos varies from village to village, as does the prominence of the bull.

The dance sets may occur in different orders and combinations in different villages. Despite this diversity, the performance tradition within each community is said to remain fairly stable, although a careful observer will see situational variation and improvisation from year to year. Any given version contains usually from seven to nine sets. Their choreographic patterns and motifs correspond very broadly to the formats diagrammed by Gertrude Kurath (1949:106) on the basis of a sample of twelve Old and New World societies; these nine patterns are reproduced in figure 1.

The music for the Matachines dance is typically performed by a fiddler and a guitarist. Several melodies and approximately nine dances have been identified for the Río Grande Matachines (Robb 1980; Champe 1983). The tunes tend to be short, varying from four to twenty measures in length, and subject to multiple repetitions. Most are done in duple or triple count and feature conventional harmonies in dominant and tonic chords on the guitar, while the fiddle carries the melodic line in A or D. Percussive effects are added by the dancers' rattles and foot stamping and in some cases by a drum (Robb 1980:738–39).[2]

Many communities hold the Matachines dance at Christmas, although some do it in the summer, and at least three villages—Arroyo Seco, Alcalde, and El Rancho—have danced it in both seasons. As shall be seen, Jémez Pueblo does the dance on December 12, *el día de Guadalupe,* and again on New Year's Day, and Hispanic Bernalillo performs the dance on its feast day of San Lorenzo, August 10. As a rule, Pueblo Matachines dances occur in the winter, whereas Hispanic Matachines may take place during either winter or summer. Some Hispanic villages, such as Alcalde and El Rancho, have dance troupes that perform at home on an annual cycle as well as in other places for special occasions. Pueblo Matachines somewhat resemble the Pueblo social dances, also usually performed in winter, when outside groups are parodied.[3]

Among the Pueblo Indians, such as those of Taos, the dance enjoys religious designation while not being considered fully sacred in the "aboriginal" sense. One indication of this is that some Pueblos will allow the Matachines dance to be photographed, whereas their indigenous sacred dances cannot be. Pueblo Matachines performances tend to be organized by tribal officers or kiva groups, while in Hispanic villages it is Catholic mayordomos and certain families who carry the burden. In most pueblos the dance involves the recruitment of Mexicano musicians, dancers, and/or Penitente *rezadores,* or prayer sayers, whereas Mexicano performances do not as a rule involve Indians. Santa Clara and Jémez pueblos perform "Indian" versions of the dance, featuring Indian costumes with moccasins, along with chanting and drumming. The degree to which costumes are embellished with elements that denote specific ethnic and religious meanings varies widely from village to village.

Along the upper Río Grande valley, the Matachines dance has been incorporated into the annual ritual calendars of San Ildefonso, Tortugas, Santa Clara, Jémez, Cochití, Santo Domingo, San Juan, Picurís, and Taos pueblos and is performed in the Mexicano villages of Alcalde, Bernalillo, San Antonio, San Antonito, Escobosa, Sedillo, Cañocito, Chililí, Carnuel, El Rancho, and Arroyo Seco (the list is not exhaustive). In all these pueblos and villages the sequence of acts, the tunes, the personalities, the dramatic embellishments, the overall style, and the precise manner in which the performers and festive occasions are organized vary markedly from one community to another.

THE MATACHINES LITERATURE

References to the "matachín" dance date from sixteenth-century Europe. There are two major views on the etymology of the term *matachín:* that it is (1) of Arabic origin, derived from *mutawajjihin,* which refers to being masked, or (2) of Italian origin, referring in the diminutive to *matto,* madman or fool (Forrest 1984:34–35). Similarly, the dance is said to be of either Moorish or indigenous European pagan origin and to have begun as a sword dance symbolic of combat, involving two interfacing columns of masked male dancers and their use of sticks and bells or castanets. In any case, the dance became associated with the theme of Moorish-Christian conflict, a type of dance known in Spain as a morisca and in England as morris dances (Kurath 1949:94, 1957:262; Forrest 1984). Some version or versions of the dance type were brought to New Spain as part of a rich heritage of Iberian music, dance, drama, poetry, and other expressive culture. Many of their elements gradually syncretized into new forms in central Mexico and elsewhere along the Spanish frontier, adapting and transforming under the intensely stressful conditions that constituted the crucible for the mestizo "culture of conquest" (Foster 1960).

Versions of the Matachines dance are reported from Mexico and Arizona for the Tarahumara (Bennett and Zingg 1935), Yaqui, Otomí, Ocoroni, Huichol, and Cora Indians (Spicer 1940; Kurath 1949; Robb 1961). Their common elements include crossovers and exchanges between two lines of masked dancers who carry rattles and tridents or fans, wear high caps with streamers and feathers, and dance to the accompaniment of fiddle and/or drum or guitar. Some versions involve clownlike figures and/or young boys cross-dressed as La Malinche (Kurath 1949).

Although most scholars agree that the matachín or morisca is an Old World form (Robb 1961), those who have observed the dance in the Southwest tend to be struck by the presence of Indian elements. J. D. Robb is perhaps exceptional in his emphasis upon the Matachines's Iberian source and character, whereas Edward Dozier (1970:187), Gertrude Kurath (1949:101, 1957:262), Aurora Lea (1963–64:10), and Flavia Champe (1981:38, 1983:1) each propose a fusion of independently similar Old and New World forms in Mexico, followed by diffusion northward. Some scholars (e.g., Dozier 1957:33) have conflated the Matachines dance with *Los Moros y Cristianos,* but the latter is a separate religious drama about the expulsion of the Moors from Spain.[4] Usually involving a written script, it is still performed in parts of Mexico and the U.S. Southwest, including the New Mexico Hispanic villages of Alcalde and Chimayó, where it entails equestrian play (Champe 1981:38; Weigle and White 1988:409).

Folklorist Gertrude Kurath provides, overall, the most complete discussion of the origin, distribution, and comparative choreography of moriscas and the Matachines dance (1949, 1957) and has published choreographic notations of the San Juan Pueblo and Santa Clara Pueblo versions (1970). Her early work offers the only comparative treatment of Old and New World morisca elements and choreographic patterns. She identifies the key symbolic elements of moriscas as combat, killing, resurrection, clown, woman disguise, animal, mask or blackface, crown, bells, and feathers and provides a table showing their distribution among fourteen Old and New World regions (Kurath 1949:105). She also diagrams nine basic choreographic patterns, which are distributed differentially across twelve Old and New World examples, excluding the Río Grande, but which nevertheless correspond broadly to what is found in New Mexico (see fig. 1).

Flavia Champe's book on the Rio Grande Matachines (1983) contains the most detailed choreographic description to date, based upon the San Ildefonso Pueblo version, which Champe claims is the "clearest, longest, and most complete" she has seen (1983:1). She compares the major elements of the San Ildefonso dance with those she has observed at other pueblos, including Taos, San Juan, Santa Clara, Picurís, and Jémez, and in the Hispanic villages of Alcalde and Bernalillo. Champe's strengths are her detailed focus on one version of the dance and the fact that she approaches and describes it as a dancer herself. Her choreographic notation is simpler and more comprehensible than Kurath's. Her intent is to make the choreography understandable and therefore useful to the lay reader. She fears the demise of the dance and claims her main purpose is to provide a practical guide for those who would preserve it. The book contains choreographic diagrams of each movement or set as well as selected intervillage comparisons, numerous color photographs, and a vinyl phonograph record of the San Ildefonso music.

Musicologist J. D. Robb has added significantly to the ethnological literature on the Río Grande Matachines. His main contribution consists of sound recordings and transcriptions of numerous Matachines tunes and dances or dance sets, including eleven from Tortugas and seven from Taos, as well as others from other villages (Robb 1961, 1980). He also provides a valuable overview of the greater Southwestern Matachines tradition and its diagnostic features among pueblos and Hispanic villages, along with a fairly detailed description of the Tortugas version (Robb 1961).

AN ETHNOGRAPHIC APPROACH

Most scholarship on the Matachines dance deals with questions of origin, distribution, and selected ethnographic detail. Each of the authors just mentioned, in addition to E. C. Parsons (1929), Leslie White (1935, 1962), Edward Spicer (1940), and W. C. Bennett and Robert Zingg (1935), provides a selectively detailed description of various aspects and versions of the dance, but no single account is entirely adequate from an ethnographic point of view. For example, even though both Kurath and Champe supply detailed choreographic and musicological descriptions of all the sets within particular versions of the dance, neither treats the performance as part of an inclusive, progressive whole with a beginning, middle, and end. Like most observers of the dance, these authors have excised the collection of dance sets as the unit of study and analytically ignored the inclusive context—the feast day and ceremonial event in question—within which each individual performance is organized and embedded.

The Matachines dance is usually performed more than once for any given occasion, and sometimes several times each day for up to three days. Nevertheless, the common fieldwork practice has been to record one dance or sequence of sets seen at one point in the overall whole and tacitly to assume that all such elements are identical or somehow interchangeable rather than part of a progressive series. Such an approach obscures the dynamic, processual, and progressive dimension of the Matachines performance. It has resulted in significant oversights, such as the attribution of different colors of La Malinche's dress to degeneration or chance (Champe

1983:89–90) rather than to a progressive costume change that takes place over two or three days.[5]

This approach has also occluded recognition of the two distinct levels of reference that are interlaced throughout each version of the Matachines: first, the "generic" level, represented by the dramatic sequence within the seven, eight, or nine standard sets and their variable shuffling, and second, the "local" level, represented by the dramatic and thematic embellishments improvised by particular performers, including clowns. Previous studies of the Matachines have focused exclusively on the first level and missed the existence of the second altogether. They treat the dance only generically, that is, in terms of its presumed "universal" meaning. But only together do local and generic levels make up the mixed, frequently ironic meaning of the dance. These two levels of meaning should be explored systematically. The regional, or generic, is encoded in the common elements of structure and content observed in all performances, and the local consists of the particular way the dance is carried out in a given village, including its elaboration of specific characters or elements, the festival occasion in which it is embedded, and year-to-year variation and change.

Every Matachines performance therefore needs to be examined not only as a sequence of distinct dance sets accompanied by certain tunes but also as a one- to three-day ritual event made up of multiple performances carried out in a meaningful sequence toward a certain completion, with an identifiable and patterned beginning, middle, and end. It should also be looked at through time, from year to year, as well as from one decade or generation to the next. This view enables the observer to discern the existence of an important, revealing subtext woven by performers out of local elements and meanings. It can also reveal the nature and direction of ritual change.

The Matachines should be studied as a dance sequence framed within a specific ritual setting. A properly contextual, ethnographic reading, moreover, must examine the specific features of each local version in terms of the historical, ecological, and social particularities of the community in question. This involves what Victor Turner (1967) calls the operational, exegetical, and positional levels of analysis, with systematic focus on observed behavior, native explanation, and consideration of the symbols in relation to one another and their overall sociocultural and environmental contexts. As a method, it requires field observation and recording, conversation and interview, and analytical synthesis of these with all other available documentary materials on the phenomenon and setting in question.[6]

THEORETICAL FRAMEWORK

> In ethnography, the office of theory is to provide a vocabulary in which what symbolic action has to say about itself—that is, about the role of culture in human life—can be expressed.
> —Clifford Geertz, *The Interpretation of Cultures*

This study is driven by two questions: what does the dance mean to those who perform and celebrate it, and what does its performance reveal about the people who do it? The first question inspired my research and looms large throughout my engagement with the subject matter, but this study better achieves an answer to the second question. It is interpretive rather than linguistic, based primarily upon observation and conversation rather than upon the systematic elicitation and semantic analysis of native categories. This work is predicated on the proposition that the Matachines dance communicates symbolically and metaphorically about the history and character of Indo-Hispano relations in the community that performs it. My approach follows in the anthropological tradition of trying to decipher, through the systematic analysis of symbols and behavior, the social meanings encoded in ritual acts.

Ritual behavior provides an enduring focus for the anthropological quest to discover cultural meaning, understand human social process, and account for patterns of variation and similarity. Ritual is a prolific propagator, transformer, and user of symbols. Ritual symbols have the power to rivet the imaginations of those who apprehend them, be they celebrant or analyst. Symbols tell about the people who use and create them. Or, as Geertz puts it (1973:23), they "present the sociological mind with bodied stuff on which to feed." For such an appetite, the Matachines provides a succulent feast.

Because my theoretical perspective is more implicit than explicit in the ethnographic descriptions that follow, it may be helpful to provide a brief account of the basic intellectual landscape out of which my somewhat eclectic approach arises. Three broad anthropological schools of thought inform my approach to the Matachines dance. They can be characterized as symbolic or interpretive, ecological, and political-economic. Indeed, this study represents an effort to synthesize key aspects of these sometimes divergent perspectives in order to arrive at a deeper anthropological understanding of the Matachines dance than scholars have previously put forth.

The descriptive task of ethnography is to interpret the flow of social discourse, an effort that consists in "trying to rescue the 'said' of such discourse from its perishing occasions and fix it in perusable terms" (Geertz 1973:20). The ethnographer shuttles between careful microscopic scrutiny and ambitious grasp at the overview, interpretively using small facts to speak to large issues (Geertz 1973:23). The practical, political, and epistemological precariousness of this mission, mercilessly deconstructed in recent years, does not negate the scientific desirability or possibility of a good, "thick" ethnographic description. Nevertheless, however well informed through a variety of field techniques (participant observation, interview and oral history, questions, mapping, genealogy, diagramming, photography, audiorecording, quantitative measurement, archival study, etc.), such a description is ultimately the anthropologist's own construction "of other people's constructions of what they and their compatriots are up to" (Geertz 1973:9).

Focus on symbols is but one part of an adequate account of any given flow or segment of social discourse. The temporal process or flow of a ritual event, with its simultaneous effect on participants, is another important aspect of such behavior. This issue is addressed by Turner and others who emphasize the processual nature of ritual and its location in behavioral and dramaturgical time. Hence my insistence that the dance be analyzed as part of a progressive ritual event and that it be considered with reference to its particular sociocultural, political, ecological, and historical settings.

Attention to context is a tenet not only of performance theory but of all contemporary linguistic and ethnographic interpretation. Gregory Bateson (1972) is credited with the concept of interpretive or metacommunicational frame, a concept elaborated upon by Erving Goffman (1974), in reference to a set of communicational markers that instruct recipients of a message in how to interpret that message (Baumann 1984:15; Briggs 1988:9). The concept of a metacommunicational frame enables one to make an analytical distinction between levels of meaning. This approach is implicit in my distinction between local and "generic" or "universal" levels of meaning, and also in the proposition that local meanings contain (or are the vehicle for) what James Scott (1990) calls a "hidden transcript," which is always juxtaposed against but embedded within the "public transcript" of manifest, universal (in this case, regional) meaning.

To what degree are different participants conscious of the full discursive import of a hidden transcript or subversive subtext embedded within a larger text/context of compliance with tradition/hegemony? Degrees of awareness exist, as is acknowledged in the distinction between manifest (conscious), latent (marginally aware), and hidden (completely unconscious) meaning (Turner and Turner 1978:246). Another axis of differentiation to keep in mind when considering the polyvocality of symbols is that of social positionality—different people have different understandings of the same event or symbol, by virtue of who and what they are. Such diversity, giving rise to what Bakhtin calls heteroglossia, is a function of social differentiation.[7] Relations between levels or contrasting views are dynamic and typically fraught with tension.

The recurrent elements in the upper Río Grande Matachines complex constitute dominant or key symbols. These symbols are the focus of this study. Not surprisingly, the dance's underlying symbolic structure involves bilateral opposition, which is reflected in the two symmetrical columns of dancers, in the pairs of Monarca and Malinche and of the Abuelos, and in the choreography itself. As ritual process, the movements enact interchanges among paired and opposed personae, resulting in symbolic transformation of the whole: Malinche and Monarca's conversion and/or "marriage," El Toro's demise, the Abuelos' routine, the crossovers between the danzantes. As will be seen from the case materials in the following chapters, symbolic oppositions and reversals abound in virtually all Matachines performances. Oppositions and reversals are a major vehicle for meaning in both regional and local contexts, operating, in addition, at manifest, latent, and hidden levels.

This symbolism is both a reflection of and a response to the historical conditions of mutual opposition and subjugation and of enduring resistance that characterized Indian-Hispano relations and, later, Mexicano-Anglo and Indian-Anglo relations. The Matachines dance has survived not because of people's pious adherence to tradition but because it continues to hold meaning or "to work" for those who perform it, Indian and Mexicano alike—or, more accurately, not quite alike. The ideological, social, and symbolic "work" the dance accomplishes among its participants takes place at a multitude of levels. The dance affirms and enacts the individual's faith and commitment as well as the faith and unity of the group. It proclaims ethnic boundaries and identity by juxtaposing symbols of indigenous and European origin. Today, both Mexicanos and Indians have long histories of oppositional survival under adverse conditions—histories they differentially project, however consciously or unconsciously, onto this ritual dance of forced conversion.

Two more lines of anthropological thought contribute to my reading of the New Mexico Matachines dance. The first draws on Fredrik Barth's ecological model of ethnic boundary maintenance, which proposes that, like species, ethnic groups occupy ecological niches, and thus the nature and character of relations (symbiosis, competition, antagonism, nonengagement, etc.) between ethnic groups depends in part upon their relative positions within the larger, inclusive ecosystem and macrosocial environment (Barth 1969). Boundaries assert differential claims to resources and serve to structure relations among groups within a given setting. Their permeability, rigidity, or intensity varies through time according to circumstance and is affected by demographic or technological change, climate, catastrophe, and so on. This approach applies easily to the historical, sociological, and even prehistoric record of social relations in New Mexico, as it does elsewhere in the Southwest, where water is everywhere the limiting factor. It serves to clarify what drives face-to-face ethnic relations in the Taos valley and elsewhere in New Mexico, and thus helps to inform my analysis of the Matachines.

Barth's ecological approach to ethnic boundary maintenance is a necessary but not sufficient ingredient for a coherent theory of ethnic relations in the semiarid upper Rio Grande valley (Rodríguez 1987). It must be integrated with a focus on political economy, attending to who holds power and who controls the land and water, or, as Marxists say, the means of production. This focus helps to locate the microcosm of face-to-face relations within the historical macrostructure of colonialism and incorporation into a mercantile and then modern capitalist nation-state. Fusion of boundary theory with a neo-Marxist world system perspective thus informs my ethnographic treatment of how class position interacts with ethnic identity in specific local settings of ritual dance organization and performance. It serves to contextualize local analyses of symbolic opposition and ritual transformation in the Matachines dance and helps to explain why and how the Matachines continues to be so compelling and important to those who perform it.

DIDACTIC OF THE BOOK

This study pursues a "thick description" of three geographically proximate Matachines performance traditions, which are compared with seven additional cases, more thinly described (Geertz 1973). My basic interpretive method will be developed with reference to the Taos Pueblo material in the first case study (chapter 2) and then applied to Arroyo Seco (chapter 3) and Picurís Pueblo (chapter 4), all located in Taos County. The same approach is applied, albeit much more superficially, to a southward progression of seven additional case examples (chapter 5). The final chapter draws some conclusions from the preceding materials and offers a few propositions about what the upper Rio Grande Matachines dance has to say to whom.

A few words must be said about the style of discourse employed in the following descriptions. It has been common in anthropology to couch ethnographic descriptions of human behavior in the present tense, or "ethnographic present," especially with reference to recurrent patterns or events such as rituals. Although this device can convey a sense of immediacy and concreteness, it also fosters an ahistorical and distorted impression of static practice and unchanging essence. Any ethnographic account of ritual is caught squarely in the crux of this dilemma. The description the ethnographer constructs is based upon individual informants' claims and explanations, hearsay, and direct observation of specific, discrete instances of behavior located in time and space. In the final analysis, anthropologists presume to construct authoritative descriptions of cultural practices and texts on the basis of careful and yet finite, fragmentary, and fleeting sets of data.

This study distinguishes conceptually between general or generic meaning and particular meaning in the dance. It therefore becomes necessary to address the problem of whether or how a specific element or performance is idiosyncratic or regionally characteristic or both. The rhetorical decision to use either the present or past tense to construct an analytic description of a specific performance and performance tradition cannot, under these circumstances, remain casual or unconscious. The most difficult part of writing this book was deciding when to stop. Because every local dance is dynamic and constantly changing, its carefully deciphered "meaning" can never hold true for long. Ethnographic description of specific events should properly be cast in the past tense, because by the time it reaches paper it is over. Yet the past tense becomes boring and awkward when one strives for analysis and generalization. Several common measures are used in the following pages to deal with this dilemma. Specific dramatic episodes are dated but nevertheless written in the present as well as the past tense. Generalizations about the dance, based upon direct and secondary observation, are written in the present or sometimes subjunctive tense. Discursive shifts between past and present tenses are a way of indicating historical specificity, on the one hand, and analytic insight into the general rule, on the other.

Plate 1. La Malinche dressed in pink, Taos Pueblo, December 25, 1986.

Plate 2. La Malinche dressed in yellow, Taos Pueblo, December 26, 1986.

Plate 3. La Malinche dressed in blue, Taos Pueblo, December 26, 1986.

Plate 4. La Malinche dressed in green, Taos Pueblo, December 26, 1992.

Plate 5. "Pregnant" Perejundia, or La Abuela, Taos Pueblo, December 26, 1986.

Plate 6. El Abuelo displays the first of twin "offspring," Taos Pueblo, December 26, 1986.

Plate 7. La Perejundia, Taos Pueblo, December 25, 1992.

Plate 8. El Abuelo with "baby," Taos Pueblo, December 26, 1992.

Plate 9. The Maypole, or closing segment of the Matachines dance, Taos Pueblo, December 26, 1986.

Plate 10. The Abuelos, Picurís Pueblo, December 24, 1985.

Plate 11. La Abuela leads La Malinche, Picurís Pueblo, December 25, 1985.

Plate 12. La Malinche pinned with money, Picurís Pueblo, December 25, 1987.

Plate 13. The Maypole, Picurís Pueblo, December 25, 1985.

Plate 14. Danzantes, San Juan Pueblo, December 25, 1989.

Plate 15. Danzantes, San Juan Pueblo, December 25, 1989.

Plate 16. El Abuelo leads La Malinche, San Juan Pueblo, December 25, 1989.

2 · TAOS PUEBLO

Mestizaje and Chile con Candy

Taos Pueblo is the northeasternmost of all the pueblos, the only remaining northern Tiwa village besides Picurís, its closest relative and Pueblo neighbor, which lies some twenty-five miles to the southeast. Taos sits on the Río Pueblo de Taos, a tributary of the Río Grande, where, according to archaeologists, it was established during the fourteenth century (Bodine 1979:258) in what is probably the optimal location in the greater Taos basin. The village straddles the river and is divided into moieties known as north-side, or winter, people and south-side, or summer, people.[1] Even aboriginally Taos seems to have been a contact point between people from the south along the Río Grande corridor and groups from the eastern plains, a fact reflected in its material and ceremonial culture.

Long known for its conservatism and history of violent as well as legalistic resistance to assimilation, Taos Pueblo was the starting point for the 1680 Pueblo Revolt as well as a participant in the 1847 Mexicano revolt against American occupation.[2] Its 1970 victory in the Blue Lake case after a 64-year legal struggle with the federal government has become a landmark in American Indian legal history (Bodine 1978; Gordon-McCutchan 1991).[3] Although Taos Pueblo is famous for its closed, conservative character, it has also been the focus of intense interest generated by the tourism industry during this century and has in many ways been profoundly affected by the romantic mystique it began to acquire in the early days of the Taos art colony (Rodríguez 1987, 1989, 1990). Its five-story adobe construction has made it one of the most photographed and painted architectural structures in North America.

A major theme today and throughout Taos's history has been its continuous struggle to preserve its physical integrity, including claims to surrounding land and water resources and traditional use areas, against the unceasing encroachments of Spanish-Mexican and American settlement and counterclaims. Spanish colonization of Taos Pueblo began in 1598, when the mission of San Gerónimo was imposed. Hispanic settlement radiated outward from the pueblo in successive rings as the colonial population grew, steadily occupying the lower Taos watershed and other adjacent watersheds in the Taos basin. Eventually, at least sixteen Spanish-speaking villages, including the town of Don Fernando de Taos, crystallized along eight mountain streams within a twenty-mile radius of the pueblo, all imposing, to one degree or another, competing demands upon increasingly scarce arable lands and surface waters. The precise geography of this layout and the particular patterns of proximity, conflict, reciprocity, and cooperation it gave rise to are important to any detailed understanding of the character and nature of Indian-Mexicano-Anglo relations in the Taos area.

THE DANCE

At Taos Pueblo the Matachines dance is usually performed at Christmas every other year, alternating with the Deer dance. It is the only (public) masked dance at Taos, and the only one in which Mexicanos actively participate. The Taos Matachines has a long history of continuous performance, although it lapsed for several years during the 1970s after the longtime musicians Adolfo Frésquez and Tranquilino Lucero died, and it lapsed again between 1986 and 1992.[4] Taos Indians say the dance was brought to them from Mexico by Montezuma. It is not considered religious or sacred in the same sense as their "own" dances, and they typically disparage it, wish it away, or complain that it will push aside the Deer dance—sentiments noted also by Parsons (1936:95).

If the Taos people perform the Matachines grudgingly, they nevertheless perform it with great care and lavish extraordinary attention and expense on it in terms of costume, complete and proper execution, and feasting. The Taos performance is an elaborate, visually striking production that probably costs the governor's office well over a thousand dollars and new performers up to two or three hundred each. Yet it brings significant revenue into the governor's office in the form of entry, parking, and camera fees charged to outsiders.

The performers include twelve danzantes, El Monarca or "Monanca" (sometimes called "Malanca" or "Maranca"), La Malinche, El Toro (sometimes called the buffalo), two Abuelos, and two musicians. The Taos music is traditionally played by hired Mexicano musicians—in recent years by a father and son from the Valdez rim in Des Montes who auditioned for the job. At present all performers except the musicians, Abuelos, and occasionally the Toro, are Indian.

The dance usually takes three days to complete, starting around noon on the day before Christmas and concluding around sundown on the twenty-sixth. It begins and ends each day in front of the church, and during the second and third days it proceeds through a prescribed order of dancing of selected sets in front of officers' and dancers' houses.

The Taos version contains about eight movements or sets, depending on how they are grouped, and seven different tunes.[5] The movements include the following:

1. *La Procesión.* The dance begins and ends with a musical procession and recession, done to the same tune.

2. *La Malinche,* parts one and two. Malinche, escorted by the Abuelos, takes Monarca's palma (trident) and then his rattle and travels with them, weaving within and between the two rows of dancers, while he sits at one end facing them all. Then Monarca and Malinche travel together along the rows.

3. *El Monarca,* or *Brincando las Palmas.* Monarca rises from a seated position, where the Abuelos briefly stroke his legs, to dance among the two rows and jump or wheel over the downwardly extended palmas of the kneeling (*La Cortesía*) danzantes.

4. *La Corona* and *La Cruz.* The two rows of danzantes execute patterned crossovers and wheel in groups of three, and then assume a crosslike formation (fig. 3).

5. *El Toro.* Toro chases after Malinche when she waves a handkerchief at him; the danzantes then cross sides while encountering the Toro.

6. *El Zapatazo* or *La Patada.* The danzantes do a stamp dance with a kickback step.

7. *La Indita de San Juan,* by the Toro and Abuelos. The Abuelos wrestle Toro to the ground and castrate him.

8. *La Faja,* or Maypole. The dancers interweave around a central pole held up by the Abuelos and Toro, braiding long belts attached to its top (plate 9).

Figure 2. Night procession on Christmas Eve, Taos Pueblo, 1986.

RITUAL PROGRESSION

Each day the Matachines begins with a procession to the churchyard followed by a full dance performance, and each day it concludes with the Maypole in front of the church followed by a recession. The entire production is both repetitive and progressive. On Christmas Eve the dance is performed before vespers in front of the church. After mass comes the night procession around the plaza illuminated by *luminarias*. This dramatic nocturnal event is attended by throngs of townspeople and tourists, some of whom are bused in from the nearby ski resort. A large canopied bulto, or statue of the Virgin, dressed in white, is paraded clockwise around the plaza along the path of luminarias, accompanied by one or two smaller saints carried by women singing *alabanzas,* or hymns. The musicians and other performers join in the procession, which is led by a man carrying a giant torch (*hachón*) and several men who fire rifles into the air at intervals (fig. 2).

During the second and third days, selected sets are performed at various

Figure 3. The portion of the Matachines dance known as La Corona, Taos Pueblo, 1986.

locations alternating between the north and south sides of the pueblo. These follow a prescribed order, beginning on Christmas day with performances in front of or near the houses of tribal officers, who must feast people including the dancers and their attendants and other guests. The performers appear at the homes of the cacique, governor, lieutenant governor, war chief, Monarca, Malinche, and the two head dancers (or *Capitanes*) of each column. The dancing and feasting take all day. On the next day the performers dance in front of each of the remaining *danzantes'* houses.

The family of each dancer performing for the first time must put up a feast for everyone, and like the other hosts, each selects the dance set(s) to be performed in its honor. Ideally there is a balance between new and old dancers (the latter do not have to provide a feast), because otherwise the feasting can make the dance run into an additional day. On the third day each new dancer is *entregado*—"delivered" or carried—by the Abuelos and Toro to the dancer's house, where his family greets and blesses him before

Figure 4. The *entrega,* in which a new dancer is delivered to his own house for feasting. Taos Pueblo, December 26, 1986.

the entourage enters to feast. His face is covered entirely with a *paño,* or scarf, for the *entrega,* and upon arrival his family is asked if they recognize him (fig. 4). Inside, the family women serve the dancers and other guests in shifts at one long table, while the Abuelos amuse the crowd in front of the house. The Malinche, Monarca, and even the Abuelos and Toro also undergo entregas, the last three being feasted by the governor, lieutenant governor, and war chief, respectively.

RECRUITMENT AND ROLE REQUIREMENTS

Participation in the Matachines is a substantial undertaking for all who perform, as well as for their immediate families. The dance places considerable material and physical demands on all of the performers, especially the Monarca, Malinche, and new danzantes. Rehearsals begin about a week in advance, after the governor's office decides to hold the Matachines, and are conducted at night in the community hall. Recruitment follows different routes for the different roles. New dancers generally volunteer on the basis of a personal oath, or *promesa,* sworn during a time of duress such as an illness or wartime service overseas. In other cases individuals, usually including El Toro, are asked (or sometimes pressured) to dance by the governor's office. El Monarca may be recruited either way, but he is preferably an experienced and skillful dancer and may play the role more than once. La Malinche seems to be both chosen and pledged by her family and is a different little girl every year. Voluntary participation brings honor and blessing to the performer's family and the community in general. The Mexicano Abuelos, like the musicians, are hired.

The governor's office selects the Abuelos, who typically are Mexicano or "Spanish," although some have been Indian. The Taos Abuelos make up a pair of very lively clowns. In the late 1970s the Abuela ("grandmother," sometimes known as La Perejundia) and then Abuelo roles were played by a dwarf from Valdez, who was invited, despite being considered "really too short," because he was so funny. During the 1980s the Abuelo, who also started out as the Abuela, was an individual from El Prado, and in 1992 the new Abuela was from Don Fernando de Taos. Mexicano Abuelos usually seem to come from families that have married into or have other close ties with the pueblo and to be mostly from neighboring villages that border on Indian land, such as Arroyo Seco, El Prado, or the town of Taos. These Abuelos often speak some Tiwa, a preferred feature because their imperfect delivery amuses the Indians. In the old days the Abuelos were given food, including a lot of bread, but today they are also paid. In 1986 the Abuelo received $360 and a great deal of bread; in 1992 the Abuela received $300, plus another $400 in tips.

Taos Abuelos sometimes run in families. The Abuelo in the 1980s from El Prado was married to a Taos Pueblo woman. His grandfather, who was "born and raised at the pueblo," was also an Abuelo. He was first recruited by his wife's uncle, who evidently taught him some of the jokes and routines, which he embellished in his own versions. In 1983 his partner was an Indian, and in 1986 he picked his brother-in-law, another Mexicano from El Prado whose father also once played the Abuelo and whose Hispanic wife, the Abuelo's sister, was raised at the pueblo. This Abuelo brought mischievous gusto to the role. He was a born-again Christian who saw his role as a calling, saying he hoped to play the Abuelo "until the day I die." He did not like playing the Abuela and indicated that it was a less

Figure 5. El Toro and Los Abuelos, Taos Pueblo, 1986.

desirable role, probably because of its transvestism. In 1992, after a lapse of the dance since 1986, new Abuelos were chosen, and the Abuela became the more prominent member of the team.

Evidently the Toro is not currently a particularly prestigious role either, since he gets thrown on the ground and castrated. El Toro wears horns and a cow or buffalo hide over his regular clothes (fig. 5). Nowadays this performer is usually Indian. Many years ago the Toro was played by a Mexicano from Arroyo Seco whose rendition became so popular he was nicknamed "Torito." His father played the Abuelo. Older informants recall how the two clowned with an inflated animal bladder and how the Toro was shot with a cap pistol. It appears that these roles can become imbued with the personalities or styles of those who play them, and performance details vary accordingly through time.

The costumes involve much work and expense because they are very fine and are changed several times over the course of the three days. Each day the danzantes, El Monarca, and La Malinche change clothes, in some cases twice. The danzantes and Monarca wear good creased pants, vests, colored dress shirts, and heeled boots, in addition to gloves, scarves, shawls, and pins. The frame for the cupil, or headdress, may be borrowed or constructed, but each year it is decorated anew. The Taos cupil involves a velvet facing overlain by a silver-and-turquoise necklace and other jewelry. The matachines' clothes have grown progressively fancier over recent years, so that it is now about the most expensive dance to dress for, and the dancers feel some pressure to meet the high standard. Usually the women in their families help assemble their costumes, and much intrafamily borrowing of items goes on. In the old days, when people dressed more "traditionally" and few owned non-Indian–style dress clothes, they would borrow the garments from Mexicano neighbors and friends.

La Malinche wears five different costumes, each a different color. On the first day she wears white. On Christmas morning of 1986 she wore white with a pale green trim; that afternoon she wore pink (plate 1); on the morning of the third day she wore yellow (plate 2), and that afternoon, pale blue (plate 3). The sequence in 1992 was different: white, pink, blue, yellow, green (plate 4), and pink again. Her costume includes a veil and matching tights or socks and necklace, and white shoes and gloves. Malinche is dressed by her mother, who, assisted by female kin, closely attends her from the sidelines. The dance is probably most difficult for Malinche because she is so young, usually around six or seven, although in 1986 she was only four (having begun practice earlier that year), and in 1992 she was five.

All performers, except for perhaps El Toro, are attended from the sidelines by family members who, for example, provide little pads for the danzantes to kneel on, straighten their ribbons, and make other costume repairs. The Abuelos will have a wife or family member carry their large pillowcase bags for bread and other goodies, and musicians may bring a family apprentice. The long hours of dancing in the cold, broken only by intervals of feasting, make for an arduous three days, and usually by the end everyone, including the musicians, is visibly exhausted. It is customary for friends and relatives in the audience to pin dollar bills on the Malinche and sometimes the danzantes during a performance. The Abuelos and musicians are slipped tips as well.

THE ABUELOS' ROUTINES AND BIRTH BURLESQUE

The Abuelos are the most distinctive characters in the Taos Matachines, and of all the performers, they have the greatest latitude for improvisation in their masks and other details of their routines. At the same time they are carefully supervised by tribal elders in charge of the dance. They are a raucous couple consisting of a gruff *pícaro,* or male trickster, accompanied by a man cross-dressed as La Abuela, his paramour or "wife." The Abuelo wears heavy boots and fatigues and/or dungarees and carries a *chicote,* or whip. His "wife," La Perejundia, is portrayed as a husky woman in a wig, long dress, and boots. In 1986 the Abuelos looked white and she was called "a sexy blond." In 1992, new actors portrayed a Mexican in a sombrero and an "Indian" woman in moccasins and braids.

At Taos both Abuelos are masked, but their masks vary from year to year. During the 1980s they wore mostly modern rubber head masks. One year the Abuelo was instructed to wear a traditional rawhide mask like the Abuelos used to wear in the Hispanic villages, but it inspired less "respect" among the children than the rubber masks he favored, which he claimed disguised his identity better.[6] In 1992 the masks were made of plaster. Other details of the clowns' costumes, such as a skirt, jacket, poncho, or hat, may vary from day to day during a given performance.

Two separate accounts of the Taos Pueblo Abuelo routines follow. The first is based upon casual observation during the late 1970s and early 1980s followed by close examination of the 1986 performance. It captures the general character of the Taos Pueblo Abuelos as well as the particulars enacted by one set of clowns. My theoretical understanding of the Abuelos' role in the Matachines dance originally derived from a detailed analysis of the 1986 Taos Pueblo performance, substantiated by more casual observation of the same Abuelo in previous years. The change that took place in 1992 reminded me how fleeting every version is, despite my having reified one particular version into a useful conceptual model. Nevertheless, both performances exhibit common thematic elements. The second account is based upon the 1992 performance, the first Matachines done at Taos Pueblo since 1986, after lapses in 1988 and 1990.

The precise reason for this hiatus is known only to those who enforced it, although I will offer some speculation later. In any case, the break signaled the end of one Abuelo tradition and possibly the start of another. Whatever their reasons for starting afresh with new Abuelos in 1992, one consequence was to restore control of the clowns' repertoire to the pueblo elders in charge of the dance, thereby erasing a slate on which to reinscribe another slightly modified version of an old drama. The contrast between the 1986 and 1992 versions reveals that certain elements remain constant while details of style, sequence, and execution vary in significant ways, reflecting changes in personnel and circumstances. A satisfactory account of the Taos Pueblo Abuelo complex must combine ethnographic immediacy with temporal specificity and identify thematic continuity within a chronological perspective. I attempt to achieve this by allowing the narrative to shift between present and past tenses throughout the following two descriptions.

The 1980s Abuelos In 1986 the Abuelo wore a rubber mask of an aged white person, and the Abuela a gooey-looking science fiction mask and curly dark blond wig. The Abuelo was a compactly built man smaller than the Abuela. He wore a dark blue jumpsuit. She wore a kerchief over her wig, a shawl, and a long, brightly striped skirt. The Abuelo's major functions were to call out the dance steps and tunes ("¡Vuelta!"; "¡Arrúganse!"; "¡Corona!"; "Play it again, Sam!"), keep the audience back, and provide comic relief. The Abuela was less verbal than her consort, although she frequently called him "honey" in falsetto or a loud male voice. The two entertained the crowd between sets while the dancers ate and rested inside. They appeared before the opening procession to summon the dancers in the mornings. They danced and sang, acted out, skirmished with each other and the bull, and teased people in the audience.

Some people privately disapproved of some of the songs this Abuelo sang—for example, when he chanted in Spanish about Chinamen, Jews, and pigs' feet while the danzantes executed the choreographically complicated Maypole: "Chino, chino, pata de cochino, chino, chino, pata de marrano" (literally, Chinaman, Chinaman, pig's foot, Chinaman, Chinaman, swine's foot). *Marrano* is also a term used in New Mexico to refer to "crypto" Jews, or conversos—Christianized yet still practicing Jews. In colonial times, *chino* was a *casta* term referring to an "India-Mulato" hybrid (Bustamante 1991:144, table 1). Nevertheless, this Abuelo evoked laughter. He joked, made innuendos, and terrorized dogs. Joking about their size, he handed the castrated bull's "testicles" to the war chief amid great mirth.[7] At the midpoint of the Maypole (just before unwinding) he would ask the crowd, "Is this a good American [or, alternatively, Japanese] candy [or sundae]?"

Just as they mediate between performers and audience through discipline and teasing, the Abuelos mediate the relationship between Malinche and Monarca and between those two and the matachines, as well as between all of these and El Toro, whom they finally dispatch. The Abuelo directs the proceedings under the unobtrusive purview of the governor's staff, and by his own account takes care of the Monarca "like my own son." The Abuela takes care of the Malinche like a chaperone, guiding the little girl through her transits and weavings along the two rows of dancers. They escort her between them, Abuelo in front with La Perejundia behind, during her interwoven journey between the two columns, to and from the seated Monarca.

The Abuelos accompany the Malinche and preside over her "marriage" or interchange with Monarca, when he sits facing the rows of dancers while she stands facing him, rotating her arm around his, taking and then returning his palma and his rattle. In 1986 the Abuelo chanted, "¡Engáñalo, mijita! ¡Engáñalo, mijita! como engañó tu mamá, tu papá. ¡Engáñalo, mijita! No more chile con candy." This literally means, "Deceive him, my child! Deceive him, my child! as your father deceived your mother [or vice versa]. Deceive him, my child! No more chile with candy!" (fig. 6). This Abuelo told me the part had been taught to him, and elaborated:

> Yeah, they told me what it was, it was like he was cheating with . . . before . . . well, he was dating this girl. The Monarca was dating this girl, ok, ok, and on top of that he was cheating on the girl. He was seeing another woman, that's what this means when you say it in "¡Engáñalo! ¡Engáñalo mijita!" That's what . . . his parents were cheating on each others, *his* parents, Monarca's parents, that he was seeing another woman, the father, and the mother was seeing another man, instead of being mother and father, together. They were cheating on each others, and that's why they . . . the song, when I'm saying, "¡Engáñalo! ¡Engáñalo mijita!" . . . And it's "Tell him, daughter! Tell him, get after him, that way he won't cheat on you again!" See . . . it's like almost, them two were supposed to get married, but they won't, they don't, see.

He learned the chant from his wife's uncle, and translated *engáñalo* as *talima* in Tiwa, meaning "stick it."

Yet the man at the pueblo in charge of directing the dance told me it is not *engáñalo* at all, but *gayalo,* which he said meant "to keep on making the turning motion with her hand." He also remarked on the need to

Figure 6. "¡Engáñalo, mijita, engáñalo!" Taos Pueblo, December 26, 1985.

supervise the Abuelos and keep them from taking too much time during the dance. This "heteroglossia" (Bakhtin 1981, 1984), or discrepancy and tension between the Abuelo's seemingly privileged interpretation of his own *engáñalo* lines and the contrary view expressed by the Pueblo elder, reflects the radical divergence of perspectives in the plural, stratified world of Taos. As shall be seen, *gayalo* was replaced by *callalo* in 1992.

The dramatic climax of the 1986 Taos Pueblo Matachines was a burlesque between the Abuelos involving the Perejundia's progressive pregnancy and, as the grand finale on the third day, vigorous delivery of twins who were then mock-baptized with Indian *padrinos,* or godparents, pulled from the audience. Each day her stomach grew bigger (plate 5), until finally she fell to the ground groaning and the Abuelo acted as midwife. Evidently this theme has been part of the Taos performance for more than fifty years.[8] Locals invariably say the dance is always done the same way.

In 1981 the Abuelo wore a rubber Planet-of-the-Apes mask and the baby was a teddy-bear–like chimpanzee doll, while the Abuela wore a dark blue ski mask. In 1986 the Perejundia gave birth to very white, blond "twins":

a Strawberry Shortcake doll and a large, pinkish rag doll (plate 6). A brief mock marriage took place between the Abuelos on the first afternoon. The "baptismal" padrinos were the cacique and his wife, while the Abuelo joked in Tiwa that the *taboona*, or governor, was the real father.

The Abuelos in 1992 The pueblo was scheduled to perform the Matachines dance in 1988 and again in 1990 but instead did the Deer dance for five consecutive years. So even though 1992 would "in theory" be a Matachines year, it was by no means a foregone conclusion that the pueblo would deign to do "the Mexican dance." When the governor's office announced the Matachines about a week before Christmas, some said it was to mark the Columbian quincentenary. Another reason was that someone had made a promesa to do it. Although the musicians and a few of the danzantes were the same as in 1986, all of the other principals were new, including the young Monarca and the Abuelos.

The new Abuelo's mask was a mestizo caricature with a large, bristly handlebar mustache, wispy beard, and elongated, ragged white teeth. He wore a wide-brimmed straw hat, a neon-striped serape, dark leather coat, gloves, and boots and carried a bullwhip. His paramour was a large, exuberant figure with glossy black braids, long skirt, and enormous breasts. Her mask had a large open mouth with bright red lips, aquiline nose, and dark brown complexion. She wore a tight beige sweater that revealed her nipples, a bustle under her skirt, and a brightly flowered shawl. She carried a horsetail whip and wore lace-up boots refashioned with moccasin soles (plate 7).

Perhaps the most striking contrast between 1986 and 1992 was the Perejundia's dominance, in the sense of being not only bigger but also louder, more vocal, and more interactive than the Abuelo. By the third day she had become the crowd's darling, carrying on a lively banter of Tiwa jokes and friendly if aggressive horseplay. Her routines included a constant stream of risqué innuendos, grabbing and lifting people, shrill ululations, and an elk mating call that invariably evoked paroxysms of laughter from the Pueblo women.

The birth burlesque came on the second day rather than the third, around noon, in front of the governor's house. It took place as a sudden, oddly underplayed gesture when the Abuela quickly dropped a tiny doll onto the ground from under her skirt. The baby, a tiny black troll with little red horns, was presented to the governor. He was summoned along with other blanketed men for the mock ceremony, after which people filed into his house to eat. The Abuelos sat around under a ramada holding the baby while guests feasted inside. The baby reappeared the following afternoon, again in front of the governor's house, but this time as a larger, old-fashioned baby doll with molded black hair and dark skin, wearing a blue dress and swaddled in a little pastel-striped blanket (plate 8). The Abuelo carried it throughout the remainder of the afternoon, briefly surrendering it to a blond woman in the audience during the last Maypole (plate 9) inside the church yard.

Although more subdued than the Perejundia, the Abuelo was a distinct presence nonetheless. He called out the songs and occasional dance instructions such as "¡Vuelta!" or "¡Arrúganse!" and repeated "¡Engáñalo! ¡Engáñalo!" during the Malinche-Monarca guaje-palma exchange. He cracked his bullwhip violently against the ground like a crazed slave driver and mock-sodomized a male tourist who was crouched on all fours to videotape the dance. He called the Abuela "mahoney" and squeezed and patted her. He lifted her skirt during the Maypole to peek underneath. At the conclusion of the Maypole, he asked the audience, "¿Te gusta?" Late on the third day he used a small orange for the Torito's balls and squeezed juice from it. During an earlier performance someone lent him a pair of fragrant elk testicles. The Abuelos took turns carrying the Malinche over muddy ground, and in the mornings each patrolled one side of the village, calling out in Tiwa for the dancers to come and begin.

The Abuelo and Abuela were chosen separately. Neither knew the dance or was familiar with the previous Abuelos' performance. Each was recruited somewhat differently and given piecemeal instructions about what to do and say and roughly what to wear. The Abuelo was recruited first and during the first days of practice was accompanied by a Taos Indian Abuela, who fell sick, however, and was subsequently replaced by a man from the town of Taos. This Abuelo was an Aztec dancer (practitioner and instructor) from Mexico who has lived in the Taos area for about a decade and is married to a woman from Arroyo Seco.[9]

He was initially approached by friends from the pueblo familiar with his Aztec *danza*. This man had danced twice before at Taos Pueblo for King's Day (January 6), when various kinds of dancers may be invited to dance house-to-house for ritual food-giving. He was familiar with the

Matachines dances in Mexico but had never seen or participated in a Río Grande valley version. His recruiters told him something about the dance at Taos Pueblo, instructing him mainly to "have a lot of fun." He was assured at the outset that he would be provided with a costume, mask, and the necessary accouterments. But after several days of practice, when asked if he had these yet, he realized he would have to assemble his own costume. He borrowed an unfinished mask from a friend in Arroyo Hondo and ended up making the Abuela's mask as well. He was guided by his own sense of Abuelos as *indigenista,* or pan-Indian protectors of tradition and religion. The elder in charge of the dance was his main instructor in what to do and say, although he also picked things up from other participants as they went along.

Interestingly, his interpretation of the *engáñalo* line was that the Malinche should try to trick the Monarca during the guaje-palma exchange, in the sense of coquettishly offering and then snatching away an object, to fool him into grabbing for and missing it. He said the other term was not *gayalo* but *callalo,* meaning to "hush (it)" or "quiet (it)," with reference to the rattle, because its sound is a signal for the musicians to start playing. An experienced and accomplished dancer in his own right, this man said he found the role of Taos Pueblo Abuelo intensely challenging in its complexity, scope, and sheer physical demand. It was difficult but rewarding. Months later he said, "The whole experience was great for me, as an individual and as a dancer. . . . It is something I will carry with me for a long time in my life." He was impressed by how respectfully he was treated, noting that when the first Abuela had to quit, they "bothered to ask" him how he felt about their second choice, a young man from the town of Taos who had grown up with a number of "old buddies" from Taos Pueblo.

The young man who played the Abuela in 1992 comes from La Loma, an old *placita* and barrio west of the Taos plaza that is now a gentrifying neighborhood within the town. He is known as a virtuoso flamenco guitarist, an ambitious businessman, and a bon vivant. If the Abuelo was selected for his skill and dedication as a dancer, the Perejundia was probably chosen because his gregarious, wildly playful personality seemed ideal for the role of trickster. He was approached by the war chief and vaguely instructed in what he would need and what to do. Over the course of the three days he devised, with encouragement and coaching, a repertoire of gags that evoked robust laughter and applause.

He compiled a list of Tiwa words and phrases, including commands such as "lick them!"; "suck them!"; "feel them!"; and "look at it!"—all uttered while aggressively presenting his ample bosom to men in the audience. He yelled "get back!"; "come here!"; "let's go"; and so on, all in Tiwa. Another word he repeated was *quanah,* or "rusty nail," a Tiwa term that refers to the Spanish. He was told to say "Whe-wa" when the Abuelos stroked El Monarca's legs before he rose to dance, but not what it meant. Whereas most of the Abuelo's utterances were in Spanish, the Abuela spoke mainly in (broken) Tiwa, but they communicated with each other in Spanish. The Abuelo fashioned the Abuela's mask from a plaster of paris mold of his face. The Abuela then put together his own costume from borrowed items, except for his moccasin-boots, which he called "beketticups," a shoe form rarely seen on non-Indians. A Taos friend had previously given them to him because he frequently visits the pueblo in areas where hard-soled shoes are not permitted. They were made from an old pair of his lace-up boots.

It seems the Abuela learned only piecemeal that he would have to dress like a woman and give birth to a doll. At first he was told something like, "You're going to need a skirt," and later, "You'll need a doll" (which was provided), and finally, "Go have the baby in front of the governor's house." The birth episode was rushed, he indicated, because it embarrassed him, a sentiment that seems at odds with his otherwise easy flow of borderline vulgarisms. He picked up words and routines as he went along, garnering $400 in tips over the course of the three days, in addition to the $300 the Abuelos were each paid. Both were also given the customary bagfuls of bread and food.

In sum, the major dramatic elements in the performance, including the Abuelos' tasks and the birth burlesque, remained much the same in 1992, although their timing, sequence, and individual performance styles changed. Whereas in the first case the clown offspring's gestation was portrayed, in the other its growth as a neonate was shown. Similarly, the Malinche's color change sequence was altered from 1986, apart from white on the first day. Although the specifics may vary, perhaps the nativity and color change alike refer to cyclical temporal transformation.

On the first day the dancers were visibly rusty and the Abuelos did not yet know quite how to do things, so they all required unusually overt and explicit supervision by the older men who watched over the dance. But as time went on their rendition improved, and on the third day they performed the last dance perfectly. On the last day there were also a good many entregas, including those for the Abuelos and Toro. Among the new dancers was the young Monarca, who danced to fulfill a promesa for the healing of an injury. His vow included luminarias for the second and third night processions, a special feature of the 1992 Christmas celebration.

There were more people at the Christmas afternoon Matachines than I had seen there before. Thousands were packed solid in a dense crowd, many trying to follow the dancers as they proceeded from one site to another. Hundreds arrived on big buses and barely knew where they were or what they were seeing when they got out to look around. This kind of tourism, which brings several thousand people to the central plaza at Taos Pueblo, all wanting to see the dance, transforms the social atmosphere of such events. A palpable sense of strain, tension, and joylessness seemed pervasive, because there were too many people many times over to allow anyone to watch the dance. Nevertheless the tribal office must have taken in many thousands of dollars, at the rate of $5 per car and $10 per van or bus with $1 per passenger, and $5 per still camera and $10 for video. Things lightened up on the third day when the crowd was much thinner, and feasting became more open in terms of inviting visitors in to eat. The tribe feasted into the fourth day, there being a lot of food left over, but the pueblo was closed to the public.

ANALYSIS

Even though they will discuss it more freely than they will discuss indigenous dances, individual Taos Indians profess little knowledge of or interest in the Matachines or its meaning. Indeed, there seems to be scant speculation aloud as to meaning among the Pueblo population, although people will recall who performed the dance when, how, and where. In any event, one must bear in mind the Pueblos' notorious disinclination to discuss such matters with outsiders. In pursuing the generally indirect, passive ethnographic approach one must adopt at the pueblos, I have encountered little commentary as to what the movements or sets represent individually, and only broad notions of what the dance as a whole stands for.[10]

Throughout the Taos area, as elsewhere, the dance is commonly said to commemorate Monarca's conversion to Christianity and the coming of the Virgin to the Indians. The innocent young Malinche is associated with the Virgin Mary, the Monarca with Montezuma or "someone with power." The twelve danzantes symbolize, most people will say, apostles or soldiers.

The dance as a whole is characterized by oppositions: two rows of danzantes, Malinche/Monarca, Abuelos/Toro. Its dramatic structure is informed by a dialectic of opposition and resolution, culminating in the birth of offspring. The most ready association here is with the birth of the Christ child, since the dance is done at Christmas. But why should this be portrayed in burlesque?

For the Pueblos, the coming of Christianity is a profoundly ambivalent event because it was central to their subjugation. Many are devout Catholics, a fact reflected in the extreme honor attached to the role of Malinche and the intense care given to her costume and proper comportment. Nevertheless, as one Taos Pueblo woman commented, the gunfire during the Virgin's procession symbolizes the brute force the Spaniards used to bring her. At Taos, the link between Malinche and the Virgin is hinted at in the little girl's change of costumes, reminiscent of the seasonal color changes the Virgin's bulto undergoes at the hands of the Guadalupanas (a Catholic women's society) every year inside Taos Pueblo's St. Jerome church.[11]

Like the Abuelos, La Malinche is a mediating figure between two opposing sides, but unlike them she is solemn and pure. The dissonance unleashed in her paradoxical "wedding" or exchange with Monarca bursts forth in symbolic particulars played out by the Abuelos. These tricksters preside over her conversion of Monarca while urging her to deceive him, and they protect her from the bull while parodying the birth of bizarrely crossed offspring. The Abuela and Abuelo act as reversed counterparts to Malinche and Monarca and together invert whatever holy union the dance overtly proclaims.

Because she is the only child dancer, La Malinche receives special attention from participants and audience alike. Yet she brings the same degree of seriousness to the performance as any adult. All the dancers, especially her "chaperones," the Abuelos, along with the governor's staff, solemnly undertake the ceremonial obligation to care for her and return her safely to her family. Together with her mother and other women, they guide and even carry La Malinche through a week of practice and three days of dancing and processions.

The dance is both appreciated and resented. Ironically, it is perhaps the most costly public ceremony the pueblo performs, although nowadays it brings in considerable revenue as well, at the tribal level. It is certainly the only ceremony whose execution requires direct involvement of, dependence upon, and business exchange with Mexicanos, along with major use of European music and paraphernalia. Almost never is the Matachines dance mentioned without invidious comparison to the Deer dance, which is said to bring more snow. Nevertheless, the Matachines's colorful beauty and infectious music are always remarked. Its opposition to and alternation with the Deer dance, perhaps the quintessential "aboriginal" dance within the Taos animal, or winter, ceremonial cycle, is significant and seems to underscore its ambivalent, ambiguous nature.

The Matachines "says" something metaphorical about the pueblo's mixed attitude toward Christianity. But this reference does not exhaust the range of possible meanings. There is also a great deal of bilateral commentary going on about the relationship between Indians and their Mexicano neighbors, in-laws, and co-participants in the dance. The performance serves as a richly nuanced cultural barometer of the year-to-year complexion of these ongoing relations. Thus even its lapse between 1988 and 1992 seems charged with unspoken meaning; it coincided with intensified litigation between Taos Pueblo and its neighbors over land and water issues, about which I will say more later. These ongoing interrelations are registered in traditional content and in year-to-year situational and idiosyncratic variation.

LAND, BLOOD TIES, AND ETHNIC BOUNDARIES

While the birth motif may parody the holy nativity, it also contains parallel subtexts that refer to paradoxes of paternity, intermarriage, miscegenation, and marital infidelity. Thus, although the pantomime can be read as a pagan's subversive mockery about the unlikelihood of virgin birth, there is also the joke about who the father really is, or about what the child or children look like—during the 1980s they tended to look like the Abuelo or "real" father, whose mask nevertheless changes from year to year. There are the Abuelos' veiled allusions to Indians, "rusty nails," and other ethnic punning, always paired with their subordination to the tribal officers. In the cases of the chimpanzee (1981) and the pinkish white (1986) and black (1992) dolls, racial references seem clear-cut, especially in light of Taos's pervasive system of racial stratification and attendant color bar.

Like certain other parts of the Southwest, metropolitan Taos exhibits a basic three-tiered system of ethnic stratification, with Indians at the bottom, Mexicanos in the middle, and Anglos on top. The local ethnic boundary system is compounded by the universal American color bar, which stratifies people automatically according to skin pigmentation and other phenotypic features but which is also crosscut and modified in major ways by class. In northern New Mexico, ethnicity is a master status that enables and constrains each individual's pattern of social access and interaction. In Taos a peculiar interethnic dynamic, which Bodine (1968) named the "tri-ethnic trap," evolved during the twentieth century as a result of several factors. These include incremental Mexicano land loss, successful Indian land claims, and Anglo control over the increasingly important tourism economy based originally on the art colony (see Rodríguez 1987, 1989). As elsewhere, different local stereotypes and attitudes attach to different ethnic groups, including Indians, Hispano/Mexicanos, Anglos, Jews, Japanese, Chinese (or the casta by that name), and African Americans, all alluded to by the Abuelos.

As shall be seen, in no other Pueblo Matachines performances do the Abuelos have a more prominent and verbal role than at Taos. The Abuelos are drawn from a mixed sector intermediate between Hispanos and Indians: intermarried couples and interethnic in-laws, compadres, *criados* (grown adopted infants), and friends. Today and within living memory they seem to have come mostly from those villages that border directly on Indian land: Arroyo Seco, El Prado, Taos, and Cañón.

Although Indians maintained active trade and other relations with non-contiguous communities such as Ranchos, Valdez, and San Cristóbal, the pueblo's most intimate contact, in terms of daily interaction as well as ongoing litigation over water and land, has been with these four bordering neighbors. Historically this contact has been a mixture of alliance and conflict, the inevitable consequences of contiguity and subsistence within the same watersheds.

The quality and intensity of these relations have no doubt changed over time. In the "old days," or several generations back, the contact seems to have been more intimate. People borrowed clothes and visited one another's homes on foot or by wagon or horseback, bringing gifts, trade goods, and food and staying overnight. Today older people on both sides lament the passing of closer, friendlier relations and comment on how distant Indians and Mexicanos have become and how little they now interact. Mexicanos involved in the pueblo's Matachines dance relate to Indians more equally and closely than many other Hispanos in similar class positions.[12] Yet racism and segregation persist, compounded by the ubiquitous dynamic of Anglo domination, alongside the old intervillage conflicts over land and water.

In each case of pueblo-neighbor relations the shared watershed is different. The town of Don Fernando de Taos shares the Río Pueblo itself, which originates at Blue Lake, bisects Taos Pueblo, and supplies the town and part of Cañón with irrigation water. The town overlaps onto the so-called "pueblo league," an old bone of contention still not laid to rest. A pueblo league or grant is a square of approximately 18,000 acres of land, 5.2 miles on a side, usually measured from the cross at the center of a pueblo's cemetery. The precise source of this measure remains nebulous, inasmuch as no original or authentic pueblo land grant documents are known to exist, even though the league forms the core of most actual Río Grande Pueblo landholdings (Hall 1987). As can be seen from map 1, Don Fernando de Taos and El Prado both encroach on the Taos Pueblo league. All of the non-Pueblo–owned lands that fall within the boundaries of the league or other Pueblo land have gone through the process of court settlement, in many cases more than once. Every tract has a history thick with litigation. So when a particular community is said to "border" on Pueblo land, this refers to actual, present-day boundaries rather than the more-or-less theoretical league boundary. The long and tortured history of Pueblo land encroachment and litigation continues today in the recurrent issue of the pueblo's claim to the streets of Taos as well as certain county roads and tracts of land.

El Prado sits on the Río Lucero, which lies north of the Río Pueblo and feeds rich meadowlands between the two communities. As late as 1978

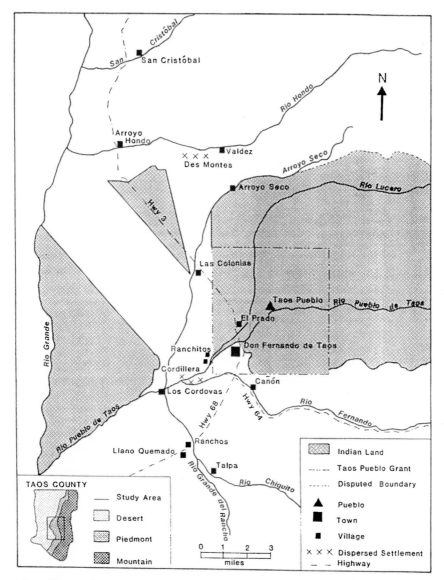

Map 1. Taos Pueblo and its neighbors — and sometime adversaries over land and water rights.

a Mexicano family was ejected from Pueblo land in El Prado along the Río Lucero. Arroyo Seco, several miles to the north, trespassed onto the Tenorio tract upstream from El Prado and diverted water in the upper Río Lucero watershed. As I will explain in the next chapter, Mexicano settlers were ejected from this land south of the El Salto road during the 1920s and 1930s. And in 1991, the pueblo won its suit for the road itself, above Arroyo Seco to El Salto. In addition to these long-standing litigations, another perennial and currently major issue is the federal and state adjudication of ownership of all water rights in the greater Taos basin (and throughout New Mexico), which pits the pueblo's claims against those of all its neighbors.[13]

Thus there are old and bittersweet ties between Taos Pueblo and its neighbors, and some of the most enduring tend to be with settlements that border or trespass on Indian land. It is also these communities that seem to have supplied a significant proportion of Mexicano participants for the Matachines dance, at least in this century, frequently individuals who are married into the pueblo, have friends there, and/or have a family history of participation.

CONCLUSION

I propose that the burlesque nativity in the Taos Matachines performance came to be enacted by an ethnically mixed sequence of Abuelos sometime prior to living memory and that it expresses, among other things, ambivalence about the bonds that both unite and divide local Indians and Mexicanos. The piquant irony of this dissonant alliance is captured by the former Abuelo's odd admonition to Malinche—"No more chile con candy"—paired with an exhortation to trick her partner, the king. These lines might have a thousand other meanings as well, although in 1994, their future seems as nebulous as their source.[14] In any case, the mere attachment of the Abuelos' farce to the Taos Pueblo Matachines helps us to interpret the overall meaning of the dance, just as it helps to create it.

The Taos Pueblo Abuelos enact an eloquent burlesque, rich in commentary about local ethnic relations as they and their instructors perceive them. This commentary takes the form of reversals. In this their performance resembles the Pueblo clowning that occurs in other ritual settings and would seem to fulfill similar multiplex expressive, equilibrating, and transformative roles (Crumrine 1969; Hieb 1972; Ortiz 1972; Babcock 1978; 1982; 1984; 1986; Handelman and Kapferer 1980; Sweet 1980; 1985; 1989). Even more significant than their obvious syncretizing of aboriginal and European components is the fact that the Abuelos are a mixture of living, intergenerational elements that ritually embody, through burlesque and their association with the Matachines dance, the very making of that mixture. But whatever their origin and despite their mostly Mexicano constituency, the ongoing character of the Taos Abuelos shows the unmistakable influence of the Pueblo clown tradition.

Alfonso Ortiz (1972:145–46) pays particular attention to the role the Pueblo clowns and other reversals play in depicting, commenting on, and symbolically containing such socially dissonant circumstances as deviance, internal breaches, and relations with other groups. Indeed, symbolic reversal would seem to constitute the very idiom in which the socially problematical is actively rendered in Pueblo ritual: burlesque that simultaneously mocks the sacred and fulfills a multitude of adaptive and expressive needs in the process. The meanings inherent in any given instance of reversal are multivocal and contradictory, and they draw their substance as much from the particulars of everyday life as from the verities of ancient myth. Thus Pueblo clowns enact all manner of bizarre and forbidden scenarios, ritually juxtaposing the obscene with the sacrosanct. They parody outside groups, including different tribes and a wide variety of non-Indian social others encountered in contemporary life.

Anthropologists and others describe Pueblo society as egalitarian, at least in contrast to "white man's" society, even though the internal workings of Pueblo society are shaped by the inequities that result from its subordinate, peripheral, yet incorporated position in the world system. The Matachines dance is of interest because it embodies both the historical and the living intersection of these two societies. Drawing on Pueblo (mostly Zuni) clown materials, Louis Hieb (1972:192) proposes that whereas caste societies or those structured by inequality create *communitas* through reversals resulting in symbolic equality, egalitarian or clan societies generate *communitas* through "symbolic inequality in which the ritual clown reverses, inverts, and transposes the normal patterns in such a way that humor and laughter are a result." In the case of the Taos Pueblo

Matachines, both kinds of society are involved, and both equality and inequality are symbolically reversed and commented upon by the clowns' machinations.

Like the Mexicano musicians, the Abuelos reverse the local order by working for the Indians rather than the other way around, although it is uniquely their charge to traffic in reversals throughout. They are subordinated to the governor's staff and yet make fun of them, and they routinely protect the solemn religious meaning of the dance while they subvert it. There is constant tension between the pueblo's authoritative structuring of the event and the creative license enjoyed by the Abuelos to embroider their own subtext onto the ritual whole. Again, ironically, the reversal is compounded because the Indianized Hispanics are the clowns while the Hispanicized Indians are "the system." This jarring intersection of Indian and Hispano worlds, and the myriad mestizo complexities it continuously gives birth to, serve as both inspiration and medium for the clowns' expression.

John Robb (1961:93) notes that humor and clowns are a universal element of the Matachines and related ritual dances. Nevertheless, there is considerable intervillage variation in the number, character, and prominence of the Abuelos. In some villages they give vocal or other signals but are not verbal and rarely if ever utter stock phrases. Taos Pueblo may be the only place, besides Arroyo Seco, where the Abuelos recite such lines. Nevertheless, the clowns may not necessarily be the only or even the primary vehicle for the hidden transcript or local level of meaning. As shall be seen in chapter 5, in some villages the role recedes into a circumspect presence.

A skit very similar to the Taos birth burlesque is seen in nearby Arroyo Seco and is said to have been enacted years ago at Picurís Pueblo. These cases are examined in the following two chapters. Why does the Taos region show such strong emphasis on clowning and Perejundias? As shall be seen, not all traditions share this emphasis. Perhaps their importance reflects the intense and intimate character of Indo-Hispano relations in this rugged, isolated corner of the upper Rio Grande valley.

3 · ARROYO SECO
Defended Boundaries, Precarious Elites

rroyo Seco is a community of some eight hundred people, well over half of whom are Spanish speaking. It lies approximately six miles north of Taos Pueblo and eight miles north of the town of Don Fernando de Taos (map 2). According to archival sources, Arroyo Seco was established in 1815 by landless families pushed north from the burgeoning center of Don Fernando de Taos. Unlike nearby Arroyo Hondo and Valdez, Arroyo Seco was not an official land grant community. As a result, many of its residents seem to have suffered from a perennially embattled, semisquatter legal status from the beginning. Arroyo Seco is located along the northwest edge of the Antonio Martínez land grant, which the notorious British land swindler Arthur Manby tried to acquire earlier in this century (Waters 1973).

The placita sits close to the Río del Arroyo Seco, a tiny tributary of the Río Grande that lies north of the Río Lucero and south of the Río Hondo. Because this meager stream has never provided enough water to meet the needs of the entire Arroyo Seco population, over the years settlers have exerted claims, with varying degrees of success, to use rights on the neighboring *ríos*. Arroyo Seco once occupied land south of the closely parallel road and river, and its inhabitants diverted waters north from the Río Lucero to irrigate their crops. In the 1920s and 1930s, Taos Pueblo reclaimed this land, known as the Tenorio tract, and a number of Hispano families were ejected from it. Today most of this land remains undeveloped, punctuated with occasional melted adobe ruins that serve as reminders of bygone occupation.[1]

Arroyo Seco enjoys a certain prominence because it is the seat of the Holy Trinity parish and the consolidated local grade school and because it sits directly on the main route to a major ski resort. Today the village core consists of a cluster of buildings around the old placita, including

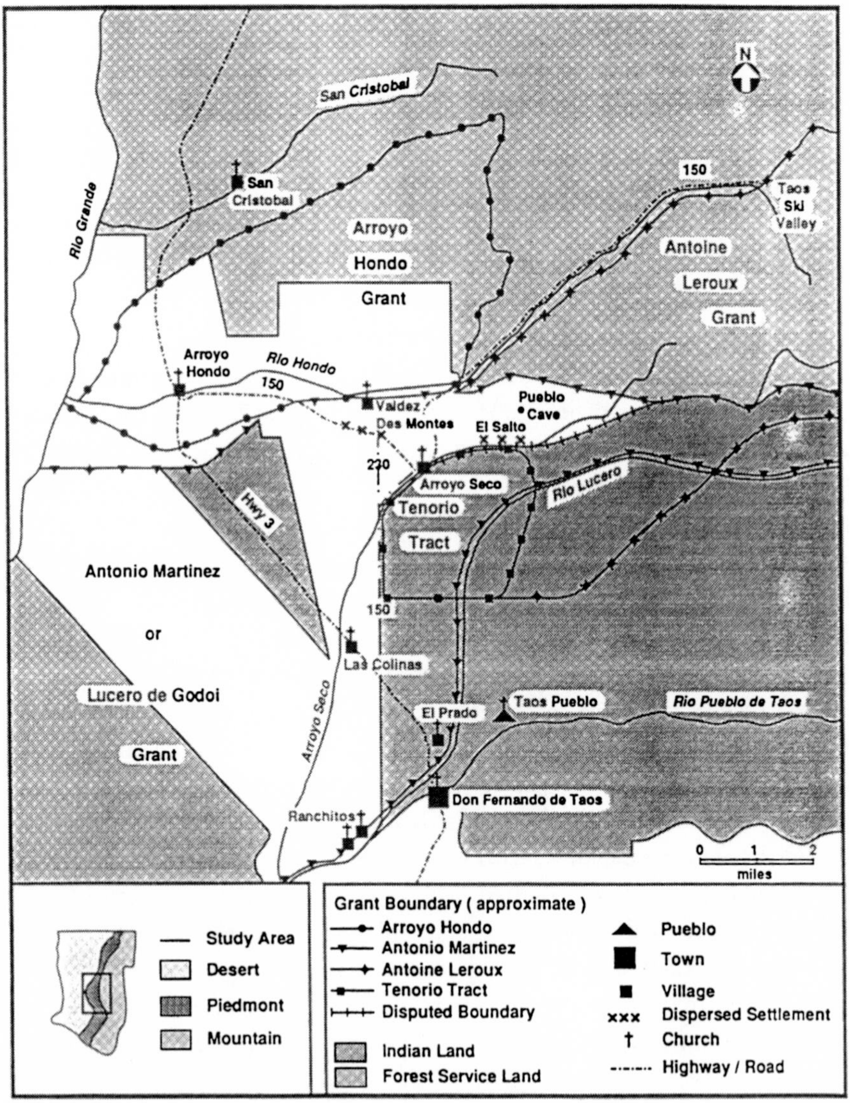
N
San Cristobal
San Cristobal
Rio Grande
150
Taos Ski Valley
Arroyo Hondo Grant
Antoine Leroux Grant
Arroyo Hondo
Rio Hondo
150
Valdez
Des Montes
Pueblo Cave
El Salto
230
Arroyo Seco
Rio Lucero
Tenorio Tract
Hwy 3
Antonio Martinez or Lucero de Godoi Grant
150
Las Colinas
Arroyo Seco
El Prado
Taos Pueblo
Rio Pueblo de Taos
Don Fernando de Taos
Ranchitos
0 1 2
miles
Study Area
Desert
Piedmont
Mountain
Grant Boundary (approximate)
Arroyo Hondo
Antonio Martinez
Antoine Leroux
Tenorio Tract
Disputed Boundary
Indian Land
Forest Service Land
Pueblo
Town
Village
Dispersed Settlement
Church
Highway / Road

Map 2. Landownership around the village of Arroyo Seco, New Mexico.

houses, the old and new churches, the post office, a cantina, a few stores, and the school. "Downtown" Arroyo Seco faces onto the road that now leads to Taos Ski Valley. It has begun to show visible architectural evidence of the progressive resort-engendered gentrification process that is rapidly transforming metropolitan Taos.

The Holy Trinity parish contains four other missions or chapels: one at Las Colonias (Santo Niño de Atocha), one at Valdez (San Antonio), one at Arroyo Hondo (Nuestra Señora de los Dolores), and one at San Cristóbal. Except for San Cristóbal, which sits on its own creek some nine miles to the north, these villages and the dispersed settlement of Des Montes all lie within the Río Hondo watershed. Each has its own character, as well as a particular relationship with each of its neighbors.

Arroyo Seco's closest neighbors are upper Des Montes and Valdez, both of which depend on the Río Hondo. Des Montes is a dispersed, unnucleated settlement scattered westward along well-drained table lands between Arroyo Seco and Arroyo Hondo. Valdez (originally San Antonio) is a placita established in a deep valley along the Río Hondo, upstream from its sister community of Arroyo Hondo, the original parish seat. Both Valdez and Arroyo Hondo have chapels, placitas, and now-defunct moradas.[2] They are linked via the river that feeds their irrigation ditch, or acequia, system. Over the years Arroyo Seco has competed with Taos Pueblo as well as with El Prado for water in the Río Lucero, and with Valdez and Des Montes for water from the Río Hondo.

Thus, within the matrix of neighboring communities, which includes Taos Pueblo, Arroyo Seco has always had to defend its fragile land base and water supply. In recent decades new developments have exacerbated old pressures, and the community has responded in a manner that reflects its peculiar internal composition and external circumstances. It was within this context of resort development and intensifying demographic pressures upon limited land and water that Arroyo Seco revived the Matachines dance.

THE ARROYO SECO TRADITION AND 1985 REVIVAL

The Holy Trinity parish seems not to have supported a continuous Matachines tradition during most of the twentieth century. Cleofas Jaramillo, writing about Arroyo Hondo during the late nineteenth century

(1974 [1941]: 49, 1955:24–25), describes the Matachines as having been danced in the plaza and in front of people's houses on the village feast day in late November. In 1986, a woman then in her late seventies remembered seeing it danced in front of the church in Valdez, probably during the 1910s (see chapter 2, note 12). Arroyo Seco has held the Matachines only intermittently since the 1920s. By 1929 it had evidently not been performed regularly for a number of years; it was performed in 1929 and again in 1934. After 1934 it lapsed until its revival in 1985. It was again performed in 1986 and 1987. Although evidently performed for a private occasion in 1993, the dance has not become a regular community event.

The traditional date for the Arroyo Seco performance apparently was New Year's Day, a week after the dance was performed at Taos Pueblo. In "the old days," the two communities shared costume items and some personnel, including musicians and dancers, as well as certain clown routines. In 1929, for example, a man from Arroyo Seco played the part of El Toro in both communities; he was nicknamed "Torito" for his regular rendition of the role at Taos Pueblo.

The 1985–86 revival occurred during a period when other, similar parish-based folk revivals were taking place in the general Taos area. These revivals were more or less contemporaneous with grassroots ethnopolitical mobilizations around issues of community water control. One question the Arroyo Seco revival raises is whether these two movements represent alternative, competitive, or mutually reinforcing forms of ethnocultural mobilization. In any case, they occurred at a time when economic change and demographic pressure on land and water intensified the selective symbolizing of ethnic boundaries in central Taos county.

The Matachines revival was instigated by a local schoolteacher who worked within the supportive framework of his large extended family and under the auspices of the local parish priest. Although its active social base was primarily restricted to one extended family, the popular appeal of the revival spread throughout and beyond the parish. The idea of reviving the Matachines had apparently been a longtime dream of the schoolteacher's mother. His father is a rancher who, along with his brothers, owns and occupies large tracts of irrigated land on the north bank of the Río del Arroyo Seco in El Salto.

El Salto is an area located along the arable incline between the Arroyo Seco placita and the mountains. The name, which means "waterfall," refers to the cave and gushing spring nestled high in the side of a hill, sacred to, and claimed by, both Taos Pueblo and Arroyo Seco. During the 1970s and 1980s, El Salto became a popular home site for middle-class as well as very wealthy "amenity migrants," including second-home owners, drawn to the Arroyo Seco area because of its spectacular vistas and proximity to Taos Ski Valley (Moss 1991; Rodríguez 1994). El Salto is reached by a narrow road that veers off the highway near the placita, follows the river, and ends after a few miles at the edge of the wilderness, where private property gives way to Indian and U.S. Forest Service land.

All land south of the road belongs to Taos Pueblo. It is fenced, posted, and the boundary surreptitiously patrolled by the war captain's staff. Several Pueblo families maintain summer *ranchitos* in the area. North of the road and river lie private lands owned by longtime ranching families, amenity migrants, and seasonal residents. At least two corporate luxury retreats also lie within this area.

In 1987, Taos Pueblo renewed its old claim to the strip of land that includes the road and extends to the midpoint of the Río del Arroyo Seco. This posed a major threat to all non-Indian residents of El Salto, most of whose driveways also lie within the contested zone. The Pueblo claim was upheld in court, and ultimately the county and federal governments worked out a final settlement of $375,000 to be paid to the tribe for public access in perpetuity to the El Salto strip. For families still bitter over the Tenorio tract ejections of the 1920s and 1930s, the 1990s El Salto suit reinflicted injury to an old, deep wound.

Why is all this history, geography, and hydrology relevant to the 1985 Arroyo Seco Matachines revival? It is relevant because of who organized it and what their position was vis-à-vis other constituencies within the watershed and parish. Even though the pueblo's El Salto suit occurred after the parish revival, it had been brewing for several years, and like the controversy surrounding uncontrolled resort development in the Río Hondo watershed, it constituted an important part of the social climate within which the Matachines dance reemerged. I will return to this larger context later.

The revival effort began with practice sessions at the organizer's parental home, involving family members who served as the musicians and majority of dancers—although it gradually grew into a community project. The organizer's maternal uncle and cousin played the music, and his parents, siblings, and other cousins made up most of the dancers. Only three participants had performed before: the elderly violinist (who had been a danzante in 1929), the 1934 Monarca, and a man who had been the Toro in 1934. The 1934 Monarca, who danced the role again in 1985–86, taught the dance steps to the schoolteacher, who in turn instructed others. Both the Monarca and the fiddler were the teacher-director's uncles. His cousin, another key collaborator, played the Abuela or Perejundia. Interestingly, this cousin's elderly mother, the director's aunt, now a retired schoolteacher, had taught Arroyo Seco students the dance in 1934.[3] In addition to their memories, the musicians apparently drew on tape recordings and records of various versions of the Matachines music. Finally, the director prepared a special instructional audiotape with narration and music and distributed copies to the dancers as practice aids.

The dance was first performed publicly on June 6, 1985, as part of a celebration commemorating the thirtieth anniversary of the ordination of the parish priest, Father Conran Runnebaum. It was part of a day-long celebration held outdoors at the organizer's family home, and it also featured refreshments and the performance of a satirical skit based on the priest's life. The festivity was a major community affair attended even by the archbishop of Santa Fe at that time, Robert F. Sánchez.

The Matachines was performed again after morning mass on New Year's Day, 1986, in front of the modern Holy Trinity church in Arroyo Seco. The dress rehearsal was held two nights before, inside the old church of Nuestra Señora de los Dolores in Arroyo Hondo, where it was privately videotaped by members of the director's family against the backdrop of the recently restored *reredos,* or altar screens. The holiday celebration was part of a parishwide series of events that included a Christmas season revival of the folk dramas *Los Pastores, Los Reyes Magos,* and *El Niño Perdido.* These, too, were organized by the young schoolteacher from El Salto and enlisted many participants from other villages within the parish.

The dance was next performed publicly at a folk music festival in June 1987 at the Museum of International Folk Art in Santa Fe, where it was photographed by museum personnel. A children's version was held in the Taos community auditorium and in Arroyo Seco just before Christmas 1987. Taos high-school students performed the dance during Lent 1990 as part of a deluxe staging of Los Moros y Cristianos under the direction of the same schoolteacher, and again in 1992 at a national conference in Albuquerque.

Although non-kin, including the Abuelo from Arroyo Hondo, partici- pated in the 1985–86 revival, it was still largely a family affair. This seems underscored by the fact that the musicians for the Taos Pueblo Matachines, who are from Des Montes, did not participate. Perhaps the enormous task of community revival after so many years could only have been accom- plished through the close-knit workings of familial organization operating under parish auspices, providing optimal conditions for a guaranteed and well-supplied support system.

The revived Arroyo Seco performance remains intermittent, owing in part to attrition, including the deaths of the violinist and the young man who played the Abuelo.[4] The dance was performed again in July 1993 for the occasion of a local family reunion. In the meantime, the director taught it to several high-school classes in town, who performed it publicly on an occasional basis. Thus the Arroyo Seco version is kept alive by this teacher through his students while remaining latently available for special performance by his extended kin within the parish.

THE DANCE

Unlike the procedure observed in most communities, during its revival the entire Arroyo Seco dance sequence was performed just once on each occasion, instead of being repeated several times over the course of one or more days. Perhaps because it has been executed on special occasions and has not become routinized with a regular date or place, there has been variation in how the Arroyo Seco version is ritually framed. For example, on New Year's Day, 1986, when it was performed after mass in front of the church, old mission bultos, or traditional wooden *santos,* were placed on a table at one end of the arena to oversee the dance, a practice common in Hispanic villages and certain pueblos. This was not done for the more secular June performance or later at the Santa Fe folk art museum, whereas the saints were "automatically" present during the Christmas 1985 dress rehearsal videotaped inside the Arroyo Hondo church.

With each performance, the production, narration, and certain cos- tume items became more polished. For example, in the original June 1985 performance, the Abuelos wore commercial masks, but by New Year's Day they had been given well-crafted handmade masks by a Latino theater group. Similarly, in June the bull, with candy-stripe foresticks, wore an artificial tan hide with large painted eyes, but on New Year's Day he wore a buffalo robe loaned by a prominent Taos Pueblo man. Because of the purely religious context of the winter production, the director placed restrictions on photography of the performance. Evidently this was related to his perception of the degree of sacredness of the setting and traditional date, which was signaled by the presence of the saints. Most pueblos and all other Mexicano communities known to me permit the Matachines to be photographed. But whereas anyone was allowed to take snapshots during the June 1985 performance, and a professional (an Anglo married to an Arroyo Seco woman) was enlisted to make a videotape of the entire occasion, not even the parishioners were permitted to photograph on New Year's Day, and only one "official" videotape was made—that of the dress rehearsal.

The Arroyo Seco Matachines contains roughly the same sets or movements seen in other Río Grande versions. Its dramatic content closely resembles that of the version danced at Taos Pueblo, although the exact set sequence and overall style differ. There are twelve matachines, or danzantes, accompanied by La Malinche, El Monarca, El Toro, and two Abuelos, one of whom is a male transvestite. The following account is based upon observation of the June 1985 and New Year's Day 1986 performances, in addition to secondary materials. These sources support a description that is analytic, historically specific, and comparative. In order to articulate these perspectives, my discussion will move between past and present tenses. The past tense locates behavior in time, whereas the present tense pursues the analysis and refers to recent observation.

The Arroyo Seco performance contains eight movements, in addition to the opening marcha. Five tunes are played, some for more than one set. As at Taos Pueblo, the first three sets in the Arroyo Seco version are called La Malinche, El Monarca, and La Corona. The first involves an escort of the little girl by the Abuelos and her exchange of palma and guaje with Monarca and their dance together. It is followed by Monarca's dance between the two rows of danzantes. The Arroyo Seco corona segment has two parts; in the first, Monarca dances beneath a canopy of upheld palmas, and in the second he dances over palmas held toward the ground by the genuflecting

matachines. Next, in *La Mudada* (the change), El Monarca leads the danzantes in a series of interweavings, crossovers, and returns between the two
rows. This is followed by *La Tejida* (Maypole) and then by the segment
known as El Toro, in which the Abuelos scuffle with the Toro and finally
castrate him, as they do at Taos Pueblo. The drama culminates in *Abuelito
de la Sierra,* in which the Perejundia goes into sudden, violent labor and
gives birth to a doll (in 1985–86, an orange-haired troll) that is then mock-
baptized with "padrinos" from the audience. Last comes *La Despedida,* or
the dancers' recessional marcha.

Several details of costume and structure in the Arroyo Seco version are
distinctive. Both Abuelos in 1985–86 dressed in long black clerical coats.
The obviously pregnant transvestite wore long dark braids and heavy boots
with bare legs. The Abuelo wore a big black hat and used a stethoscope in
addition to the customary whip. Both were masked. The danzantes wore
white shirts and black pants, like those worn in Bernalillo. Their cupiles
and pale blue, apronlike *tapa rabos* were decorated with glitter, and they
wore white tennis shoes. In 1985–86, eight of the twelve danzantes were
women, including the director's mother and other kin, dressed just like
the men. This modern innovation was pioneered at Bernalillo and is now
found in a few other Hispanic versions but is not accepted at any pueblo.

The most unusual feature of the 1985–86 Arroyo Seco Matachines was
that during the performance, the organizer-narrator, dressed in either a
cape or a monk's robe, stood among the dancers and delivered an exegesis
of the history and meaning of the dance, set by set. This narrative act is
without parallel in other villages (notwithstanding the El Rancho Abuelo's
routine described in chapter 5). It was delivered more or less extemporane-
ously, with dramatic intonation and some variation among performances.
This feature, taken with the fact that schoolteachers seem to have become
custodians of the Arroyo Seco tradition, suggests that Arroyo Seco has
evolved an explicitly didactic adaptation of the dance.

The centrality of the narrator's role means that unlike most cases, where
little native explanation is typical, in Arroyo Seco the audience and participants are provided with an elaborate, formal explication of what the dance
is about. This text is therefore an important part of the contemporary performance. It draws on a variety of sources well beyond local oral tradition,
and it represents the director's own creative synthesis. He has produced
both oral and written texts about the Matachines dance.

Before proceeding to the director's text, I will note a few similarities between the Arroyo Seco and the Taos Pueblo versions. For one thing, the Toro sequence closely resembles the same sequence as performed at Taos Pueblo. The Perejundia birth episode also closely resembles the birth skit done at Taos Pueblo, except that in Arroyo Seco it involves special music. Another feature this Matachines shares with Taos Pueblo's is the stock phrase uttered by the Abuelo while Malinche and Monarca execute their palma-guaje exchange: "¡Engáñalo! ¡Engáñalo, mijita, engáñalo!" (Deceive him! Deceive him, my child, deceive him!)

Differences between the two neighboring performances are also apparent. For example, the Abuelos are even more vocal than those in the dance at Taos Pueblo, and their skirmishing and pantomime make up a significant part of almost every set. The Arroyo Seco Toro is also considerably more vigorous and vocal than the Toro at Taos Pueblo, appearing in more than one set and often mooing loudly to the music. The noise the Toro makes, along with the Abuelos' shouting, competes at moments with the impresario's narration.

NATIVE EXEGESIS

The following history of the dance, authored by the schoolteacher-director, was printed in the six-page typescript program for June 6, 1985:

> The dance of Los Matachines is [a] very old tradition in the Hispanic Southwest. It originated in Spain toward the beginning of the Renaissance and commemorated as well as chronicled a great event of that era. Spain is a country occupying two thirds of the Iberian peninsula that has its roots steeped deeply in Roman-Catholic tradition. This heritage was threatened in the year 711 when Emir Ben-Usif of the north African coast invaded Spain and occupied it in a reign that was to last over 700 years. Almost immediately Spain began a revolt against the Moslem invaders. One of the most famous battles, La Batalla de Covadonga, occurred a short seven years afterwards, when Pelayo de Asturias made a brave stance. Of course this internal resistance continued throughout the centuries involving such colorful people as don Rodrigo Díaz de Bivar, known to history as El Cid.
>
> In 1492 the last Moorish stronghold fell back into Christian hands. The southernmost region of Spain, where this occurred, is named Anda-

lucia: so named for the Germanic Vandals who invaded the area early in Spain's history. It is here that the city of Granada is found. Just north of it is the town of Santa Fe, where the play Los Moros y Los Cristianos was first penned.

The play is fascinating primarily because its main character is the Moorish prince Selín. According to tradition, he captured and tormented some Christians in [an] effort to shake their faith. Instead, he was so moved by their fervour that he converted to Christianity. The Spanish conquerors brought this play to Mexico and presented it to the Indians in 1530, the object of course being that the Indians too would take a lesson from Selín and convert to Christianity. The message failed . . . the Spaniards had overlooked one minor detail: The Indians didn't understand Spanish. They were, however, pleased by the colorful costumes and headdresses. The Indians soon learned to imitate the ritual, but for centuries, the meaning was lost.

The following account of the dance movements is based upon observation, paraphrase, and direct quotation of a videotape of the first community performance on June 6, 1985. It also draws on published materials by the director, who writes a Spanish column on local Hispano lore in the Taos newspaper, a selection of which has been published as a book (Torres 1992). Because of its composite nature and the fact that the videotape provides a consultable visual record, I render this account in the present tense. Direct quotations and exegesis are from the videotape.

1. *La Marcha.* The musicians and other performers proceed into the dance arena and assume their beginning positions.

2. *La Malinche.* "Malinche is Moctezuma's bride, spurned by Cortés, who later became La Llorona." Holding his palma, she rotates her right arm around his extended left arm while the Abuelo advises her, "¡Engáñalo mijita, engáñalo!" translated as, "Play him for the fool!"

3. *El Monarca.* Monarca stands for both Moctezuma (Montezuma) and the Moorish king. In his dance he marches up and down between the two rows of "bishops" and "tries to reassert his power" over them.

4. *La Corona* has two parts: in the first the Monarca is "crowned" as he dances beneath a canopy of palmas held between the danzantes; in the second he "overcomes his enemies" by jumping between the downwardly extended palmas of the genuflecting matachines. On the sidelines, the Abuelos skirmish with each other and the Toro. "The Indians had a neat way of dealing with the crown, to whom they said, 'yes,

yes, yes, yes,' but did what they pleased when the Church wasn't looking. Monarca tries to reassert his claim to the throne, but when he looks away they get even."

5. *La Mudada* is the longest movement, in which Monarca, Malinche, and the matachines interweave the two rows of dancers while the Toro and Abuelos continue to frolic in the margins. In the first part the Monarca leads all the dancers in exchanging places; in the second part they return to their original positions. The matachines do a kick step. The director shouts out instructions such as "¡Vuelta!" and explains, "The absent overlord tries to re-organize his empire; he has subjugated the Toltecs, Mixtecs, every other kind of -tecs, but they go back to being what they were." [5]

6. *La Tejida* (Maypole) was "originally performed only at the beginning of the new year, which was at the beginning of April. Originally the new year began in April; when it was changed the new year moved to 1 January. Those who persisted in celebrating the spring new year were called fools, hence 'April Fools!' "

7. *El Toro.* The Toro becomes enraged and charges the Abuelos, who wrestle him down, castrate him, and then run off. In this movement the Abuelo listens with a stethoscope to the Abuela's bulging stomach in gleeful anticipation.

8. *Abuelito de la Sierra.* The Perejundia goes into paroxysms of labor and is delivered of an orange-haired troll doll proudly displayed by the "father." The "Abuelito" represents the new year. The Abuelos then dance together and pull "padrinos" from the audience for the baptism. The matachines remain in formation while the Abuelo dances with the doll to the marcha.

9. *La Despedida.* The Abuelos lead the two rows of dancers away in the recessional march.

ANALYSIS

There are several factors to be considered with respect to the problem of meaning in the Arroyo Seco Matachines. To begin with, the audience receives an explicit exegesis of its meaning and history during the performance. The director's narrative is thus part of the text to be analyzed. It yields insight into the fundamental oppositional structure of the dance. The director's account focuses on the conflict between Christian soldiers and the Moorish king, who is also Moctezuma. Malinche is "Moctezuma's bride, spurned by Cortés, who later became La Llorona." In the corona segment, Moctezuma is first "crowned" by the palmas and then "overcomes his enemies" by jumping over the palmas while their bearers kneel. Here, and with reference to positional changes in the mudada segment, the narrator emphasizes the theme of the Indians' stubborn yet indirect resistance to authority.

The Arroyo Seco Matachines shares with the Taos Pueblo version a structure whereby a social paradox is joked about: authority is surrendered to and mocked simultaneously, both within and around the metaphorical text of the dance. As seen in the previous chapter, this is acted out in the Taos Pueblo version between the Abuelos and the other dancers, the tribal governor's staff, and the audience, around themes of miscegenation and conflict. In Arroyo Seco, the burlesque nativity is present and Indians are alluded to, but the miscegenation motif so central at Taos Pueblo seems offset by other concerns. For example, the Perejundia is portrayed as an Indian (suggested by the dark braids) who gives birth to a weird-looking child, but like the Abuelo (also a doctor), she is dressed as a cleric. In addition to a riot of other elements, the Abuelos represent the Catholic church.

In the Arroyo Seco Matachines, opposition is acted out between solidary egalitarian relations, or *communitas,* on the one hand and hierarchy on the other. This is reflected in the organizer's exegetical line: Indians go back to being the way they were as soon as the overlord looks the other way. Just as the Indians/matachines revert when Monarca or the priest turns his back, so do the Abuelos and bull "go wild" during the dance while the director tries to keep things moving in an orderly fashion. The opposition/identification involving priest and Indians is thus paralleled in the contest between the raucous clowns and bull, who create chaos, and the impresario-narrator, who imposes order through direction and story line.

Three levels of community relations must be considered in deciphering the social meaning of the dance: those within the community, those between the community and its neighbors, and those between the community and external powers. Like the Taos Pueblo dance, the Arroyo Seco Matachines exhibits an oppositional structure, although the precise foci of opposition are not the same. Arroyo Seco contains its own internal contradictions, compounded by neighboring rivalries and external power relations, and all these are reflected in the idiosyncratic way the village does the dance. The revived Arroyo Seco dance seems to embody a tension between consensus and equality on the one hand and submission to elite authority on the other. The implicit consensus, sustained largely within one extended family, consists in the participants' submission to the individualized authority of the director in a friendly spirit of group cooperation, a collective act sanctioned by the church.

The inherent tension between those in power and those they must control is further attested to by the very nature of the occasion on which the dance was initially revived: the thirtieth anniversary of the parish priest's ordination. On this day the Matachines dance was followed by a comic skit, also narrated by the director (dressed in a Franciscan robe), involving a plot about the priest's ambitious climb from childhood bully (based upon an allegedly true biographical episode in which he picked on his younger sister) up through the ecclesiastical ranks to pope. Musical accompaniment for the skit consisted of guitars and a chorus sung to the tune of "Davy Crockett"/"Pancho López." The skit rendered into a comical anecdote one of the personal traits many parishioners privately noticed in the priest. It dressed personal criticism in the beguiling garb of praise and humor.

The late springtime holiday afforded an ideal opportunity to stage the revival. It assured the priest's support while effectively removing him from any direct supervisory role, which was ably filled by the dance director. The dance director stands at both ends of the equality/hierarchy continuum, depending on one's viewpoint. On the one hand, he represents the egalitarian parish congregation (vis-à-vis the priest) and affirms insubordination by describing it in his narrative. On the other hand, his impresario role (vis-à-vis the dance company and audience) is singular and authoritarian. It is noteworthy that the director has belonged to the Arroyo Seco morada for most of his life and serves as its Custodian of All Record. This linkage between the Matachines dance and the *Hermanos,* or Penitentes, surfaces elsewhere (e.g., Picurís Pueblo, Alcalde, Bernalillo, San José in Albuquerque). In any case, the overlap between dance directorship and role of Hermano is significant and underscores both the authoritarian and counterauthoritarian aspects of his position.[6]

The familial exclusivity of the Arroyo Seco Matachines revival and its concentration of leadership in a single individual symbolically enforces status boundaries within Arroyo Seco, as well as boundaries between Arroyo Seco and its neighbors. Part of what is striking about this combination is that it assumes the form of a cultural revival. It thus constitutes a symbolic assertion of Hispano ethnic identity at the community level.

FAMILY POSITIONALITY

Both sides of the director's family occupy prominent positions in Arroyo Seco. Among the larger landowners in the El Salto area, they are major *parciantes,* or water rights owners, and active participants on the local acequia, or irrigation ditch, commission. In addition to farmer-ranchers, the family includes several schoolteachers, two county extension agents, and other government workers. They are active members of the Holy Trinity parish with cordial and sometimes close social ties to the local rectory (such as between the dance director and parish priest). A number of individuals within this family wield considerable local influence.

Two aspects of this influence have bearing on the Matachines revival as a symbolic assertion of community boundaries. One aspect involves their role in the boundary dispute between El Salto landowners and Taos Pueblo over the strip of land containing the road and the south bank of the Río del Arroyo Seco. Some in the dance director's ancestral family were among those ejected from the Tenorio tract roughly sixty years earlier. Along with everyone else on the north bank, they were again implicated in the pueblo's 1980s litigation over El Salto road. The other aspect of this family's influence involves its role in suppressing Arroyo Seco participation in the grassroots protest movement against accelerating resort development in the Río Hondo watershed. Whereas the first instance concerns territorial boundaries vis-à-vis Taos Pueblo, the second involves boundaries vis-à-vis Anglo encroachment.

One incident illustrates the Matachines director's agnatic family position in the Arroyo Seco–Taos Pueblo land dispute. During the 1980s one of his father's brothers built an ostentatious stone gateway, inscribed with the family name, on a corner of land that sits inside his fence line on the river's *south* bank. This gesture implied an assertion of both ownership (vis-à-vis Taos Pueblo) and status (vis-à-vis other neighbors).

Another incident some years after the revival reveals something about the director's attitude toward the pueblo and vice versa. In his Spanish language and folklore column in the Taos newspaper, he published a piece about the Taos Pueblo San Gerónimo fiesta, which is celebrated annually at Taos Pueblo on the last day of September (Torres 1990). He related how a brief childhood encounter with the "chufunetes" or sacred clowns (who are out in force for San Gerónimo) had resulted in a nightmare he still suffers from and kept him away from the pueblo for thirty years. The article went on to present a novel history of the Taos tribe and to recount the life of St. Jerome. The following week a letter to the editor from a Taos Pueblo woman criticized the article for its historical inaccuracy and "erroneous derogation" of Pueblo religion and stated that her people hold the clowns in high regard (*Taos News,* 4 October 1990).

These episodes reveal the schoolteacher's family's social distance not only from the Indians but also, implicitly, from those Mexicanos likely to interface most closely with them. This is not to say, however, that the conflict or tension expressed in such instances is necessarily conscious or deliberate on the part of the individuals involved. On the contrary, local Hispanos tend explicitly to emphasize the more harmonious aspects of their relations with Taos Pueblo.[7] Indeed, the highly symbolic forms these expressions of tension take attest to its obliqueness.

Equally significant but perhaps more deliberate is this family's role in asserting ethnic boundaries vis-à-vis resort encroachment. In the late 1950s a private "Anglo"-owned company established a ski resort at the very head of the Río Hondo, directly upstream from Valdez and Arroyo Hondo, to the north of Arroyo Seco. Ski industry expansion and secondary real estate development have since produced significant ecological, economic, and social changes within the watershed. During the 1970s and early 1980s, downstream water users criticized the resort for polluting the river with sewage and protested its proposed expansion. Nonetheless, the resort has grown, resulting in an escalating market in water rights and irrigated and undeveloped land in the watershed. Acre feet of water rights now sell at higher and higher prices, and an increasing proportion of previously irrigated farmland is devoted to resort and second home development. Locals are unnerved by the large influx of transient and semipermanent Anglo amenity migrants who ski, start businesses, and buy or build houses, yet they express hope that these changes will result in economic prosperity for the region. But despite the proliferation of tourist enterprises and real estate activity around Taos, unemployment has remained consistently high since 1970, increasing in the late 1980s after the demise of molybdenum mining in the northern part of the county.

Organized protest against the ski valley in the Hondo watershed dates from around 1974, when the resort had been seriously polluting the river for several years. Downstream water users, including ditch officers and their families as well as Chicano youth and Anglo environmentalists, joined forces to stop the resort's proposed construction of a "700-pillow" commercial complex at the head of the canyon. This alliance persisted through another eight years of litigation, finally forcing the state and federal governments to enforce their own clean water standards. This happened only after the protesters escalated their tactics by conducting mass demonstrations and picketing the entry to the ski valley.

The peak of community mobilization against resort development in the Hondo watershed took place in 1981–82, when the demonstrations were held at the ski valley and the so-called "condo war" broke out in Valdez. The condo war was a grassroots rural protest that succeeded in stopping a large condominium development in the upper Valdez valley. The protesters subsequently worked to create a special zoning district that included Valdez, Arroyo Hondo, and even San Cristóbal—but not Arroyo Seco or Des Montes. (Neither of these communities could muster enough internal support to join.) The intent of the district, which was promptly challenged by an out-of-state development corporation and which was, on appeal, declared unconstitutional, was to protect traditional agricultural patterns of land and water use and to curtail rapid, uncontrolled development of subdivisions, condominiums, and other luxury multifamily dwellings and spas. Although active or consistent support for community zoning existed among at least some old families in Des Montes, nothing of the kind was to be found in Arroyo Seco, although the zoning issue was heatedly discussed at numerous community meetings.

A few Arroyo Seco residents have joined the Río Hondo protest over the years, but a lack of internal consensus on the matter has consistently prevailed at the level of public community discourse. Thus "the community" of Arroyo Seco, or any significant proportion of it, has never even tacitly endorsed the protest, much less publicly opposed increasing resort expansion within the watershed. This is not to say that a poll of every household would reveal universal approval of increased tourism development. It seems, however, that the most vocal opinion leaders do voice assent within the forum of community meetings, thereby effectively suppressing dissent.

These vocal opinion leaders tend to be middle-aged or older Hispanos from several prominent, politically conservative, land-rich families, and they are adamantly opposed to zoning and any other form of protest against resort development. Because they own, and still irrigate, significant tracts of land, these families remain active participants in the community acequia system. They tend to be active in the parish and, in some cases, the local morada as well. Yet unlike other staunch parciantes in neighboring settlements, who do choose to mobilize in protest against resort development, these individuals argue in favor of "progress" and the new jobs and economic growth more tourism allegedly will create. They themselves are not usually involved in tourism development. The market value of their property, however, has increased astronomically in recent years, and they see tourism development as perhaps eventually the only way to make a good living from their land in the future.

The precise sociological nature of the difference between families who quietly approve of, organize, or join the protest against development and those who quietly or actively oppose these protests is not always easy to pinpoint. It has as much to do with class orientation as with simple class position, because in purely material terms, most rural Hispano community members could be categorized as either working class, lower middle class, or middle class. Protesters as well as pro-growth advocates come from all three levels. Although it might be generally true that protest sympathizers tend to be liberal Democrats, some prominent Taos area protest leaders have been Republicans, Protestants, or even Mormons, in contrast to the more common pattern of being Democrat and Catholic. What one can say is that the "conservative," pro-development, antiprotest factions in local communities tend to be middle class, moderately well educated, business oriented, and struggling to maintain upward mobility. They are culturally conservative, sometimes Republican, and strongly Catholic. A significant proportion of them, especially the opinion leaders, belong to the local status elite. They represent an admixture of urbanizing and rural elements. And, like the most devoted protesters, they own land.

Prominent among these families is the very one that organized the Matachines revival in Arroyo Seco. As part of a small but powerful elite, the dance director's family (although not the director himself) has consistently exercised its influence against any such protest involvement in

Arroyo Seco. In light of this fact, its sponsorship of the Matachines and other religious folk dramas seems particularly significant. But if protest and parish cultural revivals appear to be activist alternatives within Arroyo Seco, they are not altogether mutually exclusive throughout the parish, because although not everyone approves of protest mobilization, most people appreciate the folk revivals. Nevertheless, the organizing constituencies of these two movements are quite distinct. And with a single notable exception, most active participants in the Arroyo Seco Matachines have tacitly or actively opposed protest mobilization as a community strategy. This was apparent again in 1986, when a large, upscale commercial subdivision began construction in Arroyo Seco and its local opposition failed to amass the kind of popular support that might have stopped it.

CONCLUSION

In Arroyo Seco, the Matachines dance has become a symbolic means of asserting ethnocommunal identity during times of heightened threat to the traditional land-water base. The dance evidently ceased to be a regular ritual event in the parish early in the twentieth century. It has been revived briefly three times since, during decades when longtime settlers' rights of landownership were challenged. The connection between the Matachines revivals of 1929 and 1934 and the Pueblo Land Claims litigation and ejections that occurred in the 1920s and 1930s is speculative. Such a link is suggested by the fact that the 1985–86 revival also took place during a time of intensified demographic and economic pressures on already overallocated water rights and land. Previously, the threat came from the pueblo, aided by the federal government, whereas today it comes also from growing numbers of Anglo resort developers and amenity migrants. Mexicano response to each of these threats is different.

It seems likely that the Matachines performance would express an ethnocultural revival only among Mexicanos. The dance affirms Hispanic ancestry as well as the basis on which their dominance was originally founded: the one true religion, backed up by guns. It self-consciously encapsulates the Iberian-Moorish legacy and projects it onto the Spanish confrontation and admixture with Indians in the New World. By definition the dance symbolizes the conquest and assimilation of Indians and the arrival of Christianity. In contrast, Indian nativism might instead displace the Matachines with an aboriginal dance, something which, as shown in the previous chapter, did occur at Taos Pueblo between 1986 and 1992.[8]

Yet the Arroyo Seco performance also expresses a certain covert identification with Indians, not only through the subtext of miscegenation implicit in the burlesque nativity but also insofar as it jokingly portrays the Indians' cunning resistance to the forces of domination. This theme must have acquired new meaning for Mexicanos after they themselves experienced ethnic subjugation (hence, perhaps, the ambiguous reference to "Tex"(an) [see note 5]). A generation or two ago the dance seems to have been based more widely throughout the parish than it is today. In the past, some of the same people, namely Abuelos, Toros, and musicians, participated in both the Taos Pueblo and the Holy Trinity parish Matachines. This suggests that its constituency was less exclusive then than it is today.

The oppositional relation between dance elements has other referents as well. These include, for example, the ambivalent relation between priest and congregation and between the narrator and the clowns and bull. The former refers metaphorically to relations between the community and the Catholic church, whereas the latter refers to status relations within the community.

Arroyo Seco's preference for one form of ethnocultural mobilization over another reveals intracommunity and intraethnic division as well as unity. Its unity consists in the fact that both sectors are ethnoculturally mobilized—one way or the other. The internal cleavages are multiple; central among them are class status and ownership of land (larger versus smaller parciantes). These two are intertwined in Arroyo Seco. Another pole of power is the Catholic church, embodied in the parish seat and rectory. The state, which today mediates Indian-Hispano relations and controls public lands and many jobs, is yet another pole of power, external to the community yet interwoven with it.[9]

In Arroyo Seco, the church and local elite have jointly sponsored the recent revival of the Matachines, each for its own reasons. For its part, the Catholic church has moved in to co-opt and safely channel heightened community-based ethnic sentiment aroused by population pressure and intensified competition for local resources. Many but not all priests discourage protest (for example, Father Conran), while only a few have been openly sympathetic (for example, his predecessor). In any case, the church has not formally disapproved such activity in the Taos area or moved to suppress it as such. Rather, it has attempted to capture and harness local ethnocultural community spirit to further its own end of promoting large, active, and devout parishes.

The elite have a position of prestige and some power to protect. Their position, like that of the community in relation to its neighbors, is in fact somewhat fragile. Because of its position, the extended family in question seems willing to assert a territorial boundary vis-à-vis Indian encroachment and a ritual or symbolic boundary vis-à-vis Anglo/resort encroachment. This differential response to separate yet incremental threats seems adaptive in a way that reflects the status and class orientation of the powerful instigating family. Given the precariousness of its land base and the pervasiveness of tourism, this dual strategy of suppressing protest and fostering revival may also prove an effective defense for the community as a whole. In any case, it expresses the interests of the elite, who are best positioned to benefit from extensive resort development by virtue of the land they own. The same land, however, or access to it, is threatened by Taos Pueblo. Vis-à-vis resort growth then, this family's class interest overrides allegiance to an activist ethnocommunal boundary. The ethnic boundary vis-à-vis Indians, however, is concrete and more bluntly asserted. But it is still conveyed in a manner that reveals a class perspective.

The ritual boundary, the Matachines dance, encodes commentary about the Indo-Hispano interface. Born of an earlier, more bipolar era of interethnic relations, today it serves to assert the community boundary under more complex and plural conditions. It now speaks to far more than Pueblo Indian encroachment. Unlike the protests, however, it does so in a socially and aesthetically pleasing manner, without ugly confrontation and without ever directly naming the opposition. In sum, Arroyo Seco's water claims and territorial integrity have been precarious from its founding, and today the community faces both new and long-standing threats. The symbolic content of the Arroyo Seco Matachines, as well as the very fact of its revival, expresses the complexity of this condition.

Plate 17. The exchange between Malinche and Monarca, Alcalde, December 27, 1989.

Plate 18. El Torito, Alcalde, December 27, 1989.

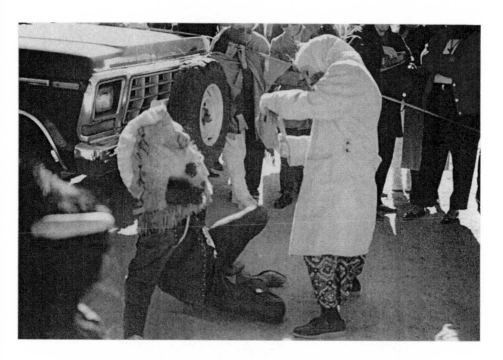

Plate 19. La Perejundia and El Abuelo, Alcalde, December 27, 1989.

Plate 20. The Abuelo, Alcalde, December 27, 1989.

Plate 21. La Perejundia revealed, Alcalde, December 27, 1989.

Plate 22. Comic foot pantomime between Monarca and the Abuelos, El Rancho, January 1, 1990.

Plate 23. The palma-guaje exchange between Malinche and Monarca, El Rancho, January 1, 1990.

Plate 24. El Torito pinned with money, El Rancho, January 1, 1991.

Plate 25. The elaborate costume worn by danzante at El Rancho, January 1, 1990.

Plate 26. El Toro and Malinche, Bernalillo, August 10, 1991.

Plate 27. Abuelo and Malinches, Bernalillo, August 10, 1991.

Plate 28. Double dance formation, Bernalillo, August 10, 1991.

Plate 29. Opening procession for the Matachines dance, San Antonio, June 9, 1990.

Plate 30. Saint Anthony dressed as a matachín, San Antonio, June 9, 1990.

Plate 31. Perejundia and Abuelo, San Antonio, June 15, 1991.

Plate 32. Male Tiwa dancers, Tortugas, December 12, 1990.

Plate 33. Female Tiwa dancers, Tortugas, December 12, 1990.

Plate 34. Danzantes, Tortugas, December 12, 1990.

Plate 35. Monarca and Malinche, Tortugas, December 12, 1990.

Plate 36. "Abuelo," Tortugas, December 12, 1990.

4 · PICURÍS PUEBLO
Persistence and Permeability

Picurís Pueblo, much smaller and more isolated than Taos Pueblo, lies about twenty-five miles south of Taos in the remote, mountainous, southeastern corner of Taos County, along the Dixon artery to the scenic "high road" between Española and the town of Taos. Its population of approximately 147 is the smallest among the living pueblos. Yet at the time of Spanish contact, Picurís is said to have been the largest and perhaps the most resistant of the Río Grande pueblos. The earliest Spanish accounts describe multistoried buildings with upper levels made of wood. Little trace of this structure has survived. Picurís history under three successive rules is one of decimation, flight and return, and three centuries of bare survival (Brown 1979). In the late 1980s this pueblo showed an intensified effort to regenerate itself.

Picurís is embedded in a community of roughly a dozen Mexicano villages, or *aldeas,* the largest and most commercially central of which is Peñasco, about two miles to the southeast. Several of these neighboring settlements, including Río Lucío, Vadito, Chamisál, and Peñasco, encroach on the pueblo's league (map 3). The history and character of their complex interrelationships have accordingly been shaped, like those in the Taos basin, by similar factors of topography, hydrology, and demography.

One apparent if paradoxical feature of modern Picurís is the high degree to which it seems both to merge with and yet remain separate from its immediate demographic surroundings. Like its neighbors, Picurís is defined by a clustering of houses around a church, placita, and cemetery. But unlike them, it lacks a morada and instead contains active and defunct kivas, ancient trash heaps, and other remains. Picurís is bounded by a reservation fence. One can still find traces of the old wooden crosses that marked passage into Indian territory along the old back road from Peñasco.

Unlike Taos Pueblo, Picurís is architecturally unimposing and, as Siegel

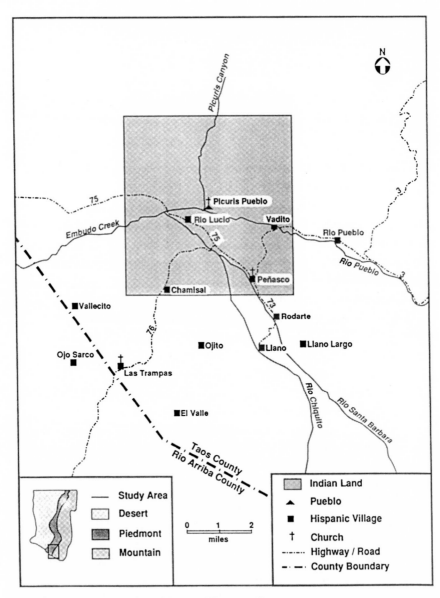

N

Picurís Canyon

75

Embudo Creek

† Picuris Pueblo

■ Rio Lucio   Vadito

75   ■ Rio Pueblo

Rio Pueblo

† Peñasco

■ Chamisal

3

■ Vallecito

76   ■ Rodarte

■ Ojito   ■ Llano   ■ Llano Largo

Ojo Sarco
■   73

† Las Trampas

Rio Chiquito

Rio Santa Barbara

■ El Valle

Taos County
Rio Arriba County

	Study Area
	Desert
	Piedmont
	Mountain

0   1   2
miles

	Indian Land
▲	Pueblo
■	Hispanic Village
†	Church
·-·-·-	Highway / Road
·— ·—	County Boundary

Map 3. Picurís Pueblo and neighboring Hispano villages.

noted (1959), appears little different from the surrounding communities in terms of a generalized rural poverty. But although it seems culturally less bounded than Taos Pueblo, Picurís remains spatially separated from all the neighboring historic encroachments by Mexicanos. To the unaccustomed eye at least, Picurís Indians seem less distinguishable from neighboring Mexicanos, in terms of cultural behavior and physical appearance, than do Taos Indians.

A major factor in shaping Picurís's strategies of ethnic boundary maintenance is its minuscule size, a long-standing condition perpetually offset only by the tribe's stubborn struggle to persist as a distinct demographic and cultural entity. The major problem facing the Picurís people today is sheer survival, in terms of population as well as a viable economic base. Their decimated condition and impoverishment are reflected, along with their will to persevere, in the way they organize and perform the Matachines dance. Perhaps because there are so few Picurís Indians, lines of social cleavage seem symbolically more submerged in their version of the dance than in either the Taos Pueblo or Arroyo Seco cases. In short, the dance constituency comes down to a matter of a few individuals, most of whom are relatively young.

THE MATACHINES AND THE SAN LORENZO CHURCH RESTORATION

The San Lorenzo mission church sits in the modern lower plaza at Picurís, just a few hundred yards from the new tribal office and community center building complex. The recent predecessor to the 1992 structure was begun in 1769 and was still under construction when Fray Francisco Atanasio Domínguez, an official canonical representative, visited in 1776, having been preceded by three earlier churches that sat away from the present plaza, the last of which had been renovated in 1746–47 (Kessell 1980:97–99). Like many other adobe missions, the structure was stuccoed, or "hard plastered," in the late 1950s or 1960s, eventually resulting in the kind of internal deterioration such walls are prone to. At first the parishioners thought a new roof and extensive repairs would be adequate, but large cracks appeared in the west wall, which then collapsed. The church needed to be rebuilt entirely from a new foundation.

At the outset the tribe had neither the manpower, the architectural expertise, nor the money to undertake this task. But loyal parishioners were already committed to the project before they realized its full extent. Reticence and noninvolvement by some tribal members notwithstanding, restoration of the church became a major community project and campaign to the outside world. Tribal officers and others recruited voluntary outside expertise, labor, and financial support. They tapped into the network of individuals, organizations, and institutions (including the Catholic church) that work to preserve and restore New Mexico's aging adobe missions. Ultimately Picurís founded its own Church Restoration League. During the entire restoration period it would have been impossible for anyone to visit Picurís and not be aware of this central, massive, visually dominant project of adobe church construction, which was finally completed in 1992.[1]

The reconstruction of the San Lorenzo church between the mid-1980s and the early 1990s had practical effects on the Picurís Matachines dance. Once the project began, all regular Catholic activities, including masses, were transferred to the community center. This created a temporary "detour" in the normal performance routine. Dancing customarily done inside the church was done instead in the community center or, alternatively, in the new museum and restaurant building known as the "Enterprise."

Customary practice is to dance briefly inside the church after mass at the start of the procession and again at the end, much as at Taos Pueblo and elsewhere, and also to dance inside during very bad weather. Locals refer to the powerful acoustical and visual effects produced by dancing inside the narrow, high-ceilinged church. Elderly Picurís remember when there were no benches and the floor was of hard mud, while those born later recall the resounding echo of the dancers' shoes on the wood floor. The reverberations, they say, could be heard throughout the village.

The collective effort to reconstruct the San Lorenzo church constituted the immediate social and historical context within which the dance was performed during the later 1980s and early 1990s. It was thus part of the context within which some Picurís themselves conceptualized the dance, as well as the frame within which I encountered it. Even if the basic integrity and execution of the Matachines remained untouched by its temporary relocation, during this interim the dance seemed to become almost emblematic of the absent church, a group embodiment of the desire once again to perform within its walls.

This relationship between the dance and the church—after all, its virtual point of origination—is captured in a painting by a prominent Picurís artist. In his late forties, this man has danced all the male roles in the Matachines performance over the years, served several times as tribal governor, and been one of the major organizers of the church restoration as well as other community projects. His affinity for the dance is well known. His painting depicts a night dance scene in front of the old churchyard gateway and facade, illuminated by firelight (see frontispiece). A similar image was reproduced for posters sold to raise money for the restoration and then was raffled off and won by a man from Louisiana during Christmas of 1985.

THE DANCE

The following account of the Picurís Matachines dance is based upon my observation of the dance in 1985, 1987, and 1988, supplemented by interviews conducted in the Peñasco-Picurís area between 1985 and 1991. Despite minor year-to-year variations and the temporal specificity of my fieldwork, my description is rendered in the ethnographic present.

The Picurís Matachines is performed every year at Christmas, beginning on Christmas Eve afternoon. Then there is an evening vespers mass, followed by a night procession with saints around a plaza circuit marked by luminarias. Afterward they dance again. Another luminaria procession takes place at dawn, followed by morning mass and dancing in the plaza throughout the rest of Christmas Day. Practice sessions begin on December 12, or "Little Christmas," and are held for several hours each night.

Performance and maintenance of the Matachines dance comes down to the governor and a handful of people who organize, participate in, and recruit for the annual Christmas event. Although organization resides in the hands of these few individuals, it does not appear that the dance exists as a describable choreographic entity in the mind of any single person, even among those who know it best. It is therefore difficult to elicit a precise enumeration or summary rendition of the different dance sets, which at Picurís no longer all seem to have specific names attached to them. The overall sequence nevertheless seems familiar or recognizable to the participants.

One peculiarity of the Picurís dance is that even though it is difficult to elicit a neat emic description of the choreography, the actual physical patterns seem extraordinarily easy to observe. Some names may be missing, but the dance itself seems clearer than it sometimes does elsewhere. So while seemingly less opulent, polished, or elaborately cognized than at least some other versions, the Picurís Matachines exhibits a striking clarity of structure. It is as if the Picurís dancers space themselves farther apart and thereby render the choreographic patterns more discernible than in cases such as Taos, Arroyo Seco, San Juan, and others, where the dance formation is denser. This visual effect seems enhanced by the comparative youth and physical smallness of the dancers.

Five movements are usually counted and named: Malinche, Monarca, Toro, the Cross, and the Maypole. Additional formations at the beginning and end can also be discerned, done to one and sometimes another of the tunes, but they do not appear to have regular names. There are up to six tunes, in addition to the Maypole, which is performed as the grand finale. Numerous tune changes occur throughout the dance, even within a single set or movement.

Although the general sequence of choreographic units seems fairly stable, there is nevertheless marked variation in some aspects of the musical sequence. For example, I observed and recorded three distinct end patterns during three different performances on Christmas Day in 1987. In one performance there were fourteen tune changes in the sequence ABACACACABDCEF. In another, the sequence ended with CBF, and tune E, similar but not identical to B, was not used. Yet despite this musical variation the choreography was the same in both cases. In the final dance, culminating with the Maypole, the sequence was ABACACACACAG.[2]

The fourteen tune changes in the first performance were tape-recorded as follows.

1. *Tune A (slow).* The dancers face forward (toward the musicians) and perform alternating kick steps while Monarca, Malinche, and the Abuela move abreast, up and down between the two lines.

2. *Tune B (fast).* The dancers stamp up and down, twirling and whirling around in place, facing forward and then to the right and left, swinging their palmas and rattles in front. The Abuela accompanies Malinche, who is led by Monarca up and down between the rows. As they retreat, each set (or cross-pair) of dancers kneels (genuflect position).

3. *Tune A.* All dancers kneel while Malinche, led by the Abuela, moves between the rows with her right arm extended toward Monarca, who sits

at the far end, extending his palma in his right hand. The Abuela, on the Malinche's left, mimics this motion with her chicote (whip).

4. *Tune C (fast).* The Malinche and Abuela rotate in one direction and then the other and curtsy after Malinche takes Monarca's rattle in her right hand. The two then weave along one side (his right) of the dancers, toward the musicians. They face the musicians, rotate, and curtsy.

5. *Tune A.* Accompanied by the Abuela, the Malinche again proceeds toward Monarca, this time with her left hand extended while she holds the rattle close to her waist. Monarca extends his palma with his left hand, by an outer prong, handle toward Malinche. Their left arms rotate around each other, twice clockwise and twice counterclockwise. She takes the palma and then curtsies, with the Abuela, who is now on her right.

6. *Tune C.* Malinche, between the Abuelos and holding the palma by the handle, weaves along Monarca's lefthand side of the genuflecting dancers, advancing toward the musicians' end, where she stops and again spins and curtsies.

7. *Tune A.* Malinche and the Abuelos then move back toward Monarca, she extending the rattle with her right hand, he taking it in his right hand.

8. *Tune C.* Malinche and Abuelos spin around, curtsy, and then proceed to weave around each dancer, this time between the two rows.

9. *Tune A.* At the end of the dance area where the musicians sit, the Abuelos and Malinche spin around, curtsy, and then return toward Monarca, Malinche extending the palma in her left hand, by a prong. Their arms again rotate around each other. (One bar of tune C: Monarca takes the palma, Malinche spins and curtsies, and Monarca stands.)

10. *Tune B.* The two rows of kneeling dancers face inward, their palmas extended downward, touching the ground. Monarca dances between the rows, pirouetting over the palmas. As he passes each pair, the dancers move away from the center and face toward the front. On his return, as he passes each pair of dancers and spins, they rise, spin, and exchange positions across the lines, going from kneeling to standing position. They then take three steps in place and stop. Malinche follows behind Monarca, with the Abuelos.

11. *Tune D (fast).* Monarca is seated; Malinche takes the rattle and palma. The two columns of dancers spin around in place. Then, as Malinche and the Abuelos move between the rows toward the far end, the dancers cross back to their original places, one in front of the trio, the other behind. The party of three then proceeds back toward Monarca, palma and rattle extended. Malinche hands them back and he stands

and moves to dance between the rows while she retreats to the sidelines. Looping around each dancer, Monarca then initiates diagonal crossovers between the two columns, leading the front left dancer to the right rear position and vice versa, down the line.

12. *Tune C.* Malinche and the Toro face each other from opposite ends of the dance lines and then move toward each other. The Abuela trails Malinche, and the Abuelo follows the Toro. Malinche dances a semi-circle around the Toro and waves her paño at him as they pass. She goes to the sidelines. Next the Monarca dances around the Toro in similar fashion, touching his left hand with palma to the Toro's left shoulder as they pass. He is followed in turn by the dancers, who in meeting the bull all cross over, diagonally from front to back, reversing the crossovers made in the last movement, each returning to his original place. The Abuelos then dance the Toro to the sidelines.

13. *Tune E (fast).* The dancers, joined by Monarca, Malinche, and Abuelos, form moving perpendicular columns which go from an L shape to the shape of a cross.

14. *Tune F (fast).* Monarca, Malinche, and the Abuela dance abreast between the two rows, advancing and then retreating, much as in the first dance. The dancers stamp lightly and do a kick step.[3]

Each tune change is signaled by the Abuelos' falsetto "hoohoo," and each set change with a "hoohoo" and a crack of the whip.

COMPARISON

As a third closely examined case, Picurís offers another step toward a regional and comparative view of the dance. Picurís, Taos Pueblo, and Arroyo Seco all perform the Maypole, a movement not found in any of the other upper Río Grande versions. Apart from this feature, however, they share the same broad ordering of choreographic elements that Champe describes for San Ildefonso and other Río Grande examples. These include an opening movement or movements followed by Malinche's journey with Monarca's rattle and palma; Monarca's jumping between the danzantes, leading to their crossovers and eventual reversal; crossovers and/or wheeling; stamping and/or a kickstep; and the Toro segment. At Taos and Arroyo Seco, the corona/cruz movement precedes the dance of the Toro, whereas at Picurís and San Ildefonso it follows the Toro. Each version culminates in some kind of finale and recessional, and each involves its own particular dramatic embellishment. There is intervillage variation in the way these "core" choreographic elements are organized and named, and even in the tunes they are linked to. Different individuals, including musicians, dancers, and outside observers, may identify some of the same dance and musical sequences differently. Moreover, as Champe notes, there appears to be no overarching system of identification common to all communities (Champe 1983:17–20).

The number of tunes a given village plays may be a factor in how people conceptualize the dance sets. There are seven tunes at Taos Pueblo and Picurís, five at Arroyo Seco, and thirteen at San Ildefonso, although not necessarily much agreement in what people call the tunes that may be shared by all four traditions. In every version there are different sets done to the same tune, and single sets that involve more than one tune. Probably the most universal of these is the slow-fast alternation that marks Malinche's dance with the palma and guaje—slow when she moves toward Monarca, fast when she moves away from him. At Picurís, the multiple switching between repeated melodies may be a factor in people's seeming to have difficulty naming and numbering the specific movements abstractly. Nevertheless, they know how to perform them "correctly," an ability that relates to the process by which the dance is remembered.

PERFORMANCE AND MEMORY

The Picurís dance seems to be remembered primarily through the collective act of performance. The sets and sequence are visually, kinesthetically, and musically reconstituted and recognized, but they do not seem to be explicitly articulated as a choreographic entity in the mind of any single participant. Perhaps this reflects a Pueblo pattern of ceremonial knowledge in which each initiate masters just one part of a complex whole that is never conceptually embraced by a single individual. In any case, the memory of the dance is encoded as group experience.

Referring to the way Picurís recovered the Maypole sequence in the 1980s, after a lapse of thirty-seven years, its principal instigator describes the mnemonic pathway into the dance as an old tune and rhythms learned as a child:

Yeah, it was in my head and that's the way it was picked up, 'cause you know you never forget things that you learned when you were young if you really were in tune with it, playing it and listening, and everything falls into place. Like with the Matachines, you dance it listening to the beat of the music. And even while playing around [as children], you're humming it and you're using sticks as violins and still humming it so it's just a thing you will always remember. The practice does help a lot; it regenerates a lot. So there automatically you're in beat with the music because you have heard it, you're listening to it, and then you fall into line. The rattles, the violin, plus the guitar, they are all on beat. And that beat is regenerated like what I was talking about a little while ago, that we practiced at the old day school which had a wooden floor. And the beats that you hear going along with the music and you stumping your feet on the floor, you know, all put into rhythm. So that part we now kind of miss 'cause the church [undergoing reconstruction] also has a wooden floor and you could create that rhythm just by stomping your feet on the wooden floor plus the rattle and the violin and the guitar, then it all falls into one where it's done automatic.

The Malinche and new dancers are trained during the practice sessions. These sessions are crucial to a smooth performance and have a sequestered, prayerful quality in that nonparticipants are not allowed to watch. Today the practice sessions are held in the community center. One old woman told me that when she danced the part of Malinche roughly sixty years earlier, they first practiced in the kiva, using only a drum and chanting. Several nights later, when a Mexicano fiddler and guitarist came, they moved outside the kiva. This suggests that the Picurís Matachines once had Indian music not remembered today.

RITUAL PROGRESSION

With some degree of situational variation, the Picurís dance is generally done once on Christmas Eve afternoon and again at night after the procession. It is usually performed twice on Christmas morning after mass and twice in the afternoon, culminating with the Maypole. Other than inside the church or its surrogates, the dancing is always done in the lower plaza just west of the church.

The counterclockwise twilight and dawn processions circumscribe this area. The choreographic structure of the procession is common throughout the upper Río Grande valley. It involves a chorus plus nucleus (in this case older men, including Hermanos, praying and singing the rosary; in other cases, mayordomos bearing the saint), preceded by the matachines, who alternate between facing them, bowing and dancing backwards, and leading the procession forward. The musicians accompany the dancers, so there are two separate yet overlapping strains of music.

The pattern of feasting is somewhat different from that at Taos Pueblo in that a single feast is given by the governor at noon on Christmas Day, when all the performers and his staff are fed along with anyone else who wishes to come. Entregas of the Malinche, Monarca, and new dancers are done after the dancing is over on Christmas afternoon, around sunset. The old order of symbolic priority has broken down and the sequence is dictated by convenient proximity. As at Taos Pueblo, the dancer may be carried the last few paces to his home, where at the entry his parents are asked if they recognize him. Years ago special prayers for the entrega were said in both Spanish and Tiwa. Today families invite the entourage inside to partake of a dessert feast of cookies, cake, coffee, punch, and sometimes (whiskey) "shots."

The Matachines costumes reflect Picurís's material poverty in that they are not as fancy as those in many other villages, although the basic accouterments of cupil, palma, and guaje are prepared with care. The Picurís headpiece, which they call the "corona," is less like a mitre and more like a crown, fashioned with two willow arcs attached at right angles, wound around and looped with colored tinsel garland. The palmas are of painted wood; the rattles are Mexican maracas wrapped inside handkerchiefs. The dancers wear anything from new Levi's to good uncreased pants, shirts, and tennis shoes, leather shoes, or boots. Some wear sweaters or vests and change clothes from one day to the next, usually dressing best on Christmas.

The Monarca dresses a little fancier than the others, and his shawl always bears the image of the Virgin of Guadalupe. He is referred to as the "lead dancer" and is usually a man who has been a danzante and knows the dance.

In comparison to those at Taos Pueblo and Arroyo Seco, the Toro and Abuelos are relatively subdued at Picurís. The conflict with the bull is understated and highly stylized, with barely a hint of skirmish or his final demise. His most constant feature is a single cane or forestick. Sometimes

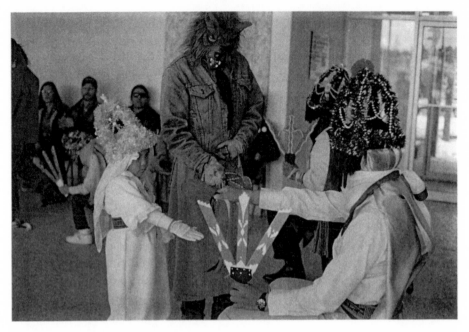

Figure 7. An Abuelo in a werewolf mask watches the Malinche-Monarca exchange, Picurís Pueblo, December 25, 1987.

he wears a set of horns, or a baseball hat backwards, or a blanket. In 1988 he wore a blanket, monkey mask, and horns on Christmas afternoon. During the years I observed the dance he was usually, but not always, played by one particular older Picurís man.

The two Abuelos (plate 10) are not as raucous or vocal as they are at Taos Pueblo or Arroyo Seco. They signal with falsetto hooting and call out to the Toro. They preside over the exchange between Malinche and Monarca, which is universal, but do not repeat the *engáñalo/gayalo* lines heard, exclusively it seems, at Taos Pueblo and Arroyo Seco. They do not currently perform a birth burlesque, but did so in the past.[4]

One or both of the Abuelos carry chicotes. Their role is demanding and requires them to know the dance. They summon the dancers (including for the predawn procession on Christmas Day), announce the dance, call the dances, keep back the crowd, accompany and sometimes carry the Malinche (plate 11), groom the dancers, and entertain the audience. In general, they seem to do these things in a much less conspicuous manner than the Abuelos at either Taos Pueblo or Arroyo Seco. Their vivacity and daring depend on crowd response, in that they usually become liveliest on Christmas afternoon, when their dress is most elaborate and the audience reaches peak size and enthusiasm.[5]

The Abuelos' costumes, like those of all the dancers, seem comparatively simple and minimalist, yet striking. They frequently reverse and exchange items of clothing and turn their masks inside out. Their selection of masks in the late 1980s showed a certain penchant for werewolves (known one year as "Teen Wolf"), apes, and witches, although a variety of other faces appeared as well (fig. 7). In the old days they wore flour sacks with faces painted on them. Such a mask was used briefly on Christmas Eve afternoon in 1988.

Usually one Abuelo is a Perejundia (a term not used at Picurís). Sometimes both are. Yet one Christmas Eve afternoon (1988) neither was, after one of the costume changes they typically undergo between morning, afternoon, and evening. Their characters and costumes thus seem even more variable than those at Taos Pueblo or other villages. The Abuela is often portrayed as an old woman with a bandanna, big purse, and overcoat. She occasionally begs from the audience, intimating just a hint of drunken seductiveness.

As elsewhere, La Malinche is a girl between six and twelve, selected by the governor from among eligible candidates in the village. She wears a First Holy Communion dress but on occasion may change into an Indian-style dress, generally a prerogative of her mother. For example, in 1987 the little girl, whose mother was from Santa Clara Pueblo, wore a Santa Clara–style white manta, or tunic, with a red, green, and black border, a red sash, and high, white, wrapped moccasins. The multiple color changes in the Malinche's dress seen at Taos Pueblo are not made at Picurís, although in 1987 the Malinche wore some pink for the Christmas morning procession, and on Christmas Eve of 1988 she wore pinkish blue. Whereas most Malinches wear a communion veil, at Picurís she also wears a corona like the dancers, wound with silver tinsel garland. Many years ago, when people were poorer, the white dress was borrowed from Mexicano neighbors.

RECRUITMENT AND PARTICIPATION

Ideally all dancers volunteer, although in some cases and perhaps especially in certain years, the governor must draft some performers. Participation brings honor and spiritual blessing to the dancer and his or her family. It happens that today most of the dance principals, including the musicians, come from Picurís, although in the past and in principle, the rules for outsider and "mixed-blood" participation seem much more flexible than they do at Taos Pueblo. Theoretically, anyone may dance who wants to, so long as the impulse "comes from the heart." Outsiders who dance have some kind of tie to Picurís, such as being married in. Thus non-Picurís Indian, Mexicano, and even Anglo in-laws may and often do participate, usually in the role of danzante. Anglos, who have not grown up listening to and watching the dance, are said to have a harder time learning the movements. Dancers from other pueblos are said to contribute stylistic elements peculiar to their home version.

Some little girls have played the Malinche more than once, in nonconsecutive years when no one else was available to fill the role. When she is chosen, the governor and his staff visit her parents and formally ask to "borrow" her, and they return her in the final entrega. The theoretical possibility exists for an outsider to play this or, for that matter, any other role. This still occurs but is less common today than it was some decades back, when *vecinos* (neighbors) attended mass at the pueblo and might petition to play a certain role in order to fulfill a promesa.

Today, the most regular participation of Mexicanos in the Picurís Matachines involves a few Hermanos who still come to pray the rosary and sing *alabanzas* (hymns of praise) for the Christmas Eve and morning processions. This long-standing custom points to a time when the bonds between the Picurís and their Mexicano neighbors were stronger and more active. Some Picurís men even belonged to neighboring moradas. A few were evidently important spiritual leaders in both religious traditions. This was the case, for example, with a now-deceased elder who was a Matachines violinist, a Penitente, and a spiritual leader in the Picurís religion. Today one of his sons is the violinist.

In the old days the Hermanos came into Picurís during Holy Week and for *velorios* (all-night watches or prayer vigils) and other functions. Neighbors also attended mass at Picurís. Today, a few older Picurís will visit certain neighboring moradas such as the one at Vadito to pray during Lent and Holy Week, but their young men no longer join the brotherhood. This history is noteworthy in light of the fact that Pueblo Indian Penitentes are not thought to have been common in New Mexico (Weigle 1976:28).[6]

Today there is no Matachines tradition among the Mexicano villages surrounding Picurís, although Vadito evidently once did the dance, prior to living memory, and one older man recalled that it was done in front of the church in Llano.[7] At Vadito they did it some five days after Picurís, probably for New Year's Day, and borrowed the costumes (headgear, guajes, and palmas) from the pueblo. An older Vadito women remembers when they burned luminarias each night beginning on December 12, adding one a night up to twelve on Christmas Eve. These were the nights when the Abuelos or bogeymen would come to terrorize the children, something many older Mexicanos and Indians vividly remember.

The Matachines Abuelos are now usually played by a pair of younger Picurís men appointed by the governor. In 1987, for example, the governor drafted his nephews. Youths known to have a piquant sense of humor or a wild streak are often picked. A few remember a short Mexicano from Llano Largo who played the Abuelo for many years. They called him "Linda," "because he didn't need a mask." Every Christmas he stayed at the pueblo, enjoying the hospitality. Apparently he lived by himself in Llano Largo and did not want to spend the holidays alone. He is said to have been buried at Picurís.

Both musicians and Abuelos have frequently been Mexicano, although there have also been memorable Picurís musicians, including the late tribal elder who was a Penitente and whose son is the violinist today. Among previous Indian musicians were an elderly couple (Ramos and Sylvianita Durán) of whom the wife, part San Juan Indian, was the guitarist. Finding musicians since these old-timers died has at times been difficult, and governors have recruited far and wide. Some musicians have come from Dixon and Chamisál. For several years Picurís even flew a Vadito man back from Nevada or Wyoming to play the fiddle. At one young governor's behest, an Anglo hippie in Llano learned the music from an old recording and served as guitarist for a couple of years in the early 1980s. Outsiders are paid.

More recently, the present violinist took over the role and then for a time recruited his brother as the guitarist. The violinist's story is noteworthy. His father was the violinist, Penitente, and spiritual leader referred to earlier, who, before his death, told his son that he should learn the music. The son did not, but his father's words stuck in his mind for years, including a long period when he lived and worked away from the pueblo. Finally, some time after he had returned to Picurís and was struggling to overcome alcoholism, he taught himself the music by listening to an old recording and practicing alone in the mountains, using the violin that belongs to the church. This process seems to have been part of a conversion experience. He has served as governor more than once and is one of the main organizers of several of the tribe's development projects.

THE SPIRITUAL MEANING OF THE DANCE

People at Picurís seem less overtly ambivalent about the Matachines than do people at Taos Pueblo. Some neutrally acknowledge two versions of the origin of the dance: that it came from the Moors via the Spaniards, and that it was brought by the Aztec king Montezuma. They distinguish between indigenous game dances like the Deer dance and exogenous social dances like the belt dance or the Matachines, but the comparison does not usually appear invidious.

All ceremonial dancing is regarded as an act of worship, which can nevertheless take different forms wherein different codes prevail. One man said he was sure that the different parts of the dance and even the procession must have special meanings, although he did not know what they were. Its basic religious meaning about the coming of Christ is nonetheless understood:

> But over here, even though we don't know the names to it, we know what it means when it's all together. Like it's a Christmas celebration and we need to continue on the traditional thing that was handed down. Keep it ongoing because it's a dance. It's already ingrained in us. And we're looking forward to that. So it's a form of worship, like going to church. It's a religious order. And anything like that, well, we probably don't look at it any different than going through the chapters in the Bible. Just, you know, one big package, like.

One difference between indigenous and exogenous dances is that gift giving, including handing money to or pinning it on the dancers, is done in the latter but not the former. Gifts to the dancers are especially common during Christmas, when dollar bills are pinned on Malinche and other dancers by people, often relatives, from the audience (plate 12). In 1987 the Malinche's mother, from Santa Clara Pueblo, handed out a basketful of gifts to all the dancers and then the audience. Significantly, the pinning of money on the bride is a common Mexicano wedding practice.

As the same individual quoted earlier put it,

> But the social dance, like the belt dance, you can go in there and give them a dollar or whatever you want to give them. But like the Deer dance, you can't. It's out of place. It's just like, uh [laughs], a Catholic priest trying to preach a Baptist sermon. . . . But since this comes from the outside, brought in by the outside, you know, newcomers, then we must follow that same order, 'cause they probably follow it themselves, giving at Christmas. You can give money any time, even to the musicians.

At the same time, both indigenous and exogenous "orders" have a common spiritual import, and at least some people claim not to value one above the other:

> No, because it [the Matachines] basically follows the same concept, but being with a different origin. And if they're religious dances, no one has no say so. It's just there. The game dances that we do here, the thanksgiving dances that we do here, the harvest dances. And all of these are, you know, in a different order but then being there with the same deal. That you are giving gratitude, by dancing. And we are always told that we are not dancing for the officers or for anyone but for yourself, and for the Great Spirit. And then it's meant as the same way. You're saying thank you, or giving your gratitude, to St. Lawrence, your patron saint, or God, or whatever.

When asked if people at Picurís feel ambivalent about the Matachines, he elaborates:

> Naw, like I've been saying before, it's a tradition, a cultural thing, and no one says anything about it. Because it goes the same order. So why would you go over there, and say well, for example, if you're reading a Bible and you say, "Well, this chapter don't belong here," and you tear it out. Now that's the kind of sense I get from [the kind of ill feeling toward the dance some people express] . . . uh, how ignorant people can be. You know when they try to separate a thing that goes in the same order. Just

for the record, I'd like to say that people like that need [laughs] to re-educate themselves or you know, learn more about what they're doing. The importance of it. So as not to go on out there and change things to their own satisfaction because they're not God [giggles]! But you hear these views around these small communities [mockingly]: "Ahhh, I don't want to dance that because it's a *Spanish* dance or *Mexican* dance!" "I have my *own* religion!" Golly, you know that kind of talk. I still hear it. . . . And you know, I think that's one area, that people seem to leave behind. That's the reason that traditions and cultures are sometimes forgotten. Some areas. 'Cause they just disregard it. It's not lived. Sure, it's practiced, but they're not really lived. That's the way we look at this. We *live* this dance. Since we can remember, and we're looking forward to it. Because each Christmas, if it wasn't the Matachines dance it won't really be Christmas!

But as his words suggest, not everyone is equally enthusiastic about the Matachines, or about Christmas, for that matter. As another, older man put it, there is no word in Tiwa for "Christmas," so they cannot wish anyone a Merry Christmas in their own language. Although he expressed no antipathy toward the dance, he indicated that some people, himself included, feel indifferent to it, and thus not everyone will come out to watch the performance. When he lived and worked away for thirteen years, he never came home once for Christmas, although he often did for San Lorenzo's Day, because it is a "spiritual thing having to do with our own religion." Likewise, not all influential men in the pueblo are active in either the dance or the church restoration. This includes the cacique.[8] As in any community, some people are more religious than others, and as at other pueblos, some people are more involved with Catholicism or Christianity than others. Some remain more active throughout their lives in Indian religion, and some, perhaps particularly those involved with the Matachines, embrace both. This latter attitude reflects Picurís's extraordinary, if necessary, degree of boundary permeability over time.

THE HISTORICAL CONTEXT

Unlike Taos Pueblo or its closest Tewa neighbor, San Juan, some thirty miles to the south, Picurís did not experience significant vecino encroachment until the eighteenth century. Missionization, encomienda

(conscripted labor), the Pueblo Revolt of 1680, and the subsequent reconquest nevertheless had changed Picurís drastically by the time Hispanic
settlers began to establish acequias, grazing areas, and placitas along the
Río Pueblo and neighboring tributaries. The population of Picurís went
from the conservative estimate of two thousand in 1680 to three hundred
only twenty-six years later, after the Pueblo Revolt and the reconquest had
ravaged and transformed colonial society.

Both Picurís and Taos pueblos contributed importantly to the Pueblo
Revolt as well as to its aftermath (see chapter 2, note 2). In 1696 the entire Picurís population fled Diego de Vargas's troops eastward into Apache
territory, where they remained at Cuartalejo for a decade before returning
home. Although all of the surviving Eastern Pueblo Indians suffered severe
losses during this period, for some reason or combination of reasons Picurís
was not only decimated but has had difficulty sustaining or increasing its
numbers ever since. So although the sparse pre-revolt accounts emphasize Picurís's large size and bellicose attitude, the majority of descriptions
thereafter convey a sense of affliction, poverty, and decline.

Along with Taos and Pecos, Picurís sits along the eastern edge of the
northern Río Grande valley and engaged in contact and exchange with
nomadic plains tribes even prior to colonization. Both hunting and trad-
ing were important to their subsistence, inasmuch as their mountain niche
sustained a short growing season. Following their return from Cuartalejo,
the Picurís allied with the Spaniards against Apache, Ute, and Comanche marauders. They are said to have undergone extensive admixture with
Apaches as well as other nomadic groups and certain Pueblo Indians,
although not especially with Taos. Their relations with San Juan are reputedly easier and friendlier than those with Taos Pueblo. Overt resistance
against Europeans ceased after the reconquest, and Spanish-Pueblo relations were tempered. French traders established contact with Picurís in
1739, engendering commerce which the Spanish government later tried to
thwart.

During the eighteenth century, Picurís Pueblo was gradually surrounded by a network of Hispanic settlements encroaching on its league.
The earliest *merced,* or royal land grant, in the general area was the Embudo grant, several miles to the west along the Río Embudo, made in
1725 (Ebright 1980). The Las Trampas grant was made in 1751 to families
from around Santa Fe; it was populated to reinforce a buffer zone be-

tween the Santa Fe and Santa Cruz areas and the open territory of the raiding nomads (deBuys 1981). The original settlement of San Antonio del Embudo (now modern Dixon) was evidently abandoned prior to establishment of the Trampas grant. The Trampas documents mention another settlement, Santa Barbara, which was abandoned and then reoccupied when the Santa Barbara grant was made in 1796, when Llano and Llano Largo were also established. Santa Barbara is now known as Rodarte, lying southeast of Picurís beyond Peñasco.

A third grant was made in 1832, during the Mexican period, to forty-two local families, including a number from Picurís (Bowden 1969:997–1002). Although a community by the name of Río del Picurís or Río del Pueblo was well established on this grant by the time of American occupation in 1847, the Court of Private Land Claims rejected the grant. Today this community is called Placita. It lies east of Picurís on the other side of Vadito, which is said to be the pueblo's most intimate neighbor, even though Río Lucío, to the immediate southwest, is geographically closer.

According to Donald Brown (1979:271), the twin struggles against territorial encroachment and against the erosion of political autonomy became the dominant themes of Picurís-Hispano relations during the nineteenth century. Peñasco, Chamisál, Río Lucío, and Vadito all trespassed onto the league, and even settlers of the Mora grant (1835), twenty-eight miles to the east, laid claims to Picurís's land and water. As they did elsewhere in the region, civil authorities upheld the pueblo's claims while the fact of encroachment continued, a process of unequal compromise sustained through an unending chain of negotiation. Its modern legacy includes a "checkerboard" pattern of ownership outside the pueblo grant, involving many tracts which the tribe leases to Mexicano neighbors.

Despite a persistent thread of conflict and tension, the character of interethnic relations in the Picurís-Peñasco area *seems* to have been largely nonviolent and comparatively mild. Writing of the late 1960s, Frances Leon Quintana (1990:292–94) generally rates Indian-Hispano relations in the Peñasco valley as poor, and yet she describes the delicate balance of diplomacy and tension whereby irrigation waters are allocated among the pueblo and its neighbors on the Río del Pueblo de Picurís. Compadrazgo, intermarriage, mutual help, and interdependency between Indian and Mexicano families developed over the generations. Indeed, because their population is so small, miscegenation seems extremely common among all

Picurís families in every generation. Like the people of other tiny pueblos such as Tesuque and Pojoaque, the population has interbred with immediate neighbors as well as other regional groups. In a word, the population appears extremely mixed, a pueblo of coyotes (half breeds) and mixed marriages. It nonetheless remains a distinctly bounded sociocultural and political entity.[9]

INTERCOMMUNITY RELATIONS

Today locals will tell stories not unlike those told around Taos Pueblo of bygone days of greater intimacy, exchange, and mutual regard between Indian and Mexicano vecinos. One hears many accounts of people harvesting, slaughtering, plastering, threshing, and praying together not so long ago. The degree to which locals perceive a history or a present of interethnic tension seems partly a function of ethnic positionality, in that subordinates tend to express greater awareness of the face-to-face dynamics of inequality than do members of the dominant group. Thus Mexicanos tend to underplay the importance or intensity of antagonism in their relations with Indians and to stress the amicable side, whereas Indians will more readily recall or point to the negative or oppressive aspects of local society.

Position determines interpersonal perception in a stratified system as well as, of course, the inclination or ability to voice such perceptions. For example, when asked about the quality of local Indo-Hispano relations, most Mexicanos living near pueblos will say relations are very good but there is less contact than before. Even neighbors with little personal contact with Picurís today will refer to an ancestor or older relative who married in, was raised there, had compadres there, lived on Indian land, or is buried there.

Many Hispanos have childhood memories of visits and fiestas at Picurís, personal texts that reveal an overt sense of conviviality laced with a subtle undercurrent of tension and mistrust. One man from Llano, in his sixties, recalled that he often went there as a child with his grandmother to visit her compadres. His two outstanding memories centered on meals. In one instance he was quite young and had trouble chewing the skins on cooked haba beans, and the comadre took away the bowl, saying, "Este niño no tiene hambre" (this boy isn't hungry). In the other, the compadre had slaughtered a calf and invited them to eat. Before its demise the calf had followed the owner around "like a dog," and so when they were eating, he joked, "Que sabroso ésta carne de perro" (how tasty this dogmeat is). The little boy took him literally and would not eat the food.

One persistent gripe many Picurís have about Peñasqueros is over the matter of the San Lorenzo fiesta on August 10, which the pueblo celebrates with a foot race and pole climb, similar to the festivities of San Gerónimo Day (September 30) at Taos Pueblo, with dances in the afternoon. San Lorenzo's Day also happens to be the anniversary of the Pueblo Revolt. Vecino families from the surrounding communities have traditionally come for the mass and feast. But Peñasco celebrates the fiesta quite independently, as a secular though nonetheless very popular event, by setting up a three-day carnival along the highway to the pueblo. Many Picurís resent this as an opportunistic exploitation that undermines their feast day by distracting their youth and draining business away from craft and snack booths set up at the pueblo. Peñasqueros nevertheless warmly consider San Lorenzo their fiesta too, and every year many who live away come home for it. Ironically, it draws a much larger crowd than does Peñasco's own saint's day celebration of San Antonio on June 13, which is observed in simpler fashion with a mass.

Just as Spanish penetration of the Picurís valley took a bit longer than that in other parts of the Río Arriba, or upriver area of northern New Mexico, the full impact of Americanization was felt later also. According to locals it hit just around the turn of the century, when a government day school was established at Picurís in 1899 and major commercial timber operations damaged ditches, shrines, and other use areas. Agriculture still flourished at the end of the nineteenth century among Mexicanos in the Peñasco valley, when U.S. Cavalry Captain John G. Bourke noted a marked contrast between the "neat, trim, and elegant look of the Mexican settlements in the neighboring valleys" and the "slouchy, down in the heel look" of Picurís Pueblo, which Bourke visited in 1891 (Bloom 1936:281). After the early 1900s, agriculture declined dramatically among both groups, although it did persist, while substantial outmigration became increasingly prevalent.

Americanization brought economic underdevelopment, partly through massive land appropriation of the surrounding wilderness into the federal "public domain." While the four Mexicano placitas remain on the pueblo grant, some families were ejected and compensatory exchanges made as a result of the Pueblo Lands Board hearings in the 1920s. As elsewhere throughout the northern region, World War II signaled a final shift away from agricultural livelihood to universal wage dependency. Yet even today this part of Taos County retains a much more rural, agricultural, isolated character than either the Taos basin or the Questa-Costilla area.

From the standpoint of metropolitan Taos, the Peñasco-Picurís-Rodarte multicommunity area has the reputation of being rough, backward, and dangerous, an image that adheres particularly to Peñasco, long notorious among Taoseños for its shootings and dance hall knifings. Taos Indians sometimes refer disparagingly to the cultural breakdown at Picurís. For their part, some Picurís see their Taos Pueblo cousins as aloof and inhospitable, while Peñasqueros see Taos *políticos* as apt to neglect the southern part of the county. Although it garners less civic attention than the central part of the county and remains peripheral to the mainstream tourism economy, the Peñasco area nevertheless pulls a certain weight in county electoral politics, to which it has contributed a number of prominent players over the years. Peñasco sits almost as close to Española as to Taos, but its political, economic, and social orientation remains more toward the latter, partly because Española resides in another county (Río Arriba). Yet many Peñasqueros and their neighbors have close ties to Chimayó and commute regularly to Española or Los Alamos.

Although Anglos and other non-native groups (including French mill owners and Lebanese merchants) have long been present in the Peñasco valley, their numbers never reached the proportion they did in the Taos valley. Thus southeastern Taos County, which according to the 1980 census contained a population of approximately forty-five hundred people, remains strongly rural and around 88 percent Mexicano. Anglos constitute a powerful numerical minority; a number of them work for the Forest Service.

While neither Peñasco nor its sibling villages have made much effort to cultivate a local tourism economy, Picurís has strived in recent years to tap into the New Mexico tourism market. During the past twenty-five years this attempt has been driven by the pueblo's push to regenerate itself economically and culturally. Because of its tiny numbers and somewhat ramshackle architecture, Picurís has never enjoyed the aura of mystique Taos Pueblo became so famous for. This subregion in general has been far less visited and studied than others in the Río Arriba, although since the 1960s, significant archaeological excavation has been carried out at Picurís. This process of tribally endorsed archaeological excavation, as well as the example of Taos's touristic success, seem to have contributed to the pueblo's renaissance and concerted appeal for external support.[10]

Today Picurís seems more energetic and hopeful than when observers described it in previous decades. Since the 1960s, federal funds have helped provide a new community center, low-income tract housing, tribal offices, a commercial center and trout pond, and a small archaeological museum. Although the extremity of its situation remains apparent and there exist widespread unemployment, poverty, alcoholism, and family disintegration, the tribe is actively engaged in several ambitious, long-range projects that offer promise for its social and economic future. New tribal enterprises include a local store and restaurant and partnership with a corporate developer to build and operate a major hotel in downtown Santa Fe. Broadly concurrent with these ventures have been the revitalization of certain ceremonial practices, including revival of the Black Eyes clown society and their pole climb on August 10, and, most significantly with regard to the Matachines, restoration of the San Lorenzo church.

CONCLUSION

At Picurís, performance of the Matachines dance seems to express an integral part of the inhabitants' self-identity as a people with two distinct yet inseparable religions that constitute, in the words of a person quoted earlier, "one big package." The dance, like the mission church and the religion it symbolizes, is a vital part of who the Picurís are. But the symbolic preoccupation is not with miscegenation, as at Taos Pueblo, nor with hierarchy, as at Arroyo Seco. In a sense, Picurís is beyond miscegenation, just as it is beyond much hierarchy. The great puzzle of Picurís is that it has fused with the surrounding social world precisely in order to remain a demographic entity separate and distinct from it. This it has just barely managed to do.

One aspect of its small size that makes Picurís very different from Taos and other, larger pueblos is the leveling effect it has on face-to-face relations within the community and between community members and outsiders. It makes for both formal and informal role density because there are so few individuals available to carry out necessary functions within the tribe. In other words, the burden of maintaining tradition and governance falls to comparatively few individuals, who therefore tend to fill more than one role at a time and a multitude of roles through time. As at other pueblos, attenuation of certain traditions has occurred because there were no longer personnel to perform them. Tribal organization seems pared down to the bare bones of essential operation at Picurís. Thus the division of labor within the ritual and civil structure cannot be either very broadly dispersed or very hierarchical. This lack of extension magnifies the general accessibility of those in authority, such as the governor himself, and allows for a degree of informality in interpersonal dealings with officers and elders not possible at a pueblo like Taos, where protocol and hierarchy seem paramount.

Perhaps this demographic "thinness" enhances the clarity of choreographic structure noted earlier, seemingly accentuated by the broad physical spacing of dancers in the Picurís performance. Unlike the case at Taos Pueblo and especially Arroyo Seco, the dance is not mnemonically "carried" (formally or informally) by designated individuals. Rather, it is remembered through the collective act of performance in which every actor fulfills a necessary role in the overall reconstruction.

Although ever-present, even factionalism seems submerged by the exigencies of sheer survival and the push to regenerate.[11] Picurís represents a living paradox in that its high degree of boundary permeability has simultaneously been a key mechanism for the pueblo's persistence. The effort to regenerate is both galvanized and mirrored by ritual activity. And while religious compartmentalization is easily seen at Picurís, there is also evidence of fusion, as well as what Florence Hawley Ellis (1954) called the "amalgamation" or absorption of Catholic elements.

The reigning, if slightly antiquated, typology of acculturation in the greater Southwest, initiated by Edward Spicer, identifies five distinct patterns exhibited by different Southwestern Indian populations in response to Europeanization. These include compartmentalization among the Eastern Pueblos, fusion among Cahitan peoples such as the Yaquis, reorientation among Athabascans (Navajos and Apaches), complete assimilation among the Southern Pueblos (Piro) and Opata, and complete rejection among Western Pueblos (Hopi) (Spicer 1954). Fusion and compartmentalization are the most theorized of these, based on Spicer's work among the Yaquis, on the one hand, and the work of Pueblo ethnologists, on the other. Compartmentalization is the "coexistence of native and Catholic systems within the framework of Pueblo culture" (Barker 1958:450), whereas fusion involves the blending of native and Catholic forms and meanings into new, hybrid combinations (Spicer 1958:434).

Edward Dozier (1954:681) confirmed compartmentalization in the Eastern Pueblos by noting how indigenous religious practices remain separate from and devoid of Christian symbolic elements, with the possible exception of the Matachines and Horse dance ceremonies, in which "there appears to be a fusion of Spanish or Mexican-Catholic elements with native Pueblo features." Ellis (1954:678) posited another possibility—"amalgamation," or the "absorption of Catholic elements"—and claimed it was more prevalent among the Eastern Pueblos than compartmentalization. The concept remained vague, however. If one is to imagine these modes along a hypothetical continuum with compartmentalization and fusion at its opposite extremes, "amalgamation" would seem to refer an intermediate situation in which exogenous elements remain identifiable as such and yet have become integrated into the living cultural fabric. In any case, the Matachines dance seems to involve all three, and in any given pueblo one or another of these modes will be discernible or prevalent.

Without clarifying the distinction between "fusion" and "amalgamation," George Barker (1958) contends that fusion and compartmentalization are demonstrably separate and distinct processes, on the basis of a comparison of Catholic processions among the Yaqui and among the Eastern Pueblos. Among the Pueblos after the revolt, he argues, native religion was allowed to coexist, in covert form, alongside overtly expressed Catholicism, and the two have since persisted as separate yet manifestly linked systems. Such compartmentalization is reflected in the fact that a saint's procession, featuring gunfire, drums, a chorus, priests, and the canopied saint's image, both precedes and follows an indigenous dance and thereby remains entirely distinct from it: "Among the Pueblos," according to Barker (1958:453), "this process may be described as analogous to a mechanical action in which two elements are combined without losing their separate identities." Perhaps the distinctive structure of Matachines processions, in which the dancers alternately face and bow to and then lead the santo and chorus, reflects its origin among the Pueblos under conditions of hostile confrontation. Symbolic opposition becomes submission, which becomes incorporation into a single stream.

Among the Yaquis, on the other hand, both Lenten or penitential and festive Catholic processions have become completely integrated into new ritual forms created through the process of fusion: "Among the Yaqui, the process is more analogous to a chemical action in which fusion of the two original elements produces a new compound" (Barker 1958:453). This happened, according to Spicer (1954), because the conditions and programs of Christianization were so different in the two cases. In contrast to the somewhat relaxed post-revolt program the Franciscans imposed on the Pueblos, the Yaqui elders invited the Jesuits in and enabled a process of rapid acculturative conversion that resulted in new, hybrid forms. It thus seems significant that there are no public Lenten processions, so important in neighboring Hispanic villages, at the pueblos (Barker 1958). Yet at Picurís, men who belonged to the Penitente brotherhood joined in the Holy Week processions and activities of nearby moradas.

This somewhat dated taxonomy for differential incorporation seems to point nonetheless to an observable truth about how distinct groups have dealt differently with the conditions of their oppression. Accordingly, there is also variation among the Río Grande pueblos with respect to degree or even combination of so-called compartmentalization, fusion, amalgamation, and probably other patterns as well. Picurís history has resulted in a high degree of amalgamation and even fusion, although compartmentalization (arguably predominant at Taos Pueblo) seems evident as well. This history involved the early decimation of a large, resistant population, followed by centuries of struggle to maintain a self-reproducing tribal population. Both "fusion" and "amalgamation" are manifest in the Picurís Matachines. Indeed, they constitute its very subject matter. Like the Maypole in which it currently culminates (plate 13), the dance is a living composite of diverse received and improvised multicolored elements, braided together through the collective act of performance.

5 · FROM ALCALDE TO TORTUGAS

A Journey Downriver

The three Taos County cases examined in the previous chapters are instructive not only about the Matachines dance but also about Indo-Hispano (and, implicitly, -Anglo) relations in the area. Moreover, the Taos County materials provide a basis for interethnic comparison as well as for an analysis of how status and class can affect dance performance and participation. There are several axes along which to analyze and compare the Taos Pueblo, Arroyo Seco, and Picurís Pueblo Matachines examples. These include symbolism, ecology, historical and contemporary political-economic context, and performance. The Taos County materials reveal a configuration of traits that one can compare and contrast with patterns to be encountered southward along the Río Grande valley.

This chapter reviews the Taos County findings and then examines seven more cases between San Juan Pueblo and the Mexican border. The same methodology developed in the Taos research is applied to these additional materials. Each is dealt with, however, much more superficially. Whereas the goal in each previous chapter was to achieve ethnographic depth, here the aim will be for comparative breadth.

THE THREE TAOS CASES

The Taos Pueblo and Arroyo Seco Matachines performances are separate and yet related, in the past as well as today. They are, like the Matachines performances of Alcalde and San Juan or, probably, El Rancho and San Ildefonso, or Bernalillo and Sandía, companion traditions. Their comparison, especially when added to the Picurís material, suggests that whereas in Indian versions the primary symbolic preoccupation seems to be interethnic cleavage (in both opposite senses of "to cleave"), in the

Hispano case the oppositional lines expressed by the dance tend to be internal and largely, it appears, of a class or status nature. The Arroyo Seco dance shows the unmistakable influence of Taos Pueblo in terms of form, content, and music, but the central preoccupation, at least today, is not with Indians or the Indian-Hispano interface, even though this relation is certainly referred to. The Picurís Matachines resembles the Taos Pueblo version in several ways also, although it presents some interesting differences as well.

On the basis of this Taos comparison, one may postulate that in general, Pueblo and Mexicano versions of the Matachines dance differ in their patterns of preoccupation. Because the dance came to the Indians via the Spaniards and symbolizes their subjugation and transformation by them, Pueblo Matachines tend to foreground the Indian-Hispanic relation and to express ambivalence about it. As the contrast between Taos and Picurís pueblos suggests, the degree and form of this expression varies according to historical and current circumstances. In Pueblo versions, aboriginal and Christian religious traditions are symbolically juxtaposed and commented on, and Mexicano performers are included.

In Mexicano versions, the ancestral legacy is unitary and chauvinistic, and Indians and Moors are symbolically conflated and contained. Indians do not participate. The central preoccupation is internal and primarily along class or other hierarchical lines, including the relation between church or clergy and village. Intraethnic rivalries and oppositions are what get foregrounded. This may have been otherwise during the colonial period, when the fact or memory of interethnic warfare was immediate. It may even have been the case in Arroyo Seco in 1929 and/or 1934, during the period of the Pueblo land claims trials and ejections.

Whereas the contemporary association of the Matachines with Hispano ethnocultural revivalism makes perfect sense, one would not expect to encounter the dance as a manifestation of Pueblo ethnocultural revivalism — on the contrary. This expectation is born out by the Taos Pueblo example, in which ethnocultural revival seems to suppress the Matachines dance. Yet Picurís quickly poses an exception to this proposition, even while it seems to confirm others. The revivalistic aspect of the Matachines dance at Picurís, concurrent with the church restoration and enacted among a significant but not universal portion of the tribal population, becomes understandable in light of that pueblo's history and present demographic relation to neighboring communities. Both Christianity and the dance that symbolizes it have undergone intensive fusion and amalgamation with indigenous elements at Picurís, visible right alongside the common Eastern Pueblo pattern of compartmentalization.

The way in which dance participation and performance interact with class position seems to differ between Indians and Mexicanos and, like the dance itself, to reflect divisions within colonial as well as contemporary society. For example, in Taos County it is lower-status Mexicanos who tend to participate in the pueblo's Matachines dance, whereas higher-status elements organize the dance within the Mexicano community. The internal divisions reflected in Mexicano Matachines performances tend to be of a class, status, and/or factional nature, whereas in the two pueblos the most salient internal opposition seems to be religious-ethnic: Christianity is always symbolically juxtaposed to Indian religion, and Pueblo people seem drawn to this particular dance according to the intensity of their Catholicism. The dance is maintained and organized by distinct if functionally analogous institutions in Pueblo and Hispano cases: by the governor's staff or kiva groups in the pueblos, and by church mayordomos and certain families in Mexicano communities.

As a group, the Taos County dances share several features that set them apart from other Río Grande examples. These include the Maypole, done only in these three communities,[1] and the general character of the Abuelos. In all three cases the Abuelos include a transvestite, or Perejundia, who, at Taos and Arroyo Seco and apparently in the past at Picurís, gives birth to a doll or two. As shall be seen, Perejundias are not universal and tend to accentuate the clowns' burlesque quality. Yet the significance of these traits may lie less in their simple presence or absence than in what the details of their actual performance reveal about the particular people involved.

In sum, the Taos case materials suggest a few propositions about how Pueblo and Mexicano Matachines performances differ, about how class affects participation, and about the nature and role of clowning and reversals in the symbolic discourse of live performance. With these ideas in mind, I shall now embark on a journey down the river to look at seven more Matachines dances.

RÍO ARRIBA AND RÍO ABAJO

The upper two-thirds of the upper Río Grande valley contain northern and southern portions known as the Río Arriba and Río Abajo, respectively. Their transition zone is called La Bajada, a steep gradient on the road between Albuquerque and Santa Fe. The Río Abajo (lower river) extends between La Bajada and Socorro. Van Ness (1979) has identified the Río Arriba and Río Abajo as distinct ecological zones characterized by differential patterns of Hispano economic adaptation: the Río Arriba consists of river and mountain corporatelike villages, and the Río Abajo of more dispersed ranching communities. The majority of cases to be looked at in this book are located in the more mountainous Río Arriba. Bernalillo and the Tijeras complex fall within the wider, more open Río Abajo (map 4). Tortugas sits below the Río Abajo, near the border between the upper and lower Río Grande valleys—between New Mexico and Texas and between Anglo and Latin America. There, the Matachines's completely mestizo character embraces both New Mexican and Mexican elements.

The particular selection of communities presented in this chapter is the mixed result of design and chance, dictated initially by the practical need to expand my scope beyond the sporadic Taos Pueblo version. The prominence or distinctiveness of certain versions (Jémez, Bernalillo, Tortugas) directed some choices, while simple opportunity offered others (El Rancho, San Juan-Alcalde, San Antonio and its neighbors). Even though it lies farther south than Alcalde, the tour will begin with San Juan Pueblo because of its reputed primacy as a site of Christian-Moorish ritual drama.

Although I have tried to convey an accurate sense of the character of each particular version, it is seems likely that I have overlooked important aspects of each of these traditions. Only the most obvious features of each performance tradition are touched on. The reader will notice some unevenness in the degree of contextualization I have been able to provide in each instance, dictated largely by circumstance and by the availability of secondary source materials. Each amounts to a quick study. A closer examination of all the following cases, as well as of other Matachines traditions, is warranted.

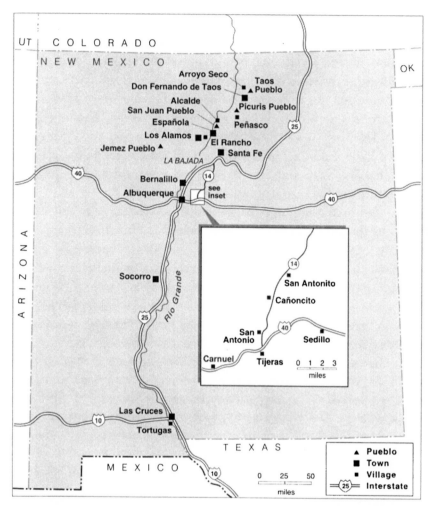

Map 4. Towns and pueblos in the Río Grande valley whose Matachines performances are discussed in chapter 5.

SAN JUAN PUEBLO

San Juan is the largest, northernmost Tewa-speaking pueblo, located in Río Arriba County about ten miles north of Española and thirty miles southwest of Picurís. San Juan was the site of the earliest Spanish settlement colony and thus bore the first brunt of occupation, although the capital was transferred to Santa Fe in 1610. Along with Taos and Picurís, it was one of the major instigators of the Pueblo Revolt and was the home of Popé, the best-known revolt leader. The first performance of Los Moros y Cristianos in New Mexico, sometimes confounded with the Matachines, is said to have occurred across the river from San Juan Pueblo to commemorate completion of the San Gabriel chapel in 1598 (Villagrá 1933; Dozier 1958:446; Ortiz 1979:281). Today San Juan performs the Matachines dance but not Los Moros y Cristianos. My account of the San Juan Matachines is based upon published materials, my own observation of the dance on Christmas Day 1989, and Brenda Romero's recent dissertation (1993) on the Alcalde and San Juan traditions.

The San Juan Matachines is performed on December 24 and 25, followed by the Turtle dance on the twenty-sixth, a prelude to which is held after the Matachines on Christmas evening. Romero (1993:246) reports that dance practice begins on the thirteenth and continues for ten days. According to Parsons and Kurath, the Matachines begins on Christmas Eve morning with a mass and procession that involves separation and reunion between two groups, one bearing santos and singing alabanzas, the other composed of the Matachines dancers and musicians. They meet along the road between the church and the graveyard. The return procession is punctuated by intervals of dancing in front of specific sites, including a small kiva (Parsons 1939b:852ff., cited in Kurath 1970:265). They dance three or four times on the twenty-fourth and perform the ritual circuit from the church to the central and north plazas and back, and then break until the vespers procession (Romero 1993:242, 257). The *vísperas* includes "Gregorian recitative-like chanting." Luminarias and occasional gunfire mark the evening procession. A group of women carry statues of the Holy Family while a few older men, probably Hermanos, chant the rosary (Romero 1993:258).

The dance begins in front of the church on Christmas morning, right after mass. The dancers proceed to various locales, up to a total of eight dance stations, which Kurath (1970:258) says include the Catholic priest's house, the north plaza, the south plaza, and the houses of El Monarca, La Malinche, the summer cacique, and the winter cacique. They may enter houses for a refreshment and brief rest, but the governor's feast is held off until after the dancing is done. Preparations for the Turtle dance have already begun inside the village by the time the Matachines is over, almost as if to sweep away all trace of what went before.

The Matachines falls under the jurisdiction of the pueblo's Spanish-style officials, including the governor's office, which also collects camera fees. The *Towa é* (an apparently indigenous level of Tewa political-ceremonial officers) preside over the Turtle dance (Ortiz 1969:61–77, 158), which cannot be photographed. The Matachines's proximity to this important aboriginal solstice ceremony posits a clear oppositional link between the two religious systems, a theme further underscored in the way Indian elements are woven throughout the fabric of the dance.

As at both Taos and Jemez, the costumes at San Juan exhibit a lavishness not seen at Picurís or, for that matter, in most Mexicano villages, with the exception of El Rancho. However, unlike the case at Taos or Picurís, there is a strong Indian cast to the San Juan Matachines costumes, which include beaded moccasins, feathered cupiles (an eagle feather on each side), plains-style beaded vests, kilts and fancy felt leggings, jewelry (including arm guards or *ketoh*), arm bands, and sleigh-bell belts (plates 14 and 15). The San Juan palmas are brightly painted with Indian designs, and the guajes are gourd rattles. The dancers have a polished sartorial quality somewhat reminiscent of Taos Pueblo's with its intense colors, good clothes, and tall cupiles (although the San Juan cupiles are slightly shorter and more slanted to the back). But the feathers, bells, and moccasins create a very different effect. The dancers' soft-soled footwork is bouncier and brings them closer to the ground, while their body movements seem just a bit looser than those at Taos Pueblo. Absent is the acoustical conquest symbol of hard soles upon the earth, so prominent in the Taos and Picurís performances. Kurath (1970:263) noted how the San Juan danzantes simultaneously move their palmas horizontally and their guajes vertically, an impressive feat of coordination. Romero (1993:262–63) reports that the danzantes sometimes tie their ribbons back on alternate days and wear white shirts on one day and colored shirts the next.

The Malinche wears high, white, wrapped moccasins and a rhinestone diadem. Although color change appears not to be a regular feature of her costume, scattered references to yellow (Parsons 1939b) and blue (Champe 1983) dresses suggest that it may be observed on occasion. The Monarca wears light-colored creased pants and a pale ribbon shirt, and no feathers in his corona, which is tipped with a small cross. The Toro is a young boy, dressed in a Guernsey (brown and white) cowhide and helmet with horns attached. Another young boy beats a drum when the Toro is killed and castrated, while a rifle is fired into the air. As elsewhere, the Malinche, Torito, and other dancers are pinned with or handed dollar bills throughout the course of the event.

There are two Abuelos, both male figures in boots, with chicotes and distinctive sorts of masks. They do not include a transvestite, or Perejundia. Their conelike headpieces are fashioned out of either hide or some stiff synthetic material onto which a face and other features such as flap ears or fringe are either painted or affixed. The expressions on these masks today seem more startled or whimsical than dreadful, and they belong to a type found also at Alcalde and Jémez.

Kurath (1970:257) erroneously refers to the Abuelos by the Tewa term *tsaviyo,* which Ortiz (1969) calls "Tsave Yoh" in reference instead to the masked whipper kachinas who appear in the Turtle dance. Kurath (1970:262) describes a range of familiar Abuelo antics such as mocking the dancers and musicians, and she mentions a third clown in 1964 who wore a feathered camera and emulated "the blank expression of a tourist photographer." Their jovial but guardlike manner weds entertainment to crowd control.

One Abuelo seems more prominent than the other, guiding Malinche in her dance (plate 16) and interacting with the Monarca in a gambit, seen also in the Taos County cases, that involves a short sequence in which the squatting Abuelo strokes Monarca's knee or pulls on his leg or foot, in some cases when the latter rises from his chair to dance. It is done in a variety of ways. At San Juan in 1989 it took place during Monarca's dance when all the matachines were kneeling, which they do on both knees (in contrast to the Taos cases). The Abuelo touched Monarca's extended foot with his looped chicote (fig. 8).[2] The first Abuelo occasionally teases people in the audience, mostly women. Typically he will pull a white woman (Indian women run away) from the sidelines to dance with him or will hand her the castrated bull's pretend testicles, represented in some 1989 sets by a walnut.

San Juan's music is similar to Alcalde's and includes seven tunes and five movements. Romero (1993:250) reports that the tunes are sometimes called "octaves" and lists a total of eight sequences between the two neighboring repertoires (La Entrada, La Cortesía, La Malinche, El Monarca, La Cruz, La Mudada, El Toro, La Cerrada de la Danza), although neither San Juan nor Alcalde performs all eight of them. A drum is used at San Juan to

Figure 8. Foot pantomime, San Juan Pueblo, December 25, 1989.

accompany the arrival of the dancers at the beginning, and again when the Torito is killed and a rifle discharged. There is some overlap in musicians for the San Juan and Alcalde versions, and occasionally among the Abuelos as well. Although there are differences between them in terms of both performance and costume, the San Juan and Alcalde versions are quite similar and, like the historically linked cases of Taos and Arroyo Seco, should probably be studied as a pair. As companion traditions, these two versions might be expected to hold a rich store of information about the historical and contemporary relations between these neighboring communities and thus about the Indian-Hispano contrast in general.

ALCALDE

The Alcalde Matachines dance is embedded in a web of social relations and religious meanings that overlaps at certain points with that of San Juan. The two dance traditions nevertheless belong to organizationally separate constituencies. Just as the Turtle dance picks up after the Matachines at San Juan, so does the Alcalde Matachines follow the Turtle dance within the larger intercommunity context.

Alcalde lies about three miles north of San Juan and seven miles north of Española, in Río Arriba County. It sits on the northern edge of the town of Chamita land grant, made in 1724, which also encompasses San Juan Pueblo. Alcalde performs the Matachines on December 26 and 27, starting the first day with a vespers mass and night procession, followed by dancing and feasting on the second day. Kurath (1970:257) noted that Alcalde used to do the dance occasionally on July 25 for the feast of Santiago, although this is no longer the case. The event is spread out over a fairly broad geographical area centering on two churches located about two miles apart. My description is based upon observation in 1989 and secondary materials, including Romero's dissertation (1993).

The dance begins around three in the afternoon of the twenty-sixth and is followed by vespers and a procession along an unpaved back road from the old chapel of San Antonio in the Alcalde placita north to the new church of Santa Ana, just off highway 68. They carry their saints from the placita chapel to the church on the first night and return them after dinner on the second night, reversing the route. The procession resembles those at Picurís and San Juan in that a few Hermanos may accompany the saints and sing the rosary. They are preceded by the Matachines dancers and musicians. The dancers alternately advance, facing ahead, and skip backward, facing the saints.

The dancing begins after morning mass on the twenty-seventh, inside a cordoned area in front of the Santa Ana church, and continues throughout the day at selected sites around the village of Alcalde, including in front of the old morada (Romero 1993:279). Dance sites include the homes of certain older people, or *viejitos,* the mayordomos, La Malinche, and El Monarca. The mayordomos host a noonday feast.

There are social dances on both nights, held at a popular dance hall where the Matachines rehearsals and the day's final dance set take place. Practice sessions are held for five or six days and end on December 23 (Romero 1993:279). The Alcalde Matachines is an important festive event that draws locals and visitors throughout the day, including musicians and other *folkloristas* from nearby communities. Players who know the Alcalde–San Juan music may join in during the last sets of the day, as some

Figure 9. The exchange of guaje and palma between Malinche and Monarca, San Juan Pueblo, December 25, 1989.

did in 1989, when two violinists and two guitarists played for the grand finale.

The dance sequences are broadly similar at Alcalde and San Juan in that both begin with a set in which Monarca wheels between the two lines of kneeling Matachines. At San Juan, Monarca wheels between pairs of danzantes before they kneel, whereas at Alcalde, he wheels between them after they have risen (Champe 1983:96). As at San Juan, the cortesía segment is done on both knees. Next comes Malinche's dance, when she takes and returns Monarca's palma and guaje. At both Alcalde and San Juan they stand during this exchange (fig. 9; plate 17). A brief Abuelo-Monarca foot pantomime follows (fig. 10). Then comes La Cruz.[3] The fourth set is the Toro. The fifth involves more quadrillelike crossovers.

Throughout the dance the seven tunes are alternated in certain sequences that differ slightly between the two villages and probably vary within villages at different times. In any case, elusively different musical

Figure 10. Foot pantomime, Alcalde, December 27, 1989.

orders are said to distinguish the two versions. In the words of one Alcalde violinist, "To me it seems like they [San Juan] dance it backwards instead of . . . you know, like we start from one part and they start from the middle but dance it twice, double. So it is a little bit longer than ours."

As might be expected, the Alcalde version is devoid of the overtly Indian elements so striking at San Juan. Alcalde's ten danzantes wear clothes ranging from suits to shirts with creased pants and street shoes. El Monarca wears a light-colored suit and corona. Some palmas have rounded or almost arabesquelike lines. Malinche sometimes wears pink on the twenty-sixth, but white on the twenty-seventh. As elsewhere in this region, the Toro is a young boy, who in 1989 was even younger than the boy at San Juan and wore a small buffalo hide with horns (plate 18).

The dance starts out with two clowns, and more may appear throughout the day. In 1989 the initial pair included a Perejundia, portrayed as an old woman in a coat, bandanna, long skirt, and gloves, carrying a purse (plate 19). The Abuelo was very similar to the ones at San Juan, with a homemade, fringed cone mask and long, lariatlike whip (plate 20). That afternoon two more Abuelos, in jumpsuits with ape and clown rubber masks, joined in, and at the end, yet another appeared. The Perejundia, usually played by one particular local, wore a pale, wrinkled rubber mask with a mat of white hair. Around noon she removed her coat to reveal a brightly colored dress with modest padding beneath (plate 21). Shortly thereafter she was ushered out, due to her inebriation—just as in 1988, when the same performer had come dressed as a harlot. Some years ago another Abuela had a tendency to utter too many "bad words" and evidently had to be "reined in."

One noteworthy aspect of the Alcalde tradition is its association with the Penitentes, attested to, as at Picurís, by their role in the rosary and procession. The Hermanos sing the rosary to San Antonio on the first night and to Santa Ana on the second night. One of the Matachines tunes and sets is known in Alcalde as the Rosario. Intensive ethnographic research would be needed to plumb the meaning of this and other images important to the Alcalde and San Juan versions.

In 1989, the first dance of the morning was followed by *Los Comanches,* a scripted folk play performed on horseback. Composed in the eighteenth century, this drama depicts a battle between Mexicanos and Comanche warriors led by their chieftain, Cuerno Verde. It is based on historical events and modeled on the Moro-Cristiano format of Iberian reconquest dances.[4] In the 1920s Alcalde also performed Los Moros y Cristianos (Austin 1928, cited in Weigle and White 1988:409), but it does not do so today. It revived Los Comanches in the middle 1980s, with the help of a local folklorist-violinist and professor of languages who procured a script for community use. Alcalde is said to have borrowed capes and swords from Chimayó, which also recently revived its Moro y Cristiano tradition.

Los Comanches involves approximately ten men on horseback, divided into two opposing groups, who ride toward each other, face off, and engage in a mock battle narrated by their spoken—or shouted—lines. The central character is Cuerno Verde, who narrates the dance and exhorts the audience. In 1989 Cuerno Verde wore a concha headband with a green feather and a brightly banded Mexican serape as a cape, draped across the back of his horse. One side of his face was painted white, the other black. The other "Comanches" also wore feathers and war bonnets, while their Spanish or Mexican adversaries wore hats and carried lances. The play lasted about forty minutes, after which everyone drove back from the Santa Ana church to Alcalde to have lunch and wait for the Matachines to resume.

The Matachines dance is an important annual obligation for the people of Alcalde, who express warm pride in it and for whom it embodies a self-conscious sense of cultural heritage and continuity. Today most of the dancers are in their teens or early twenties. Their mentors, mostly middle-aged organizers of the dance, praise their effort and recall that a few years ago the bond of cooperation and mutual reliability between generations had begun to break down. Primarily older men danced then, but they would get drunk and not show up, so the dance devotees decided to train the boys instead.

Despite difficulties and a period of waning interest, Alcalde has maintained the tradition more or less continuously. The present violinist, who has participated in the dance since he was a teenager, remembers only once when the Matachines was not performed, the year the mayordomo's son died. He told me that when they reorganized some years ago they made all the hats at the same time and copied the San Juan cupil, departing from the style used previously at Alcalde. This was a corona covered with flowers, similar to the Monarca's crown. He hoped to reinstate the old form, which, like the Picurís corona, is made with green willow branches.

As in so many Mexicano communities, the musicians of Alcalde are the repositories and custodians of the Matachines and other oral-musical traditions. They are the sine qua non of performance and regeneration. A number of present-day musicians who know the music, including two active violinists, concentrate on playing for Alcalde and San Juan respectively. Because it carries the tune, the violin is the key instrument for the Matachines. The Alcalde musicians are not paid to perform in their own village, whereas San Juan pays its Mexicano violinist. A generation ago Carmelito Torres, a violinist from San Juan known for his mastery of the subtle differences between the two versions, played for both communities. Today's musicians express a sense of connection and apprenticeship to him and to others, including the now-retired folklorist-violinist mentioned earlier, and to those they themselves instruct.

Enthusiasm for the dance has increased in recent years, partly, some say, in response to publicity generated by an Anglo photographer who moved to Alcalde in the 1970s. Today almost all men in the community have participated in the dance at one time or another, and there is a significant contingent of young dancers available to perform on other occasions as well, at other locales, which they do as a traveling troupe. Thus, like those from El Rancho, the Alcalde Matachines dancers will perform on special occasions at other places for a fee or "donation." Such occasions include fiestas, special events, and cultural demonstrations for tourists.[5]

EL RANCHO

El Rancho is a Mexicano community located between Pojoaque and San Ildefonso pueblos in the Pojoaque valley in Santa Fe County. It sits along a paved road off highway 502 to Los Alamos, roughly twenty-three miles northwest of Santa Fe. This community appears to have been settled at the beginning of the eighteenth century and sits inside the boundaries of the San Ildefonso Pueblo grant, a perennial cause for litigation ever since 1762 (Snow 1991:3).[6] In her study of the San Ildefonso Matachines dance, performed on Christmas, Champe (1983) makes no mention of the El Rancho performance, possibly because it lapsed for about twenty years between the 1950s and 1972, when it was revived by a number of younger men who formed a dance troupe that now also performs elsewhere for special occasions.

Today the Matachines may be performed in El Rancho up to three times a year: on New Year's afternoon, on San Antonio Day (June 13), and for La Santísima Trinidad in October. It may be held in at least two locations: in the placita in front of the old chapel on *el día de San Antonio* and in the parking lot of the local cantina and dance hall on New Year's afternoon. The former instance is embedded in the usual routine of mass and procession, whereas the better-known January 1 performance seems to have a more secular air in that it takes place adjacent to a cantina. As much as "secularization," this move reflects the shift from the old to the new functional "placita" social space of the living community (Levine 1991; Snow 1991). Most outsiders witness only the New Year's Day performance (as in my case). My description is based upon secondary materials and observation in 1990 and 1991.

Lapse of the El Rancho Matachines seems to parallel those in other Hispanic villages during roughly the same period. In any case, as elsewhere, the dance made a comeback in the 1970s, undergoing in the process a modification in its basic organization. Several individuals and their families, including men who had lived away and returned, played key roles in regenerating the El Rancho Matachines. Today older boys are easily recruited. The revivalists drew on their own memories of the dance and consulted elders, including a man at San Ildefonso Pueblo, who taught them the steps (Lynn 1988).

One member of the new organizing generation plays the Abuelo and serves as the principal interlocutor for the El Rancho Matachines performance. Although less central and authoritarian, his role is vaguely reminiscent of the Arroyo Seco impresario's in that he announces and explains the dance to the audience. As a well-known aficionado of the dance, this man proclaims a wish to see the Matachines universally revived throughout northern New Mexico.

According to the Abuelo's account, the dance depicts the arrival of Cortés in Mexico and his conversion of Malinche to Christianity. The Abuelo claims it originated in Spain, where the masks were developed to protect the anonymity of Christians during the Moorish occupation. He states that the figure of the Abuelo, however, is not Iberian but comes from the Pueblo clowns, or *koshare*. There are nine sets, which he describes as follows: (1) La Marcha, or procession of the dancers to the dance site; (2) *Entrada;* (3) La Cruz, or "the introduction of Christianity to the Indians"; (4) Las Palmas, or "instruction in religion"; (5) Capitanes, or sword dance; (6) Malinche, in which "the Abuelo introduces Malinche to Monarca (who gives her his guaje and palma) and then to each half of the population, after which the Abuelo pays homage to Monarca" through the leg pantomime; (7) Torito, in which the bull, "symbolizing evil, is converted into a steer"; (8) *La Cuna,* a slow, waltzlike movement with two U-shaped lines moving in opposite directions; (9) *La Vuelta,* a dance in which the two lines form a cross and then a circle, signifying that "everyone has been Christianized and united in harmony." Next follows the marcha and despedida, which reverse the entrada.

In the procession, the dancers, led by the main Abuelo, emerge from the back of the dance club where they change clothes. They march along the road, circling around to enter the parking lot from the opposite direction. They reverse this route during the recessional. When the weather dictates it, the dance ground is prepared in advance with a dry layer of dirt or sand. Although some argue that performance of the Matachines next to a cantina "secularizes" its meaning (Snow 1991), it is evident that the procession, which begins and returns to a place very close to the dance area, symbolically circumscribes a ritual space set apart from the everyday setting. A close analysis of the full El Rancho Matachines cycle might well reveal how the Abuelo and other figures mediate such contradictions between symbols of past and living practice.

At present there are usually two violinists, two guitarists, and three Abuelos, including the master of ceremonies. In 1990 there were twelve danzantes plus a small boy dressed as a matachín, who danced at the front of the righthand column facing the musicians. The Abuelo introduced him as the youngest apprentice in one of the custodial families. The practice of having one or two child danzantes is not uncommon in other communities.

The main or impresario Abuelo dresses in a suit and tie. He has a grizzled beard and wears a custom-made, gold-colored mask with bushy eyebrows over the upper half of his face. In 1990 and 1991 all three Abuelos were male figures with masks or wigs and paint, carrying chicotes. They teased people in the audience, stole shoes and purses, grabbed women to dance, and hoisted children into the air. The El Rancho Abuelo stands out not only because he is a master of ceremonies but also for his aggressive targeting of women and children in the audience, which gives him a somewhat predatory air. In 1990 he spun around a child in a wheelchair, and the next year he threw a young boy to the ground and proceeded to strip off his shoes, socks, jacket, and sweater.

The leg pantomime is turned into a comic routine in which the kneeling second Abuelo hugs and kisses Monarca's knee and then, pretending to be kicked, somersaults backward (plate 22). The first Abuelo does likewise (fig. 11). This act follows Malinche's palma-guaje exchange with Monarca, which is just a quick snatch, with none of the protracted arm rotation seen elsewhere (plate 23). The Torito is a young boy dressed in a tunic of soft, artificial brown fur, with a cap with horns. One side of his face is painted white, the other brown, and he uses a single stick or cane (plate 24). His castration and demise at the hands of the Abuelos is graphic, his testicles in 1990 being represented by a small, droopy leather bag offered to a woman in jest.

El Rancho's Matachines costumes are the most elaborate I have seen in a Mexicano village. They are made by the women. They have an opulent, brocaded, layered quality with lots of glitter, gold ribbon, embroidery, and ruffles. The Monarca and the four Capitanes, or corner dancers, are specially arrayed with coronas instead of cupiles, and with *fundas de almo-*

Figure 11. Foot pantomime somersault, El Rancho, January 1, 1990.

hada, or embroidered pillowcase leggings. Their garlanded coronas are ornamentally tipped with rings, a bird, or a cross. The danzantes' layered effect is enhanced by an extra shawl around the head, which encompasses the ribbons that flow back from the cupil and give the figure a distinctive "Moorish" cast (plate 25). The little dancer is dressed as a miniature capitán. All the dancers and Malinche wear white gloves.

Money is pinned to all the dancers, including the Abuelos, and an older man passes around a slotted box for donations. As at Alcalde, the audience applauds after certain sets. The New Year's Day performance lasts a bit more than an hour and is followed by a party in the cantina–dance hall.

Several features of the El Rancho dance seem to have parallels in what Champe (1983:51) reports for San Ildefonso. For example, she notes that there is a thirteenth young matachín apprentice and that the Abuelo "makes a speech that delights the crowd" during a brief intermission before the Toro enters. She reports one principal Abuelo accompanied by a variable number of secondary clowns who usher the procession into the dance area. The Toro is usually a young boy with one cane, whose face may be painted (Champe 1983:15–16). The four capitanes and Monarca all share the same kind of adorned coronas and fundas, or pillowcase leggings, seen at El Rancho (Champe 1983:10). All the Matachines wear gloves.

Champe also indicates some differences. For one, the secondary clowns at San Ildefonso sometimes include an Abuela (she does not use the word *Perejundia*), who on one occasion wore a long raincoat and carried a toy trombone (Champe 1983:14). There is no Abuela in the El Rancho version today, and she may or may not have appeared there in the past. It seems that the Malinche-Monarca palma-guaje exchange is more drawn out at San Ildefonso (1983:39). Research on both versions is needed to uncover the relationships they evolved in the past and experience today.[7]

JÉMEZ PUEBLO

Jémez is a Tanoan, Towa-speaking pueblo located in Sandoval County, roughly thirty-five miles northwest of Albuquerque and forty miles southwest of Santa Fe. Its nearest Mexicano neighbors are Vallecitos (now called Ponderosa) and Cañon. The nearest pueblo is Zía (Keresan).

The full Jémez Matachines dance is traditionally performed on December 12, or Día de Guadalupe. Its most striking feature is that "Indian" and "Mexican" or "Spanish" versions are performed by the Pumpkin (or Squash) and Turquoise moieties, respectively. The two versions, usually performed alternately at least three times throughout the day by two different dance groups, are choreographically similar but musically and stylistically distinct. The Mexican, or Turquoise, version precedes the Pumpkin version. The Turquoise and sometimes the Pumpkin version is repeated on New Year's morning. Sometimes the Turquoise version is accompanied by another dance performed by the Pumpkin kiva, such as the Buffalo dance or Shield dance. Both versions are very elegant in terms of costume and execution, but the Pumpkin Matachines seems particularly stunning, perhaps because it is so rare—Santa Clara's (done on Christmas Day) being the only other completely "Indian"-style version. My description is based upon observation in 1985, 1988, and 1989, in addition to secondary materials.

The Jémez Matachines has eight movements. The "Mexican" version involves eight tunes played by violin and guitar, and conventional European-style clothing. The "Indian" version features Indian costumes and drumming and chanting, with several, possibly eight, different songs. These are chanted by a chorus of men with a small drum who stand near one end of the dance circle. Their faces are streaked with red paint, and one man carries a small American flag.

The dance begins around ten in the morning, after a mass held in the San Diego mission church. The congregation and dance company proceed from the church to the dance plaza, where a shrine for the Virgin and other saints is set up under a ramada on the northwest side. They enter from the east and later on, in recession to the church, exit at the west. The long-stemmed crucifix carried in the procession is planted in front of the ramada, which is bowered with fresh evergreen branches and flanked in front by two Christmas trees. The walls are hung with blankets, and chairs are placed along the sides for honored guests. The saints are displayed on a table altar at the back, with candles and offerings of corn meal placed to receive homage and bestow blessing. They are visited by worshippers throughout the day. This includes the Turquoise dancers, who file past them at the end of their dance. Bread, coffee, and other refreshments are provided for guests in the ramada throughout the day. The dance usually begins with the Turquoise version, followed by the Pumpkin. Everyone then breaks for lunch, and guests are invited to eat in people's homes. In the afternoon usually two dances of both versions are performed again.

The Pumpkin dancers' costumes are more Indian than those at San Juan. The dancers wear moccasins, white crocheted tights, and fringed shawl kilts held by concha belts. They wear brightly colored shirts with armbands and jewelry, including a ketoh on one wrist and a shell bracelet on the other. They also wear belts dangling with shells, and shell pendants. Their high moccasins are white with black soles and ankle pieces of skunk fur. Tied around each calf is a skein of yarn, green on the left side and red on the right. The backs of their hands are painted with a cream-colored clay with diagonal hatches scraped across. Three feathers tip each cupil. In general, they seem to have more ribbons and scarves than the Turquoise dancers.

Both Pumpkin and Turquoise cupiles involve velvet facing with turquoise jewelry. The Turquoise danzantes wear shirts, shoes or boots, creased pants, and, like the others, fringed shawl kilts held by concha belts. The four capitanes and Monarca wear either fundas or lace leggings. A single downy feather is affixed to the top of each cupil. The palmas of both groups have five rather than the customary three prongs and are looped with tinsel garland pinned with bows. Their guajes are maracas held in the naked hand pointing down. Their eye fringe (fleco) is variously colored. Each Monarca is dressed like his capitanes except that he wears a four-sided, peaked cloth cap decorated with turquoise.

The Jémez dance style is notable for its balletlike quality, especially pronounced in the Pumpkin version, in which, as at San Juan, the difference made by the dancers' wearing moccasins is striking. The dancers enter the plaza lightly prancing, and their entire execution has a bouncy, light-footed vigor, characterized also by broad, smooth, sweeping arm movements. Although highly controlled, the kinesthetic style seems much less constrained and more exuberant than that in other versions I have seen.

The Monarca is a virtuoso whose prowess rivets audience attention. He rises slowly from a crouching position after Malinche's dance, and while an Abuelo pulls on one leg, he dances along on the other. The exchange between Malinche and Monarca involves the usual arm rotation and her weaving along and between the two rows. She is led by an Abuelo who dances backward, facing her along her transit.

The sequence of tunes and named sets in the Turquoise version seems to be (1) Entrada, (2) Monarca (short), (3) Malinche, (4) Monarca (fast), (5) La Cruz, (6) Toro, (7) *Paseo de Calles,* and (8) another Paseo. The Pumpkin names for these movements and accompanying chants are not generally known. Because the first Monarca set is short, Malinche is the first long dance, followed by the Monarca's second set, which in turn leads into La Cruz. Here, Monarca and Malinche wheel with groups of three danzantes, their wrists linked by a strip of cloth. The four capitanes exchange positions diagonally, and the two lines then move into the form of a cross. In the Toro segment, Malinche uses Monarca's palma instead of a paño to wave at the bull, and similarly, all the dancers swipe at him with their palmas as they skip past him in diagonal lines between rows. They swing their large, five-pronged palmas horizontally. The final Paseos begin with a cross formation that reassembles into rows and culminates in a slow, waltzlike movement. In both versions, one or two men in headbands walk along the rows of dancers, touching a pinch of cornmeal from a small leather bag to the inside shoulder of each.

The Pumpkin Malinche wears a black manta or shift with one shoulder, high white moccasins with black soles, jewelry, and a crown of tropical feathers. Her Turquoise counterpart wears the customary communion dress with a veil, a turquoise necklace, white tights, and gloves. Like all Malinches, both appear extremely serious.

El Toro, played by a young boy, is prominent at Jémez. In both versions he is carefully outfitted, and all over the plaza he chases and is chased by Abuelos and a rowdy gang of little boys. The Pumpkin Torito wears white moccasins, white crocheted tights, and white kilt and shirt, and his hands are painted brown. Like the Turquoise bull he wears a Holstein (black and white) cowhide, in his case fitted with evergreens and tropical feathers between the horns. His canes are of semifinished wood with leather handles. The slightly less elegant Turquoise Torito wears regular clothes with boots and a similar hide, but his face is painted white.

The Jémez Abuelos are different from those described so far, although their headpieces are vaguely reminiscent of those noted in the Tewa basin. Instead of being cone-shaped, however, they sport two hornlike cones and are fashioned out of hide, with flap ears and eyebrows and mustaches of fur. Their faces have an almost winsome expression. The sides and backs of their masks are painted with "Indian" designs such as cloud symbols or corn plants, lightning, or animals. Quadrants of their faces may be painted in blocks of primary color; a few ribbons stream from their horns.

The Abuelos dress like cowboys, with plaid shirts, vests, chaps, boots, gloves, and spurs. The main Abuelo, considered the dance director and sometimes called "Monanca," wears high, yellow leather gloves and carries a lariatlike whip. He usually wears a corduroy suit jacket. The others have cowbells attached to the backs of their belts. Now and then one will ride a stick hobby horse.

There are usually at least three Abuelos, generally quite similar but with some differences. For example, the main Pumpkin Abuelo wears plains-style, ochre-colored gloves with high beaded cuffs and carries a small American flag. The main Turquoise Abuelo wears similar gloves but carries no flag. This Abuelo accompanies Malinche and Monarca, whereas the other two are in charge of the bull. Their interaction with the bull continues throughout the course of the dance, when they chase after him and the gang of children outside the dance circle, eventually capturing him with the lariat. The Abuelos call out dance sets in falsetto, using a mixture of Spanish and Towa words. They also hand the pillows the dancers use to kneel on during Monarca's dance back to family members in the audience.

All dancing is done in the same central plaza area, more or less in front of the ramada shrine. As elsewhere, circumstantial variation occurs in performance details from year to year. For example, in 1985 both dance groups numbered fourteen danzantes, seven per row, whereas in 1989 the Turquoise version had twelve and the Pumpkin eight. In some years only one moiety may perform. In 1988, for example, the Turquoise version was not done because the long-time Mexicano violinist died, a man from Ponderosa who had played for over thirty years. Instead, the Spanish version was performed by elementary-school children using recorded music and an amplifier. A new violinist (a woman from nearby Lyden) was found the following year, but in 1990 the Pumpkin group did not dance.[8]

The Jémez tradition has been less studied than other major Pueblo versions, perhaps because photography is forbidden (although it was apparently allowed some decades ago). There seems to be an implication that the Pumpkin Matachines is more sacred, or at any rate more esoteric, than the Turquoise version, in that it involves no outside musicians and thus remains beyond the sphere of non-Indian participation. On the first day of 1991, the Pumpkin moiety performed the Buffalo dance as companion to the Turquoise Matachines, which in other years might be accompanied instead by the Shield or another "enemy" or borrowed dance. The Matachines performance occupied its customary west end of the plaza, while the Buffalo dancers filled the east end, starting first but ending much sooner. Here the saints were absent, but the twofold juxtaposition of moieties and symbolized religions remained, running throughout the entire fabric of the event and defining its basic structure. Questions to answer through further study of the Jémez Matachines would be how and why this pueblo came to have distinct Indian and Spanish-Mexican versions executed by separate kiva groups. Scrutiny of the two versions through time would presumably tell a great deal about the history and character of Jémez's internal and external relations.

BERNALILLO

Bernalillo is a predominantly Hispanic town of approximately six thousand people that sits about seventeen miles north of the spreading metropolis of Albuquerque, in Sandoval County. Its nearest Pueblo neighbor is Sandía, a community of some 360 Southern Tiwa speakers that lies directly between Bernalillo and Albuquerque, providing a kind geographical and cultural buffer zone between urban and rural environments. Bernalillo is said to have been founded by reconquest leader Diego de Vargas around 1695, although local lore holds that early settlers in the area survived the Pueblo Revolt.

The Bernalillo Matachines dance is today probably the most spectacular Hispano version in New Mexico, in terms of duration, elaborateness, size, calendrical importance, and regional fame. It exhibits a particular constellation of elements that merits in-depth ethnographic and ethnohistorical research.

The Matachines is the most important annual religious celebration in Bernalillo, linked to a chain of ritual observances throughout the course of the year. It adds up, over the years, to a significant amount of time in the lives of the individuals and families who participate. By self-definition, the participants comprise the town's ongoing core population. The Matachines tradition constitutes a community-wide process that has taken shape over a number of generations and today seems indivisible from Bernalillo's symbolizing of itself as an enduring community.

The dance is performed on the town's feast day of San Lorenzo, August 10, also the anniversary of the Pueblo Revolt. Local tradition has it that the only Spanish survivors of the revolt in the neighborhood of Sandía Pueblo were a few people at Bernalillo. Because Vargas founded the new settlement and died there, Bernalillo identifies itself with him, and some locals trace the inception of the Matachines tradition to his act of reoccupation in 1693. In terms of timing as well as theme, then, the Bernalillo Matachines seems symbolically to embody the survival myth this community has evolved about itself since the late seventeenth century. The people of Bernalillo proudly claim that theirs is the original, oldest, most long-standing Matachines tradition in New Mexico.

Whereas the early context within which Bernalillo defined itself as a bounded community was shaped by proximity to Sandía Pueblo, today the dominant environmental presence is the spreading city of Albuquerque. Bernalillo's fortunes have fluctuated throughout its history. Relations with Sandía Pueblo some two miles to the south were probably a major factor during the colonial period, when, before their own church was built, Bernalillo settlers attended mass at the pueblo's San Francisco mission. A mixture of cooperation and competition doubtless persisted between these two communities for more than a century before Americanization. By the late nineteenth century and well into the twentieth, the two communities remained interdependent economically. For example, Bernalillo residents sharecropped on Sandía land, while Pueblo farmers sold crops in Bernalillo and, later on, Indian workers found employment at the sawmill there (Phillips 1987).

Before the coming of the railroad in 1880, Bernalillo rivaled Albuquerque in terms of commercial importance and size, but the quirky recalcitrance of a local landowner is said to have resulted in the railroad river crossing's being built near Albuquerque instead of Bernalillo (M. Simmons 1982:215). Thereafter Albuquerque grew into the largest city and commercial hub of New Mexico, while Bernalillo languished as a peripheralized, rural, agricultural town. A local sawmill provided employment from 1924 until 1974, when the company finally shut down completely after four decades of decline and fluctuating labor relations. The downward trend hit a low in 1958, when the new interstate highway bypassed Bernalillo, which had previously straddled the camino real. This was when the Matachines dance almost expired. But during the thirty years since then, Bernalillo has again begun to grow, largely through the process of suburbanization.

The urban expansion of Albuquerque since World War II has created new "bedroom" communities at its peripheries and has revitalized and begun to gentrify some of its older neighbors like Bernalillo. Caught at the near edge of this process, Bernalillo has managed to embark on a slow demographic and economic climb spurred by regional capital development. It is gradually repopulating through natural growth, the return of outmigrated youth, and the influx of mostly Anglo newcomers. Today people in Bernalillo often voice relief that Sandía Pueblo stands between them and the city, creating a buffer against its constant onslaught. Thus the same urban development that enabled Bernalillo to hold its ground also threatens to overwhelm it, a paradoxical situation not unlike that seen in the Río Hondo watershed north of Taos.

This recent history is mirrored in the way Bernalillo does the Matachines dance. During the town's socioeconomic descent in the 1950s, the Matachines dwindled almost to a standstill until around 1958, when pressures to assimilate and migrate out proved so great that there were no longer enough dancers available to perform. That year, dancers had to be brought in from Sandía Pueblo, which maintains its own Matachines tradition. Since that time, gradual repopulation, along with intensifying ethnic pride and awareness, has resulted in the revitalization and growth of the Bernalillo Matachines performance, such that today it involves two companies of dancers and a waiting list for future mayordomos said to be ten years long.

The turning point seems to have come during the 1970s, when some of the innovations seen today were initiated by revivalists and devotees of the dance. Among these changes were the introduction of women danzantes, the doubling of dance groups, and the taming or neutralization of the Toro and Abuelo roles. These features, in addition to the elaborated *mayordomía* system and three-day ritual structure, are what mark the Bernalillo Matachines as a distinct configuration.

Today a carnival and arts fair attend the event, which attracts increasing numbers of tourists as well as locals. The San Lorenzo fiesta lasts three days, although preparations for it go on throughout the entire year, involving monthly rosaries to the santo in the home of the sponsoring mayordomos, weekly practice sessions from the first Sunday in July, and daily practice starting in August.

Although all its component elements are familiar throughout the Río Grande region, the demanding nature and the organizational structure of the Bernalillo Matachines-San Lorenzo ritual complex seem vaguely reminiscent of the cargo or fiesta systems observed in Mesoamerica. A key theme in individual participation is the personal promesa, or vow, made in need or duress and fulfilled with a pure sense of self-sacrifice. The ideal of selfless humility in service to the saint and the community are linked practically to the extreme hospitality required of the mayordomos and to the anonymity implied by the danzantes' masks and uniform costumes.

The role of the mayordomos is especially prominent in Bernalillo because it involves a large commitment of time and resources. This married couple must maintain a shrine to San Lorenzo, patron saint of the poor, in their home for an entire year, open twenty-four hours a day to anyone who wishes to go there and pray. They host a rosary and serve refreshments on the tenth of each month, provide refreshments after rehearsals, and hold a feast for the dancers and other participants during the fiesta. In 1989 the mayordomo estimated that he and his wife provided altogether sixteen hundred meals during their year of service and said they had waited fifteen years for the honor (Trujillo 1989).

Bernalillo's seems to be the original and only major Río Grande version to have employed women matachines, except subsequently for Arroyo Seco, as well as the Tijeras, or Holy Child, complex discussed later. This practice may well have arisen out of the need to conscript any dancers at all, but it was apparently instigated by the women themselves and would seem to register a larger change in gender roles. Today one sees women danzantes every year, as well as some up-and-coming women musicians. My description is based upon secondary materials and observation in 1988, 1989, and 1991.

As at Arroyo Seco, all the Bernalillo danzantes wear white shirts and black pants and shoes. Their face kerchiefs are black, and they tie a scarf around the left arm above the elbow. Their cupiles bear pictures of saints, frequently San Lorenzo or the Virgin, or perhaps the dancer's patron saint. Monarca either wears all white or reverses the danzante color scheme with black shirt and white pants, and a floral corona.

The Toro dresses in black or red and black, uses two canes, and wears a face kerchief and red floral corona with black horns (plate 26). The Abuelo dresses like the danzantes or all in black, with a capelike paño, a flat-brimmed hat, a whip, and no mask (plate 27). He functions like an unobtrusive sergeant-at-arms rather than as the blatant clown seen elsewhere. Evidently there was a Perejundia years ago and the drama featured the usual playful skirmishing, including the demise and castration of the Toro. But these routines "have fallen by the wayside" (Kloeppel 1970:8). Today such themes are barely hinted at, through stylized choreographic passes that depict little overt conflict or burlesque. Both the Toro and the Abuelo have become sober and dignified figures.

Up to seven young girls dress like the Malinche and carry the decorated arch that precedes San Lorenzo's picture, borne by older women, in the procession. Some also fill in as Malinche during the three arduous days of celebration. Today there are also often several musicians. A drum accompanies the fiddle and guitar for certain parts of the performance.

There are twelve danzantes to each dance group, along with duplicates of each of the main cast of characters. They dance simultaneously in the same arena (plate 28). This expansion occurred in 1976 and is explained as follows: "The reason we have two [dance groups] right now is because there are a lot of men who want to dance and keep up the Matachines. So instead of turning them down, we created two dance groups" (Phillips 1987:13).

As at Taos Pueblo, the dance is embedded in a three-day progression of events with its own ritual structure. This is described in the 1989 San Lorenzo parish program and schedule of events as follows:

August 9:

2:30 P.M.	Danzantes meet at Gauna [mayordomos] Residence
3:00 P.M.	Novena
3:30 P.M.	Matachines Dance
4:20 P.M.	Promesas Dance
4:45 P.M.	Supper for Danzantes
5:30 P.M.	Danzantes meet at Gauna Residence
6:00 P.M.	Procession to Our Lady of Sorrows Church
7:30 P.M.	Vísperas (O.L.O.S.)

August 10:

9:00 A.M.	Matachines meet at Church
9:30 A.M.	Fiesta Mass in Honor of San Lorenzo
10:30 A.M.	Procession to Gauna Residence
12:00 noon	Lunch for Danzantes
2:30 P.M.	Danzantes meet at Gauna Residence
3:00 P.M.	Matachines Dance
3:50 P.M.	Promesas Dance
4:15 P.M.	Procession through Bernalillo
6:00 P.M.	Supper for Danzantes
7 P.M.–6 A.M.	Velorio for San Lorenzo
12:00 mid.	Mañanitas

August 11:

6:00 A.M.	Mañanitas y El Alba
8:15 A.M.	Danzantes meet at Gauna Residence
8:30 A.M.	Matachines Dance
8:40 A.M.	Promesas Dance
8:50 A.M.	Despedida del Santo
9:00 A.M.	Procession to Chavez [incoming mayordomos] Residence
10:30 A.M.	Recibimiento del Santo
11:15 A.M.	Return to Gauna Residence
11:45 A.M.	Entrega
9:00 P.M.	Baile (O.L.O.S. gym)

The macrostructure of the fiesta thus centers on the ceremonial transfer of the saints (two San Lorenzos: one from Bernalillo and the other, reputedly older San Lorenzo de Silva, from the small community of Llanito two miles north of Bernalillo) from the house of the presiding mayordomos to the house of the incoming mayordomos (Robinson n.d.:2). It involves several processions and a *velorio del santo,* or all-night watch over the saint, preceding departure to his new home for the coming year. *Versos,* or rhyming couplets about the participants, are sung by a certain musician during the Despedida and *Recibimiento del Santo* at the two respective homes. The major processions involve gunfire and circumscribe several square blocks in the heart of downtown Bernalillo.

The dance itself is listed as having ten movements and nine tunes:

1. La Marcha
2. La Cruzada
3. La Cambiada
4. La Malinche/La Vuelta
5. La Toreada del Toro
6. La Cruzada
7. La Tendida
8. La Patadita
9. La Promesa
10. La Corrida

The universal dance elements involving crossovers, facing off, kneeling, Monarca's dance, Malinche's dance, a kick step, and the Toro's dance are all presented, Bernalillo style.

As it is elsewhere, the Matachines dance, along with other oral and ritual traditions, tends to be preserved by musicians and their families. The music is passed from father to son, uncle to nephew, and so on. These and other long-time devotees of the dance enjoy a particular kind of prestige within the community. People begin their dance careers through a promesa to dance as a matachín during La Corrida, done in the street, when anyone may join in. From there one graduates to a position in the regular dance. Experienced dancers may then become capitanes, or corner dancers, who serve as guides to the less practiced and assist in organizing the all-night velorio. As lead dancer, the Monarca is usually someone who has been a capitán. Beginning dancers take consecutive watches over the saint during the night of August 10, and all must make a monetary contribution toward ritual costs.

All in all, the dance is a momentous undertaking. People must earn and pay for the honor of participating, with the greatest sacrifice being made by the mayordomos. The ascent is thus made from a position of self-effacing anonymity to ever-greater levels of personal expenditure and recognition. All of this points to a status hierarchy or prestige structure within Bernalillo that seems vaguely reminiscent of a Mesoamerican cargo or fiesta system, although, of course, with its own New Mexican twist. One aspiring mayordomo is said to have forfeited his place on the waiting list when he married a non-Catholic Anglo (Lawrence n.d.:29).

Another notable feature of the Bernalillo Matachines performance is occasional discord between dance devotees and parish priests, some of whom have tended to regard the town's intense pursuit as bordering on idolatry. This may or may not have to do with the rumored traditional membership of key performer-custodians in the Penitente brotherhood. In sum, although the conflation of religious and ethnic identity is by no means unique to the Bernalillo Matachines, the form it takes there would seem to offer a window onto the particular character, social structure, and historical situation of that community.

It should be mentioned that a full ethnographic analysis of the Bernalillo Matachines would probably require comparable investigation of the Sandía Pueblo version. The latter, I predict, would symbolically foreground the local Indo-Mexicano interface in some way or other, whereas Bernalillo's focus is more inward. The rich complexity of the Bernalillo case is suggested by its most prominent features. For one thing, certain elements strongly emphasized in other versions, such as ornate, colorful costumes or startling mimetic routines, appear to have receded at Bernalillo so that another element, centering on organizational structure, might receive elaboration. In contrast to the situation thirty years ago, today the "problem" for Matachines organizers is not how to recruit scarce or reluctant dancers but how to accommodate a surfeit of enthusiasts, including women danzantes. At the same time, clowning has become attenuated. The mechanism of induction combines the principle of the promesa and personal sacrifice with the prestige enjoyed by key organizers, including the mayordomos, who have a voice in selecting certain players. The Bernalillo Matachines has become a vehicle not only for collective symbolic boundary maintenance but also for a sense of personal identity and individual achievement, family solidarity, and harmonious participation within the community.

TIJERAS CANYON

A cluster of Matachines dances makes up the tradition maintained by several missions of the Santo Niño, or Holy Child, parish based in Tijeras in the eastern part of Bernalillo County, on the far, or eastern, watershed of Sandía Mountain. This complex involves performance of the dance on the feast day of each mission community, which adds up to an almost monthly round of spring, summer, and autumn observances. These widely dispersed Santo Niño (de Praga) missions include Carnuel (patron saints San Miguel and Santo Niño de Praga), San Antonio, San Antonito (patron saint Santa Cruz), Cañoncito (San Lorenzo), Sedillo (San Isidro), Escobosa (also San Isidro), and Chililí (San Juan Nepomoseno).[9]

One example of these interrelated or companion traditions will be described here—San Antonio—based on secondary material and my observations in 1990, 1991, 1992, and 1993. My account also draws on observations in San Antonito and Tijeras during the same period. The San Antonito version is very similar to San Antonio's, although details of the dance and procession differ. The Holy Child parish Matachines performances all appear to share the same musicians, Toro, and Abuelos, while each community provides its own Malinche, Monarca, and mayordomos for its annual fiesta. Danzantes are both local and parishwide. The general format of the performance in the versions I have seen is roughly the same, with implicitly significant local variations from year to year.

The first documented settlement in this area, originally known as Cañon de Carnué and now as Tijeras Canyon, dates from 1762, when an ethnically mixed group of landless petitioners from the middle Río Grande valley obtained a land grant in the name of Carnué. The village of San Miguel de Laredo, which came to be known as San Miguel de Carnué and then simply Carnué, was established near the mouth of the canyon in 1763 and abandoned in 1771 because of Apache depredations. Resettlement was marked by a new Carnué grant in 1818 (M. Simmons 1982:108–10). The present-day villages of Carnuel, San Antonito, and Tijeras are located on the Carnué land grant.

The settlement sequence and social history of these parish communities appear largely unstudied. They all lie within about twenty-five miles of Albuquerque, and today a significant proportion of their residents are employed there. But despite proximity to and a high degree of socioeconomic dependence on the city, the mountain range separating these settlements from metropolitan Albuquerque protects a strong sense of rural isolation from city life.

San Antonio (eighteen miles east of Albuquerque) has what appears to be a long-standing Matachines tradition, and indeed, its people claim theirs is the original one from which all others in the parish are derived. Día de San Antonio is June 13, and the community usually carries out the dance on the Saturday closest to that date. The celebration begins the night before with vísperas and a procession around the church, traditionally featuring luminarias and rifles all the way to the *ojo,* or spring, above the village (Sharp 1936). As elsewhere, the day of dance begins with a morning mass and procession, followed by a noonday feast, dancing in the afternoon, and a final recession back into the church. There the saint is entregado, or delivered, from the old to the new mayordomos, carried out to the singing of versos.

Several features immediately stand out in the San Antonio version: the long, well-elaborated procession (plate 29), the intense, exuberant entrega, and the fact that the bulto, or statuette, of San Antonio is sometimes dressed like a matachín with tiny ribboned cupil, palma, and guaje (plate 30). This was the case in 1990, when the Christ child he carries also wore a tiny cupil. The following year San Antonio was dressed in a little monk's robe, and the child in a hand-crocheted gown. In 1992 and 1993 San Antonio reverted to a matachín. He is borne on an arched, tule-bowered palanquin by the mayordomos, and for the morning procession is accompanied by a large bulto of the Virgin dressed in white. A chorus singing alabanzas follows closely, with its own guitarist and accordionist. The matachines (including Monarca, Malinche, and Toro) lead the marcha, advancing and then dancing backward, facing their musicians and bowing to the saints, in the same pattern seen in many other Matachines processions.

This formation creates a kind of moving *encuentro,* or meeting, between the dance and santo-bearing groups and their respective musicians. At the front of the group walk several men who carry the saint's banner, a cross, and two other standards. The procession goes for somewhat less than a mile, climbing a dirt road behind the church along the acequia up an arroyo to the spring, the community's source of surface water. The saints are set on a table altar in a patiolike area above the ojo while the matachines dance briefly. The priest offers a blessing and the congregation sings an alabanza. Frances Leon Quintana reports, perhaps of the 1960s, that the congregation brings cups to be filled with a dipper from the spring, something not done in 1990 (Quintana 1990:295). The procession returns to the church, where again they dance briefly, ensconce the saint, and break for the noon feast.

San Antonio was founded in 1819, one year after Carnué was reestablished, by people from around Albuquerque, when the Apache threat had begun to subside. Yet even though San Antonio's settlers came mostly from Barelas, an Albuquerque barrio, and from the vicinities of Isleta and Sandía pueblos, the people there today seem more conscious and proud of their Apache ancestry (Frances Quintana, personal communication, 1989). This is not so puzzling in light of the fact that their geographic orientation or watershed faces not toward the Río Grande valley but toward the eastern plains, whence came the nomadic tribes.

Evidently Apache raiding was not entirely eliminated at the time of resettlement, and a story is told about it that might shed light on why San Antonio is dressed like a matachín. The story has variants, but the common theme is San Antonio's rescue of the villagers from a catastrophic Apache attack. In one version, the matachines are just coming out of the church when the Apaches, poised to swoop down on them from an overlooking ridge, mistake the dancers for an army of soldiers and flee. In another version, San Antonio drives the marauders away with a heavenly shower of arrows. Robb gives yet another version in which a young boy dressed in blue is seen fighting beside the villagers against the Indian assailants. They recognize him as Saint Anthony and vow that if he saves them they will celebrate his feast day forever after (Robb 1961:91–92). Perhaps this is why the bulto of Saint Anthony is sometimes dressed in pale blue or lavender on his feast day.

The afternoon dancing begins at the church around 2:00–2:30 P.M., after a novena. The dancers gather in front and the mayordomos and chorus proceed outside, bringing San Antonio around to the north side of the church, where he is placed on a table altar under the canopy of an old silver maple tree overlooking the dance arena. There are twelve matachines, including occasional women dressed just like the men. Their cupiles are decorated with crosses, jewelry, or the pictures of saints, especially San Antonio. Their guajes are unusual, being metallic and shaped like two inverted triangular cones cupped together. Their age range is fairly broad, from teenagers to older men.

There are said to be five parts to the dance, subdivided at intervals by

up to nine tune changes involving perhaps six different tunes and beginning and ending with the same sequence. The dance begins and ends with
the usual formation of Malinche and Monarca advancing and receding
between the two rows. Each row then circulates in a U-like formation. A
long rendition of La Cruz, or the cross, follows. Next is Malinche's dance,
which has two parts. In the first, the little girl weaves between the two
rows of dancers, accompanied by the Abuelos. Then the guaje-palma exchange between Malinche and Monarca is enacted, rather briefly, under
the supervision of the Abuelo. Afterwards the Abuelo "searches" beneath
the (standing) Monarca's foot for the "coin or treasure which symbolizes
happiness," evidently without success. In the next set, sometimes called
La Vuelta, the danzantes do side kick-steps and whirl in place when the
Abuelo calls out "¡Vuelta!" Then comes the *Toreada,* which begins with
the Malinche waving her paño at the Toro. She then retires to the sidelines
while each of the other dancers engages in a stylized encounter with the
bull. Then the skirmishing of the Abuelos and Toro involves the Abuelo
roping the Toro, who manages to drag the Perejundia, and the Toro's final
castration and demise, which signals the climax of the dance.

A recessional returns San Antonio to the church, where he is entregado
from the old to the new mayordomos. He is carried from the altar to the
front of the church, where the incoming mayordomos are seated to receive him. Led by a local *cantador* who reads from his notebook, versos are
sung about the saint, the place, and all the individuals who have worked
together to create the fiesta. Every few versos end with the refrain "San
Antonio de Padua." The singing is done to enthusiastic cheers from the
audience, which applauds the names of participants while individuals pile
dollar bills in the collection baskets being passed around. The entrega and
the moments building up to it are charged with emotion, attested to by
the tears seen year after year in the eyes of the mayordomos and congregation. The saint is then returned to the foot of the altar for the despedida,
and the two rows of dancers line up to *despedirle,* or "say good-bye," proceeding two by two while the musicians play the opening tune. In 1992
the outgoing mayordomos placed a rosary around each dancer's neck as
he or she knelt before the santo. There follows a reception, or *brinda,* in
the churchyard or at the mayordomos' house, where cake, cookies, coffee,
punch, and beer are served.[10] A social dance is held later that night at the
land grant hall.

At the start of the day there is one Abuelo, whose only hint of costume might be a holstered cap gun or a neckerchief. The individuals who play the bull and the Perejundia appear in the morning procession without costumes. In the afternoon the Abuelo adds a hat, necktie, and faded denim overalls and carries a lariatlike whip. He keeps back the crowd, directs the dance, and calls out instructions. He is eventually joined by a Perejundia who wears a curly wig, big floppy hat, and long crepe-paper dress (plate 31). She makes a grand entrance once the dance is under way.

The San Antonio Perejundia is a striking figure paralleled in intensity and vocal behavior only by the Taos Pueblo and Arroyo Seco examples. The Perejundia plays a key role in the San Antonio version and shows several interesting features. For example, her carefully prepared costume, which is invariably torn to shreds during the course of the Abuelo-Toro burlesque, is color-coordinated with the tule bowering of San Antonio's palanquin and sometimes even with the crepe streamers placed on trees in the churchyard or flowers inside the church. Like the musicians, Toro, and Abuelo, the Perejundia tends to be played by the same person year after year. Between 1991 and 1992 the actor changed, however, from a man who had played her for more than a decade to a younger, somewhat milder man. Each brought his own personal style to the character, whose persistent features seem to be her husky flamboyance, wig and heavy makeup, hat and dress, verbal joking, and borderline naughtiness.

The former Perejundia was a long-time devotee who first got involved in the dance after he returned from Vietnam, in order to fulfill a promesa his mother had made in his behalf. Over the years he has played every role, including danzante, Monarca, Toro, and Abuelo, and served also as mayordomo. His daughter was once the Malinche and became the first woman danzante, the year he played the Monarca. His embellishments of the Perejundia role include a purse containing candy that he throws to people in the audience. Some people complained that his teasing and sexual innuendos went too far. In 1993 this man played the Abuelo.

In any case, the Perejundia is the life of the party once she appears. Her grand entrance leads into circling and "working the crowd," hugging men suggestively, shaking hands, teasing, and bantering with people—all the while attended by a bevy of delighted children. She cavorts with the Toro and Abuelo while the danzantes proceed through their movements with an air of complete serenity and indifference to the clowning. It is as if the danzantes and clowns follow separate though interwoven scripts. The two scripts intersect when the Abuelos escort Malinche and when the little girl waves her paño at the Toro. The contrast between the solemn dignity of the dance and the clowns' noisy antics is striking. The new Perejundia follows pretty much the same routine as the old one, although she is less burly and buxom, does not dispense candy, and carries on in a slightly more restrained, "ladylike" manner. Both affect a certain effeminate, lisping stereotype. Despite (or perhaps because of) its inherent risk of excess, the Perejundia role is an extremely popular part of the Santo Niño tradition. Nevertheless, both Abuelo roles are considered difficult to recruit for, requiring a delicate balance of abandon and control.

Involvement in the Matachines dance carries the connotation of a sacred office solemnly undertaken in a spirit of religious devotion and sacrifice. The degree of commitment varies with the role, being greatest for the mayordomos and the Monarca, who directs the dancers. As we have seen, devotion can run in families. For participants, dancing is a form of prayer offered in celebration of and supplication to a particular saint. This is apparent also in all-night dance velorios offered to fulfill a promesa.

The incoming mayordomos receive the saint on his feast day from the outgoing mayordomos, keep and honor him in their home for a year, and in turn tearfully surrender him to the new mayordomos. They are responsible for organizing the fiesta during their year of office, which requires them to line up the dancers, arrange for the mass and procession, host the feast, clean the church, dress the saint and decorate his palanquin, and prepare the dance grounds. The mayordoma also makes the Perejundia's dress. In the months prior to the fiesta, the mayordomos and the Monarca accompany the saint to the home of every dancer, where the invitation and promise to participate are exchanged.

Each community has its main devotees, while the parish as a whole is served by a core of individuals who assume the key roles year after year. In addition to the musicians, Abuelos, and Toro, this includes the cantador and chorus with its own musicians. The Holy Child Matachines dancers will occasionally perform outside the parish for religious fiestas or velorios. They regularly do so, for example, in the San José parish in the South Broadway area of Albuquerque. That lifelong Matachines devotees are an established tradition in the Holy Trinity parish is attested to by a poem Robb transcribed (1961:92–93), written in praise of a San Antonio dancer named José Apodaca, who was famous for his role of Monarca.[11] Neighboring parishioners frequently attend each other's celebrations, especially where kin are involved, or conversely, they may avoid certain fiestas because of feuding. Still, all of the missions' versions are symbolically united in the fiesta procession at the parish seat of Tijeras in October.

Founded possibly as late as the 1850s, Tijeras is a town of some five hundred people that also lies roughly eighteen miles east of Albuquerque, and about one and a half miles south of San Antonio. It is the major commercial center in the area, the parish seat with the rectory and the largest, most modern church building. The Tijeras, or Santo Niño, feast day of October 14 involves a grand procession that symbolically incorporates all of the missions and their saints into a celebration known as *Los Colores,* referring to all the "colors" of the seven different missions. These are represented by the bulto or banner of each mission's patron saint, paraded behind the dancing matachines and their musicians.

The fiesta begins the night before with vísperas and a luminaria procession. The saints are brought from each mission to accompany the Holy Child. After morning mass the saints are again carried from the church about half a mile to a residence atop a little rise. The yard contains a small pine arbor and flagstone patio with surrounding *banco,* where the saints are arrayed in a semicircle with the Santo Niño at the center. The priest and congregation face them, praying and singing. The mayordomos then take up the saints and retrace their steps to the church, the chorus singing alabanzas and the matachines dancing all the way. The danzantes face off toe-to-toe and palma-to-palma. Alabanzas are sung to each saint. The chorus contains an accordion, guitars, and several fine singers.

In 1990 there was no dance performance because people were exhausted from all the dancing of the previous five months. There were no Abuelos or Toro for the procession, although Malinche and Monarca led the danzantes. After the procession the noonday feast was held in the Carnué dance and land grant hall, managed by the mayordomo and president of the Carnué land grant association, who, interestingly, was also the Perejundia. As is customary, a social dance was held there that night.

The Holy Child Matachines procession explicitly proclaims that all the individual Matachines traditions are interrelated in a familylike way under the unifying umbrella of the parish seat. These celebrations are carried out with a passionate mixture of community spirit, civic pride, and hospitality. All sorts of tensions may simmer beneath the surface and around the peripheries. As in Bernalillo, they receive expression and achieve resolution in the symbolism of the dance.

One factor that can affect the climate of the parish and therefore the overall tenor of its fiestas is the personality of the priest and his attitude toward local tradition, including the Matachines. The priest is required to officiate at masses, but his presence in saints' processions, at receptions, or at the dance is a matter of personal choice. Thus the long-standing theme of variable relations between the church and local folk tradition plays itself out in this parish as in others. For example, during the late 1980s the priest had extremely strained relations with San Antonito and other villages in the parish. Under such circumstances the mayordomos' tasks were carried out less easily than they would have been with an amiable or sympathetic priest. But by the early 1990s a friendlier priest had replaced him, and the ambiance of this nonetheless irrepressible tradition seemed to grow more exuberant.

It seems that the recent history of the Tijeras Canyon tradition follows a pattern familiar in other Hispano communities, in which the Matachines performances were beginning to attenuate during the 1950s but have since undergone a general resurgence of interest and participation. Like other places in New Mexico, the Tijeras Canyon area has experienced accelerated real estate development since 1970, stimulated by the construction of a four-lane interstate highway that cut through several communities and transformed the rural character of the valley. In some cases local people have protested against the relentless pressure of development. Indeed, it seems that a sense of threat to traditional community resource domains has been a factor in the reinfusion of attention and energy into the Matachines as an assertion of ethnocultural identity.

The oppositional-preservationist aspect of the Matachines is subtly underscored, for example, during the San Antonio procession to the ojo, when the congregation must wend its way over private land, past the comparatively lavish new homes of recent arrivals. Although the ojo itself belongs to the community, the fiesta is now the only time of year when the people of San Antonio have collective access to it. Evidently the ojo went dry during a drought in the 1940s, and in the 1950s and 1960s the procession lapsed, partly because the priest was unwilling to participate. Robb (1961:92) reported that people told him the spring dried up after they let the procession lapse one year. In any event, one can see a historically layered succession of meanings inscribed upon the way San Antonio does the Matachines, spanning the years from the early days, when the dance protected them from Apaches, to the present, when it enables them symbolically to reassert their claim to their traditional water source in the face of encroaching outsiders. In sum, maintenance of the Matachines dance seems tied in parishioners' minds to the spiritual and material welfare not only of individuals but of the community as a whole.

TORTUGAS

The final, southernmost Río Grande New Mexican Matachines tradition is performed at Tortugas, 250 miles below Albuquerque in the Las Cruces area not far from the Mexican border. Tortugas is now a barrio inside the city limits of Las Cruces, lying in the Mesilla valley about one mile southeast of Mesilla Plaza. It has been characterized as a Mexicanized Tiwa, or Tigua, village (Houser 1979) founded partly by descendants of refugees from Isleta and other pueblos who accompanied New Mexico governor Otermín on his flight south after the Pueblo Revolt.

According to the single published ethnological monograph on this community, Tortugas was settled around 1851, or shortly after Americanization, allegedly by a mix of people from Isleta or Ysleta del Sur (Texas), Piro Indians from Senecú, and some Mansos (Oppenheimer 1974:240–41). The "parent" villages of Ysleta del Sur and Senecú, located in the Paso del Norte (El Paso) area, had been settled in the 1680s by Piros and Tiwas displaced southward by the revolt and its aftermath (Houser 1979:337). Alan Oppenheimer (1974:219) characterized Tortugas as a cultural "amalgam of Tiwa-Piro, Spanish-American, Anglo-American, and Mexican Indian elements." He also claimed that Tortugas history showed progressive divergence away from traditional Tiwa culture, in a pattern that supposedly bore out Charles Lange's prediction (1953) of how culture change would proceed at Cochití and other pueblos.

More recent scholars suggest a different picture: in all probability, Tortugas's "Indian" culture has become not less but more "Tiwalike" in this century, never having been especially Tiwa in the first place (Deidre Sklar, personal communication, 1992). After all, a very long time and many historical changes intervened between the Pueblo Revolt and Tortugas's settlement in 1851. Patrick Beckett and Terry Corbett (1990:6) claim the original Indio settlers in Las Cruces came from the Paso del Norte mission of Nuestra Señora de Guadalupe rather than from Ysleta del Sur. This mission group was a mixture of Piro and Manso Indians was well as some of Tiwa ancestry, and it was they who instituted the fiesta and the honoring of the Virgin of Guadalupe in Las Cruces. These settlers were joined later by families from the missions of Ysleta del Sur (Tigua) and Senecú (Piro).

Today, researchers (Sklar, Corbett) suspect that the Las Cruces or Tortugas Guadalupe Day dance organizers may have turned toward Ysleta del Sur for "Tiwa" ceremonial information only after their first cacique, from the Piro-Manso community of Paso del Norte, died in 1906 (Sklar, personal communication, 1992). Doubting Oppenheimer's notion that Tortugas represents deterioration of Pueblo culture, Sklar suggests that instead "there really is no deterioration from a Pueblo source because there really is no unitary Pueblo source" (personal communication, 1992) But while new genealogical and other findings uncover a more complex derivation than that imagined earlier, they nonetheless confirm the observation that Tortugas was and still is an extreme mixture of many different strains. Indeed, therein lies its interest.

Tortugas is not legally recognized as a pueblo and has neither grant lands nor reservation status. Its history and economy have been affected by the lack of a protected and relatively stable subsistence land base. But it does have what is known as "the Corporation," or Los Indígenes de Nuestra Señora de Guadalupe, a nonprofit corporation formed in 1914. The Corporation's originating purpose included the construction and maintenance of a Catholic church, cemetery, and other community buildings and the improvement of lots and construction of homes. Its governing officers also assumed responsibility for civil matters as well as for the maintenance of religious ceremonies, including the Guadalupe fiesta. The Corporation received title to the pueblo of Guadalupe and a deed to the church grounds and other property and buildings where their religious ceremonies are still carried out. It thus became the organizational body for the Guadalupe fiesta and its core dance groups, the Danzantes and the Tiwas or Tiguas. Today members of the Corporation conceive of their nontribal, nonreservation status as a positive rather than a negative attribute that marks their greater independence and autonomy (Sklar 1992).

Although the community was multiethnic from the beginning, some members still claim Tiwa identity, and during the 1960s, at about the same time Ysleta del Sur received state (Texas) tribal status (Beckett and Corbett 1990), one faction (which had split from the Corporation in the 1940s) initiated and today still pursues the drive to obtain official federal recognition as a tribe. Houser (1979) and others refer to the people of Ysleta del Sur and subsequent descendants in Tortugas as Tigua in order to distinguish them from their Isleta and other presumed Tiwa relatives to the north. Yet Tortugas is what one could call a *puro mestizo* community, one whose premier ritual-symbolic expression of mestizaje, the Guadalupe fiesta, clearly encompasses the several self-identified strands that interweave the whole.

The complex, multiethnic nature of Tortugeño identity is thus nowhere more eloquently symbolized than in the Día de Guadalupe celebration, which includes, among other dances, a version of the Matachines. This dance closely resembles its relatives to the north but, interestingly, is called Los Danzantes rather than Los Matachines. The term *Matachines* is sometimes applied instead to the "Azteca" dances that are done more or less simultaneously on December 12. In all, four different dance troupes perform four distinct yet broadly similar dances throughout the day.

Tortugas is said to consist of two old villages, San Juan and Guadalupe, and although both feast days are celebrated, the December 12 fiesta has become their most important and famous ritual event. It lasts for three days and exceeds even Bernalillo's Matachines in size, number of people involved, and sheer theatrical elaboration. It is said to have originally lasted for seven days, until the clergy trimmed it down in the early 1900s.[12] The event is far too complex to describe here in its entirety, and only the most general features can be mentioned. The following account is based primarily on Oppenheimer's study, Sklar's work (1991) and others' work in progress, and my own cursory observations in 1990.[13]

The celebration begins on the evening of December 10, when the image of the Virgin is carried from the church to a building known as La Casa del Pueblo or La Casa Popular. An all-night velorio del santo is held there. A rosary is prayed and the Danzantes perform, while outside rifles are fired into the air at intervals. The roof of the building is decorated with *farolitos,* or candles in paper bags, a custom attributed to the north.

Most of December 11 involves a pilgrimage to the top of Tortugas (or "A") mountain. It begins early and is followed at the summit by confessions and mass by the bishop and afterwards a picnic lunch. Special *varas,* or walking staffs, called *quiotes* are fashioned out of yucca stalks for the return procession. A rosary is held in the afternoon, and by sundown the pilgrims have descended and returned to the Casa del Pueblo, where an *ensayo real* is held, in which the "Indian," or Tigua, dancers practice for the next day (Oppenheimer 1974:101). Participation in the pilgrimage is usually undertaken to fulfill a *promesa* to the Virgin. Hundreds of people of all ages participate, including many natives who come home from out of state. Such large numbers have evidently been characteristic since World War II. At dusk, three pathways down the face of the mountain are illuminated by luminarias made of automobile tires soaked in fuel, which burn late into the night.

The Día de Guadalupe begins with mass by the bishop of Las Cruces and investiture of the new mayordomos, followed by dancing in front of and next to the church. A procession begins in front of the church and follows the familiar pattern in which dancers proceed to and fro in front of the sacred cluster, in this case made up of the bishop and other clergy. They are led by both Tigua and Danzante dancers. In 1990 the bishop was still dressed in his white vestments from mass during the morning dance, but he stripped down to black for the procession. Upon arriving in front of the Casa de Comida, the Tigua and Danzante dancers perform a large round dance together and then go inside the red-clay–colored building to feast. The meal includes a traditional meatball stew prepared by Corporation members for the hundreds of guests who line up outside the Casa de Comida to be served in relays within.

When Oppenheimer did his fieldwork in the 1950s there were a total of three distinctly costumed dance groups who performed, but today there are four. These consist of the so-called Tiwa (Tigua), or Indian, dancers; the Danzantes, who resemble the matachines farther north; and two groups of Azteca dancers, sometimes referred to as Matachines. The first two groups are evidently original to the fiesta and are the first to dance, beginning on the twelfth with the Tiwas, who also appear on the night of the eleventh, and the Danzantes, who dance for the velorio del santo on the night of the tenth. These two groups generally appear and march together and are organized through the Corporation. The Aztecas are each organized independently by different constituencies.

The Tiwa dancers consist of two lines, one of women and the other of men, who carry untipped arrows and dance Pueblo fashion to a drum and chorus (plates 32 and 33). The music is Pueblo style, with Tiwa words whose meaning is lost. The women wear Pueblo-style black mantas decorated with ribbons and tied over one shoulder, with colored blouses underneath, moccasins, and headbands with colored ribbons streaming down the back like those of a matachín. The men wear feather headbands, fake buckskin pants, and shirts made of tan cloth decorated with red fringe, and they carry bows and maracas.

The Danzantes, all men, wear cupiles with ribbons, but instead of fringe they have loops of colored cord over their eyes. They wear suits and boots or street shoes, a red sash across the chest, and white leggings layered like lace petticoats, known as *polainas*. They wear aprons with the image of the Virgin (plate 34). The palma is a kind of hoop with a handle, all wound round with colored tinsel garland, which also covers the guajes, or maracas. In 1990 there were fourteen Danzantes, two alternate Monarcas, and at least six white Malinches (plate 35).

There was no Toro, and no Abuelos as such, although there were two men who stood near or among the Danzantes, dressed much the same but with red knit caps, or *gorras,* instead of cupiles and no palma or guaje or, for that matter, a whip. Sometimes still referred to as Abuelos, these figures are considered assistants to Monarca, who is the director of the dance. They call out changes in the dance (plate 36).

Apparently none of the typical routines involving the attenuated clowns and bull take place any longer, although a brief palma-guaje exchange between Malinche and Monarca, face-offs, kick steps, and crossovers are done. Shotguns are fired into the air between sets. The music is provided by a single violinist and seems markedly different from Matachines tunes to the north.

The Toro and Abuelos seem to have become attenuated within the last forty years. Photographs of the Danzantes from the early 1900s show a masked, white-bearded figure, in one case holding a large doll (Beckett and Corbett 1990:17–18). Oppenheimer described one Abuelo in 1951 as a man in regular clothes who carried a whip, and he reported that the other, the "Evil One" or devil [Toro?], a man in overcoat and "white false-face," had been omitted that year. The movement in which the Abuelo protected Malinche from the Evil One was likewise eliminated. At the same time, the number of Danzantes expanded from twelve to eighteen (Oppenheimer 1974:334). Oppenheimer noted that some of the more conservative members of the pueblo complained that "too much was missing" from the much abbreviated and therefore incomplete performance given in 1951 (1974:335). But despite their objections, it seems that certain components of the "original" drama were indeed dropped.

While the Tiguas and Danzantes dance, a large group of red-costumed dancers begins to perform in an area to one side of the church. This group is known as the Chichimeca Aztecas, sometimes also the Matachines or (to Corporation members) Aztecas del Carrizo. The dance was introduced into Tortugas in 1925 by a man named Juan Pacheco, said to be a Mexican Indian (Oppenheimer 1974:337; Beckett and Corbett 1990:9; Sklar says that according to the family, he was a Chichimeca from Zapotecas [sic]). These dancers have a ramada with their own shrine to the Virgin of Guadalupe, and everything associated with their cult seems to be bright red.

The Chichimeca costumes seen today are more elaborate than those Oppenheimer described forty years ago, although the basic features are the same. They wear red shirts with the image of the Virgin on their backs, and long skirts opened at the sides and decorated with *carrizos,* or reed tubes, sewn onto the fabric to create a fringelike effect. They wear elaborate feather headdresses such as Plains war bonnets or high Aztecan fans. One lead dancer wears a splendid white war bonnet that reaches all the way to the ground. They carry a rattle in one hand and a stylized bow-and-arrow clacker in the other.

In 1951 there were one red Malinche and two clowns, both with white fur masks, one with a red light-bulb nose. One carried a little whip, the other a bag slung over his shoulder. Oppenheimer (1974:338–39) reported that "these clowns are the delight of the crowd. Their humorous and caustic comments never fail to elicit laughter. Other buffoonery includes such acts as dancing with a child's doll and tackling each other."

In 1990 there was just one Abuelo, who wore a red shirt, a hat, and a bearded mask. He carried a limp, furry doll. At one point the entire company of dancers circled him and he was "killed," and the doll was tossed outside the ring. There were also at least five or six little bright red Malinches. There were at least fifty red Azteca dancers, both male and female, ranging in age from children to mature adults. They danced mostly in two long parallel lines and went through several movements. The music was provided by a violin and drum. The musicians stood just inside the ramada-shrine at one end of the dance area.

A second Azteca, or "Matachines," group, also known as the Guadalupana Azteca, has formed since Oppenheimer's day. Evidently they were a splinter group led by a man named Rumaldo Paz. They are costumed very much like the red troupe except all in yellow. These dancers perform in an area below and across a road behind the church. They also have their own shrine to the Virgin, arrayed on a wooden platform and set against the backdrop of a long sky-blue panel. The drummer and fiddler stand nearby.

In 1990 this group had six or seven bright green Malinches and two clowns. One wore a gorilla mask and a pajamalike outfit. The other had a vaguely reptilian mask with a protruding snout and wore a dungaree jumpsuit. They begged and teased and slowly circled the dancers like Abuelos farther north. There were perhaps twenty-five or thirty yellow Azteca female and male dancers. Their choreography and music seemed similar to those of the other group, evidently a point of contention between the two. Some years ago the Pacheco group accused the Paz dancers of imitating its songs and filed a lawsuit to make them stop, so now their performance differs from the original. Like the Chichimeca dancers, they seem preponderantly youthful.

All of these groups dance at their particular sites throughout the day, attended by a large and fluctuating audience made up of locals, schoolchildren, visitors from neighboring communities, and tourists. The celebration draws hundreds of spectators.

The intense spirit of this feast day is explicitly Mexican in cultural orientation and derivation, just as the Las Cruces area itself, only a few miles from the border, has a markedly stronger "Mexican" character than the northern villages. Indeed, no saint's day is more important or passionately celebrated in Mexico than December 12. It is noteworthy that whereas the June 24 San Juan fiesta features just the Tiwa dancers and Danzantes, dance groups symbolizing Tortugas's Mexican Indian elements are added for Día de Guadalupe. On that day, all constituent ethnicities are represented, and the differences among them are symbolically encoded in their costumes, choreographies, and overall spatial layout. This relation was reflected, for example, in the seating pattern during the mass, in which the regular congregation all sat on the left side of the church (facing the altar), and the mayordomos and all the dancers sat on the right, each dance group arranged by row, with the Tiwas in front, the Danzantes next, and the yellow Matachines de Carrizo last, a mirror of their priority and sequence in Tortugas history. The celebration can thus be seen to symbolize rather explicitly the plural ethnic composition and heritage of the inclusive mestizo Tortugas community. The unifying symbol for this ritual bringing together of diverse ethnocultural strands is, appropriately, La Guadalupana, the Indian Virgin of Mexico.

The significance of Nuestra Señora de Guadalupe for Tortugas and for Mexicanos along the border was spelled out in Bishop Ramírez's sermon, in which he retold the familiar story of the Virgin's appearing to the humble Nahua Indian Juan Diego on a hill near Mexico City. This bishop is well known for encouraging Mexicano parishioners to embrace their Indian heritage. Speaking in Spanish with occasional infusions of English, he emphasized that because the Virgin spoke to Juan Diego in his own language, "with understanding and compassion and because she had an Indian face, he trusted her." And, as the story goes, mass conversion of Indians to Catholicism followed upon the establishment of her shrine atop Tepayec. Today, "somos todos Guadalupanos hasta los raices" (we are all Guadalupanos to the roots). The Virgin of Guadalupe constitutes what Eric Wolf (1958:34) calls the "master symbol" of Mexico's collective mestizo identity. Miguel Leatham writes (1989:36), in his summation of Guadalupe's pastoral role within the U.S. Catholic church:

> The Virgin of Guadalupe may serve as a symbol of mediation and dialogue between groups of differing status and cultural backgrounds within the church today as in the colonial period. To a large degree, the Virgin can mediate because, according to an indigenista interpretation, the image of Guadalupe encodes key elements out of Mexico's indigenous heritage while also being historically linked to the emergence of a Catholic Mexico under Spain. In this way, mestizaje, Mexicans' mixed cultural heritage, is given divine sanction, providing an ideological basis for religious empowerment and greater appreciation of the Mexican presence among the "people of God."

Las Cruces (including Tortugas), as Bishop Ramírez put it, "is the gateway through which the Virgin entered the Río Grande valley." This thought provides a kind of emic frame through which to read the symbolic message encapsulated in the entire Tortugas fiesta. The Día de Guadalupe celebration expresses Tortugeños' views about the history and social order of their community. The pilgrimage up "A" mountain reenacts Juan Diego's journey up Tepeyac. The precise location of the Matachines dance within this ritual context is significant. It follows but is nonetheless paired with the Tiwa dance, and together the two symbolize the Indo-Hispano cultural heritage Tortugas received from the north, juxtaposed in turn with the Azteca dance traditions that came from the south.

The case of Tortugas is especially interesting because of this dual or Januslike border-zone orientation. It represents a transition between the Río Grande valley Matachines and the range of variation and meaning the dance assumes in Mexico. It also says something about the symbolic framing of ethnic identity within an urbanizing, multicultural, borderland setting. Tortugas has been a crossroads for workers coming from various directions, a true crucible for cultural and social amalgamation.

A bit of sociological background on the community may help to illuminate these particular images. Tortugeños have been a consistent source of cheap labor in the Las Cruces region throughout what Oppenheimer identified as three major phases of socioeconomic change between 1851 and 1951. First, prior to the railroad, the local economy involved a combination of subsistence agriculture and wage labor, for which Tortugeños even then were known. After 1881 the railroad commercialized agriculture, brought in large numbers of Anglos, further reduced the status and power of Mexicanos, and transformed the economy in the Mesilla valley. The construction of Elephant Butte Dam in 1916 brought more change, involving a new irrigation technology that supported the introduction of cotton and a concomitant reduction of agricultural diversity. Agribusiness labor practices intensified workforce competition between locals and Mexican nationals.

Another factor that contributed to the Corporation's turn toward its presumed Ysleta del Sur (and by implication Isleta Pueblo) cultural roots early in this century was the climate of anti-Mexicanism that accompanied the push for New Mexican statehood. Advocates of statehood sought to downplay the mestizo genetic composition of the state's non-Anglo demographic majority. At the same time, the emergent tourism industry was beginning to promote images of "pure" or "unspoiled" Indian and Spanish ·American cultural exotica. The adaptive fiction of Tiwa ancestry among certain elements of the Corporation took shape in this context.

It is interesting that Oppenheimer identified a "status inversion" at Tortugas, whereby prestige within the community was directly related to the perceived degree of "Indian" or "Tiwa" identity. He explained this state of affairs as follows (1974:353):

> The people of Tortugas believe that there are more status rewards in being Indian than in being Mexican or Spanish-American. Prestige in the village goes to those with the knowledge of Indian practices. Those who are considered Indian "by blood" are jealous of their position. The Anglos of the valley feel that Indians have more romantic appeal than Mexicans.
>
> This situation is to be explained by the very low status of Mexicans in the area. In the rest of rural New Mexico many, if not most of the Spanish-Americans own their own land. In the Mesilla valley they are, like the Tortugeños, landless. In the period 1881–1916 the Mexicans who were the original settlers of the valley lost their land by the subdivision of land among heirs.[14] They became day laborers on the holding of their fathers. In the period from 1916 to the present [ca. 1951] the influx of immigrant and "wetback" labor, poverty-stricken and crude, with whom the Spanish-Americans have been identified, has tended to further lower their status.

The status inversion Oppenheimer perceived in Tortugas seems to have surfaced elsewhere. For example, he notes that W. W. Hill discerned the same process at Santa Clara Pueblo after the turn of the century (1974:353), which in turn resembles Bodine's "tri-ethnic trap" of Taos. But while the argument about status inversion may suffice for the period Oppenheimer observed and wrote about, the situation has since changed, and people in Tortugas today actively embrace public symbolization of their mestizaje. This collective expression is achieved through an accentuation of the separate particularity of its constituent elements.

Yet the symbolizing of Indian identity in Tortugas seems different from that seen in other Pueblo Matachines performances. The problematic basis of Pueblo identity is reflected in the distance from and objectification of the relevant ethnic markers. Thus the Tortugas Tiwas do not speak Tiwa or dress like dancers in the "real" pueblos farther north. Instead, the men dress like Hollywood Indians and the women dress like imitation Pueblo female dancers. The dance is "Tiwa" by virtue of being meta-ethnic. In other words, it is less Tiwa than "about" Tiwa. Its very name is an emblematic symbol. The same seems true for the Azteca, or Mexican Indian, dances. The coupling of the Tiwa dance with the Matachines or Danzantes for both the Guadalupe and San Juan feasts seems to indicate that in Tortugas, the idea of Pueblo culture is inseparable from the very context of Christianization and Pueblo-Spanish conflict that occasioned migration south after the Pueblo Revolt. Their embeddedness within a larger, pluralistic festival structure bespeaks Tortugas's unique border-zone position in the cultural geography of the Río Grande Matachines.

CONCLUSION

The tour from Taos to Tortugas affords a comparative view of the Matachines among Pueblo and Mexicano populations in New Mexico, and it reveals how the dance takes on additional ethnopolitical meaning along the Mexican border. The seven short case studies, cursory as they are, seem to affirm the working propositions derived from the three Taos examples. San Juan and Jémez pueblos both symbolically foreground the Indo-Hispano or Indian-Christian dichotomy in what seem to be characteristically different ways. Each of the four additional Hispanic examples focuses internally but alludes outward, resurgent in response to changes issuing from the larger, Anglo world. Each has undergone attenuation followed by a contemporary renaissance according to its own ecopolitical situation and social character. Finally, the Tortugas material encapsulates all the lessons from the north and juxtaposes them with parallel, companion formations that symbolize ethnopolitical relations south of the border. It perches on the national divide between north and south and looks both ways, the mediating case within an inclusive geocultural context. Taken as a group, this spectrum of New Mexico Matachines performances exhibits the major features and parameters of the upper Río Grande complex.

6 · CONCLUSION
Illuminating the Hidden Transcript

Every subordinate group creates, out of its ordeal, a "hidden transcript" that represents a critique of power spoken behind the back of the dominant. The powerful, for their part, also develop a hidden transcript representing the practices and claims of their rule that cannot be openly avowed. A comparison of the hidden transcript of the weak with that of the powerful and of *both* hidden transcripts to the public transcript of power relations offers a substantially new way of understanding resistance to domination.
　　　　　—James C. Scott, *Domination and the Arts of Resistance*

In recent years, a number of anthropologists have argued that ritual dramas among Indian groups of Mesoamerica involve symbolic processes that metaphorically express, encode, and enact information and commentary about social and ecological relations, as well as about major forces that shape group history. Analysts of Indian ritual have interpreted the symbolic meanings embedded in such performances not only in light of aboriginal cosmology and community social structure but also with reference to colonial history and the political economy of Indian-Ladino relations. Victoria Bricker (1973, 1981), for example, has shown how ritual humor in highland Maya festivities pertains to the history of ethnic relations with Ladinos and other groups as well as to myth and in-group dynamics. Similarly, Gary Gossen (1986) proposes that ritual symbolism and process during carnival constitute a social commentary on the historical, political, and economic situation in which the Chamulas find themselves. He agrees with Victor Turner and others in proposing that "ritual action renders accessible and visible those truths that are basic but not customarily articulated in everyday life because they are bigger than life" (Gossen 1986:227).

Ethnologists of the Pueblo Indians, on the other hand, have continued to analyze ritual meaning largely with reference to environmental absolutes and internal social structure and to focus more on what survives than upon the historically invented. Like virtually all Pueblo scholars, Alfonso

Ortiz argues that Pueblo ritual and world view are conceptually fixed upon the eternal rhythms of nature rather than on the rough bumps of historical particularity. With respect to concepts of time, he notes that

> all of the pueblos can be characterized as ahistorical. As Parsons insightfully noted, the Pueblos, even in their myths, are not at all concerned with the first beginnings or origins of all things, just with their emergence. The Montezuma tales found just about everywhere among them hint that they grappled, after the coming of the Spaniards, with the prospect of being thrust forever into the ebb and flow of history, but this apparently was not to be. Just as an almost impenetrable moral, conceptual, and spatial organization is attributed to the cosmos, so also do the undulating rhythms of nature govern their whole existence, from the timing and order of ritual dramas to the planning of economic activities. (Ortiz 1972:143)

Among the Pueblos, the Matachines is known as Montezuma's dance, brought to them in a way that both signified and yet helped to mitigate the catastrophic advent of European penetration. In every Pueblo Matachines version considered in these pages, one reads an oppositional contrast or juxtaposition between symbols of Indian religion and symbols of Christianity. This opposition-juxtaposition linkage seems to constitute the central subject matter of the dance for the Pueblos. Ramón Gutiérrez (1989:2, 1991) has argued that the ritual dramas introduced by the Spaniards constituted an ideological means by which the Pueblo Indians were repeatedly inculcated with a historical consciousness of their own defeat. These theatrical productions were deliberately orchestrated to ritually enact the conquest of Mexico and project it as the model for the conquest of New Mexico. The use of luminarias and gunfire to announce or punctuate processions and performances such as the Matachines dance symbolically evoked the conditions of warfare that surrounded their imposition.

> In these initial conquest dramas the Spaniards played themselves as well as the defeated Aztecs while a native audience looked on. In time the actor-audience relationship of the 1598 conquest dramas was reversed. The natives then played themselves as the Spanish looked on. When the Pueblos performed the dances, dramas, and pantomimes of the con-

quest, they continually relived their own defeat, their own humiliation and dishonor, and openly mocked themselves with those caricatures of "Indians" the *conquistadores* so fancied. (Gutiérrez 1989:5)

But although conquest dramas originally enacted and recapitulated the subjugation and humiliation of Indians at the hands of their oppressors, with time some of these ritual meanings were appropriated, altered, and subtly subverted by Pueblo performers. This gradual process employed such mechanisms as "comic gestures, inverted utterances, and burlesque behavior of every sort" (Gutiérrez 1989:33). Over the generations the Pueblos made the Matachines their own, taking over its organization and filling the majority of roles. Thus, even though they enlisted outsiders, for the most part Indians ended up portraying the alien intruders rather than the other way around, and rather than themselves. Indeed, part of the ambiguous power of Matachines symbolism lies in the fact that the masked dancers are both themselves and not themselves. Incorporation of the dance into their ceremonial cycle gave the Pueblos a measure of control over how the story of their forced conversion would be remembered and told within their own communities.

It is tempting to speculate about the nature of this gradual "introjection." An account written almost a century ago by Father Noël Dumarest, a French priest who ministered to Cochiti, Santo Domingo, and San Felipe pueblos between 1896 and 1900, offers a provocative text from which to begin imaginatively to reconstruct the progression of Pueblo psychosymbolic resistance and adjustment to massive, systematic indoctrination:

Another satirical piece is presented every year, at least at San [*sic*] Domingo, to ridicule Spanish-speaking people—the dance of the matachines. *According to Indian tradition, this dance was instituted by Montezuma that the descendants of his race might have the pleasure of mocking their conquerors.* A burlesque of the matachines is performed on the Day of the Kings at San Domingo, Indians representing the bull-fighters and dressed in rags turn their heads from side to side like absentminded and distracted persons and move their limbs grotesquely and extravagantly. The queen to whom they come to pay homage, instead of being chosen from the most beautiful children of the town, is a big man who crouches down to look little. He has a wig of tow and his cheeks are painted carmine. The bull is a man covered with the hide of a bull, the horns of the bull on top of his head. At the moment when the bull is killed, the bull impersonator and the bull fighter delight the audience with obscene gestures. (Dumarest 1919:186; emphasis added)

It seems that Dumarest's informants came out and stated explicitly what today remains implicit in the Pueblo Matachines. Several other elements in his account also merit comment. First is the significance of Montezuma, the "Indian god in European clothes" (Dozier 1957:31, 1958:445), whom Richard Parmentier identifies as the "mediating symbol and temporal marker" for European intrusion into the Pueblo world.[1] As Montezuma's gift to the Pueblos, the dance simultaneously heralds alien rule and offers a hidden means to subvert it, under the protective guise of compliance. Dumarest's implied contrast between the "queen," or Perejundia, and the Malinche, or "beautiful child," is also noteworthy in light of Gutiérrez's point that the Franciscans made special use of Pueblo children in their program of ritual indoctrination. Referring to the religious dramas and dances the friars forced upon the Indians, he states that "the subtext ensconced in the generational casting (Indian children playing angels or Christians, the Indian adults playing devils, infidels, or enemies) was the defeat of Indian culture and the subordination of adults to Christianized youth" (Gutiérrez 1991:76). That Malinche is played by an innocent young girl assumes particular significance in this connection. Her escort by an Abuelo or Perejundia (like her apparent replacement by the Perejundia in the version Dumarest saw) offers a cunningly disguised satiric counterpoint to the outward enactment of Christian conversion. Other burlesque routines and elements within or between particular sets may likewise symbolize sotto voce subversion. These include the leg-pulling or knee-stroking routine the Abuelo plays out with the Monarca as the latter rises from a sitting position while the danzantes kneel.[2]

Today each pueblo embodies a distinct perspective on this compartmentalized, profoundly ambivalent colonial legacy. At Taos Pueblo, the Christianization drama is wrapped in a raucous burlesque about illicit, bittersweet miscegenation. Of all the pueblos I have looked at, Picurís seems to express the greatest degree of ethnocultural fusion and/or amalgamation in its Matachines performance, a trait understandable in light of that pueblo's history of near decimation. At both San Juan and Jémez, the dual ethnoreligious juxtaposition is firmly manifest. At San Juan, the "soldiers of Christ" are highly Indianized and the "borrowed," or enemy, dance is opened with drumming and is quickly followed by the indigenous Turtle dance. Jémez divides the Matachines into two alternating versions that together portray ethnic duality and ingeniously marry the dance's monotheistic message to a dual ritual organization. Each pueblo's Matachines performance simultaneously integrates and encapsulates the Christian presence at the winter solstice point within its ceremonial calendar. This location in the cycle underscores its external provenience and the warlike setting of its introduction. Each pueblo negotiates the consequences of Spanish domination according to the particulars of its history, ecology, and modern character. The details of this negotiation and what the pueblo makes of them are symbolically encoded in how it does the Matachines dance. Ultimately, the Pueblo Matachines must be located within each community's inclusive ceremonial cycle, a task not attempted here.

The Hispanic Matachines, on the other hand, reveals a different set of preoccupations. The Spaniards did not abandon the conquest drama once Indians took over its performance in the pueblos but instead maintained and applied it to their own needs, which changed through time. Perhaps, as the people of Bernalillo believe, they adopted it upon the reconquest, following the most momentous event of the colonial period, the Pueblo Revolt. Indian performers are not required for the Hispanic productions. Thus, while symbolic reference to the Indo-Hispano interface is apparent in each Mexicano performance, it is no longer the central concern. The focus, rather, seems to be internal, and yet responsive to pressures that are external but not directly alluded to. Mexicano Matachines dances celebrate the triumph and persistence of Catholicism with none of the ambivalence and symbolic compartmentalization so evident in Pueblo performances. It is noteworthy that each Hispano Matachines dance examined in previous chapters has undergone some form of revitalization or resurgence since about 1970, preceded by a period of attenuation. This pattern reflects larger economic trends within the state that have had broadly comparable impacts on different communities located within the orbits of different urban or urbanizing centers. The dance therefore refers not only to a given community's interethnic past but also to its living present, in terms of internal structure as well as in relation to pressures coming from without.

Internal hierarchy tends to be a principal focus in the Hispanic Matachines performance. This is seen in the case of Arroyo Seco, where the

Matachines revival is embedded in a larger context of differential ethnocultural and ethnopolitical activism, stimulated in part by accelerating resort development in the Río Hondo watershed. The dance's organizational and dramatic structures mirror tensions or schisms within the community—for example, between status or class orientations, and between clerical and lay ritual domains. And although further research would be needed to advance analysis of the dance in relation to factional structures in Alcalde, El Rancho, Bernalillo, or San Antonio, one can already see that for each, a major issue is the matter of territorially based ethnocultural continuity and survival. Ethnocommunal persistence is symbolized by the Hispanic Matachines, as it is at Picurís and the quasi-pueblo of Tortugas. The Tortugas Matachines partakes of both Pueblo and Hispano qualities and yet fuses them into something new by self-consciously juxtaposing them with influences from the south. In each case the configuration of forces, strata, and factions is distinct, as is the performance of the dance in its entirety, including the fiesta in which it is embedded.

In Bernalillo, for example, the dance has gone from the verge of extinction in the late 1950s to being a major festival some thirty years later, a festival in which the number of performers has more than doubled and ritual organization operates through a prestige hierarchy. The Matachines tradition is linked in native thought to survival of the Pueblo Revolt, Bernalillo's official reconquest origin, and its expressed desire to survive as a community today. Part of its core membership is said to overlap with that of the Penitente brotherhood. By the people's own account, the Matachines symbolizes the community's ethnocultural identity. As in the other Mexicano cases, the dance currently enjoys a surge of popularity and strong participation.

The pressure of intensifying capitalist development, which has provoked certain forms of ritual activism throughout much of New Mexico, is like the same gigantic beast with a different face for each locale. Thus Arroyo Seco has been affected by growth in Taos, Alcalde by the growth of Española, El Rancho by Los Alamos, Bernalillo and the Carnué or Tijeras Canyon area by Albuquerque, and Tortugas by Las Cruces and El Paso. Whereas the Hispanic Matachines once celebrated Spanish domination, today it also symbolizes Hispano determination to persist against the tide of Anglo assimilation.

Despite the obvious contrast between Pueblo and Mexicano Matachines performances, they nevertheless have important features in common. First and foremost among these is the basic structure of the dance drama itself, with its cast of characters and discrete choreographic motifs. The sequence, style, and emphases of these movements and roles vary among communities. If patterned contrasts exist in the way these universal elements are distributed or vary, they do not appear to be divided interethnically, at least in any simple fashion.

The most central and consistent choreographic drama in all of the dance versions I observed involves the palma-guaje exchange between Malinche and Monarca, preceded and followed by their joint and individual dance sets. The characters of Monarca and Malinche exhibit little variation, either through time or across traditions. Their pairing and face-to-face interaction is a constant of the dance. Like the danzantes but unlike the Abuelos and Toro, they are serious, conventional figures with no charter for improvisation or interaction with the audience.

The reigning metaphors of the Malinche-Monarca exchange are conversion and marriage. Conversion makes up the explicit or official metaphor for this set, as well as for the dance as a whole, a message telegraphed also by the danzantes' symmetrical formations and crossovers. Marriage is the *implicit* referent, never overtly articulated but eloquently symbolized by Malinche's resemblance to a bride. Like a bride, she is a virgin dressed in white, paired with Monarca and pinned with dollar bills. She scuffles briefly with the Toro and is escorted by the clowns.

In the upper Río Grande valley at least, the virgin Malinche—a contradiction in terms if one keeps in mind her Mexican meaning farther south—is symbolically much more pivotal than the king she supposedly converts. She is herself the first Christian convert. This Malinche resembles Cortés's famous Indian mistress, the mythic traitor and mother of mestizos, in name only—except insofar as both are mediating figures of the conquest. But she is also the Virgin Mary, the holy power that conquers and converts the Moorish-Indian king through motherly love. In sum, the entire choreographic sequence enacts an ambiguous exchange and transformation between opposite sides.

It is not surprising that marriage should be a central if unspoken motif in the Río Grande Matachines, especially in light of Gutiérrez's thesis that marriage practice structured social inequality in colonial New Mexico. Conversion and not marriage was the ideal institutional relation the Franciscan fathers envisioned between Indians and Spaniards. Marriage between social equals preserved honor and *limpieza de sangre* (purity of blood), whereas uncontrolled, illicit unions across caste lines resulted in mestizaje. But while properly sanctioned marriages remained the elite ideal, all manner of mestizaje nevertheless became the prevailing reality. The Matachines came symbolically to portray and attempted to resolve this driving contradiction at the heart of colonial New Mexican society.

In contrast to the stable, narrowly defined roles of the Malinche, Monarca, and danzantes, striking variation is seen in the personalities and routines played out by the Abuelos. This variability, in addition to the clowns' fundamental nature, can offer insight into the universal as well as the local meanings of the dance. The third playful persona, the Toro, also shows more variability than Malinche or Monarca, albeit usually less than the clowns, to whom his specific character is usually tied.

Although the Toro is of clear European origin, the symbolism of slaughter and selective meat distribution inherent in his drama enjoys both indigenous and Old World resonance. One possible aspect of its significance is suggested by yet another of Gutiérrez's ideas about how the Spaniards subjugated the Pueblos. He argues that the Franciscans preempted the Pueblos' intergenerational system of economic and religious obligation and exchange by controlling a domesticated meat supply and concomitantly curtailing the domain of the hunt chiefs, or "outside" chiefs. The padres also asserted dominance over the sacred and ritual domains of the "inside" chiefs by controlling public space, fertility (including sexual relations), and the use of force (Gutiérrez 1991:58). Accordingly, "by injecting themselves and their gifts into a system of calculated exchanges by which seniors gained the labor, respect, and obedience of juniors, the padres forged a cadre of youths who stood ready to denounce the sins of their parents" (Gutiérrez 1991:80). Like Malinche's portrayal by a young girl, perhaps the enactment of the Toro in some communities by a preadolescent boy also alludes to this history. So might the symbolic association of the Toro with the war chief at Taos Pueblo. Yet from the Spanish viewpoint, the meaning of this episode might carry somewhat different connotations, insofar as castration symbolized (male-to-male) domination, whether within or between ethnic groups (see Gutiérrez 1991:209). The transformation of this motif into a burlesque played out by the clowns shows how the struggle was contained and reinterpreted by both Pueblos and Hispanos.

Today the Abuelos range from great prominence and extreme irreverence, on the one hand, to a subdued, circumspect, peripheral role on the other. Where they are strongest and most raucous there tends to be a Perejundia, a figure found in both Hispanic villages and pueblos, yet not universally present in either. In the apparently single reference to La Perejundia extant in the literature on New Mexico, Cobos (1983:131) defines the term simply as "name of one of the dancers in *Los Matachines* (a man dressed as a woman)." Like ritual transvestism itself, the origin of the Perejundia is rooted in both New and Old World traditions rather than exclusively in either. Thus Kurath (1949:105) lists "woman disguise" as one of the key symbolic elements in both Old and New World moriscas. For the Pueblos, the winter scheduling of the dance coincides with the timing of most ritual transvestism, at changes of season or social state (Ortiz 1972:148–50). Such a figure arises out of the dynamic interface between two contrasting orders.

Today the most elaborate Perejundia routine involves her pregnancy and delivery of a doll, as seen at Taos, Arroyo Seco, and, previously, Picurís. Some Perejundias simply carry a doll, or more often a handbag.[3] Wherever she appears, the Perejundia pushes against the limits of acceptable behavior and evokes disapproval along with laughter. Among Pueblos and Mexicanos, she frequently, but not always (e.g., Arroyo Seco; Taos Pueblo 1992), burlesques a woman of the dominant group. Her partner also treads a fine line, as do certain Abuelos unaccompanied by a Perejundia (e.g., El Rancho).

Of the ten Matachines complexes looked at, five currently have Perejundias (Taos, Arroyo Seco, Picurís, Alcalde, and San Antonio, or the Tijeras complex) and five do not (San Juan, Jémez, El Rancho, Bernalillo, Tortugas). The first thing to keep in mind when considering whether this distribution is in any way significant or diagnostic is that the character and routines of the Abuelos are not eternally fixed within any given performance tradition. Indeed, they change over time. Thus Bernalillo formerly had a Perejundia and Tortugas had picaresque Abuelos, and in the early 1990s both Taos Pueblo and San Antonio, or the Holy Child parish, changed their Perejundias. It thus appears that a comparative, diachronic view of several traditions may reveal more than a single synchronic comparison.

It is noteworthy that both Bernalillo and Tortugas have dropped the Perejundia and/or downplayed the Abuelos, as well as the Toro, more or less concurrently with expanding the number of danzantes, Monarcas, and Malinches. Might this correlation register some larger or deeper change? If so, what is the nature of that change? The most obvious similarity between these two towns is that they are located close to dense metropolitan centers, and of the ten cases considered, they are probably the most urbanized and integrated into an advanced industrial or, indeed, postindustrial economy. A tentative clue to why this should help account for the expunging of burlesque elements from local Matachines performances is hinted at in James Peacock's (1968) discussion of the disappearance of clowns and transvestites from Javanese popular drama. Peacock claims this attenuation, the result of reformist Muslim, nationalist, and other modernizing influences, signals a shift away from a "classificatory" to an "instrumental" world view (1968:221–22). He draws on the Javanese material to formulate a general principal:

> The classificatory world view, which emphasizes the subsuming of symbols within a frame, nourishes and is nourished by symbols of reversal; the instrumental world view, which emphasizes the sequential harnessing of means to an end, threatens and is threatened by such symbols. The instrumental world view would reduce all forms to mere means toward the ultimate end, but symbols of reversal call forth enchantment with the form and veneration of the cosmic categories it embodies, a fixation dangerous to the forward movement, the struggle, the *perdjuangan* [an Indonesian word meaning struggle, in the sense of a gradual struggle toward some end]. (Peacock 1968:221–22)

The concept of linear progression in an individual's struggle to ascend from low to high status within his lifetime is cited by Peacock (1968:220) as the Javanese expression of an instrumental world view. How this might relate to the fading of transvestites and clowns from certain Río Grande Matachines is illustrated by the case of Bernalillo. There, the prestige hierarchy ascended by aspiring mayordomos and other key participants has become a central feature of the Matachines tradition. The dance, it seems, has grown more prestigious and dignified over the past thirty years, and those who would be mayordomos must now wait for years before they can fulfill their vow of supreme service to the community and to San Lorenzo. The unruly vulgarity of a Perejundia or of old-time Abuelo routines and Toro castration would mar the solemn dignity the Matachines has come to embody for its devoted proponents. A similar process seems to have occurred in the Tortugas "Matachines," or Danzantes, although it should be noted that while clowning has disappeared from that dance, it is still alive and well in the concurrent Azteca performances, where Abuelolike figures persist.

Further ethnographic inquiry into Bernalillo and Tortugas would be needed to determine whether Peacock's distinction between classificatory and instrumental world views or ritual arrangements helps us to understand cultural change in modernizing communities that still perform the Matachines. Such a change, writes Victor Turner (1978a:285–86), involves a shift

> from an order framed, classified, moved, and motivated by rituals based in a coherent cosmology, to a culture that contains the debris of formerly dominant religious and ideological systems, and is itself changing rapidly under the influence and pressures of various industrial forces and paradigms, both economic and ideological. . . . The new, modernizing, instrumental world view, Peacock says, threatens and is threatened by inverted symbols. Such symbols still have the agrarian quality of cyclical, repetitive ecosystems, the Yin-Yang quality of antithetical seasons and opposite biological sexes, which, once clearly defined, can be clearly reversed to cancel out the sins and errors of men who fail to correspond with the ideal delineations. Kill the inversions and you kill the undesirable world-view axioms that resist what you believe to be progress.

It should be emphasized that the Abuelo (and Toro) figures at Bernalillo and Tortugas have not completely vanished but instead have been unmasked and tamed into stewardlike figures dressed like the danzantes. Only time will tell whether these two instances of clown attenuation presage future trends elsewhere, are purely idiosyncratic, or might even be reversible. This last possibility is raised in order to avoid the rigid implication that shift from a "classificatory" to an "instrumental" world view is necessarily developmental, unidirectional, or wholesale. An alternative model posits the coexistence of diverse world views persisting under fluctuating conditions wherein one and sometimes another predominates. This leaves open the logical as well as the ethnographic possibility that the Abuelos or Perejundia might one day reappear at Bernalillo, perhaps in response to as yet unanticipated or inadequately understood conditions. Tortugas may, in fact, represent such a phenomenon. There the clowning now occurs outside the "Matachines" (Danzantes) proper, enacted by a different constituency yet still part of the larger fiesta celebration.

But even if the classificatory-instrumental distinction has some utility in accounting for why Bernalillo and Tortugas have "tranquilized" their Abuelos, it still fails to explain the range of variation among clowns where they actively persist. Why do some communities have Perejundias as opposed to male Abuelos alone? Or, why are the Abuelos costumed as werewolves or gorillas in some versions and as cowboys in others? It is by no means clear whether ritual transvestism tells us anything about gender relations in these communities, and if so, what, because Perejundias occur along a spectrum that includes both the presence and absence of women danzantes—presumably also some sort of barometer of the power balance between the sexes. In the abstract, the Perejundia's puzzling message seems a subversive-cum-conservative mix: a gender inversion in which the dominant gender mocks the subordinate gender, but not the reverse.

Possibly the neighboring cases or companion traditions of San Juan, which has no Perejundia, and Alcalde, which does, might reveal something about the comparative context of ritual transvestism. Although Perejundias cross ethnic lines, women danzantes are exclusively Hispanic. Perhaps because sacred clowns are so important in Pueblo religion and so fundamental a means by which they have coped with oppression, it seems unlikely that the Abuelos would be retired from Pueblo Matachines performances. Among Mexicanos, modern attenuation of Abuelo figures outside the Matachines context may or may not portend their future within the dance.

Whatever its future, clowning has long been integral to the Río Grande Matachines dance. This points to the common ground that Pueblo and Mexicano Matachines share, despite their obvious differences. This ground consists of the dance's basic oppositional structure and meaning: for each group it is about their encounter with the Other. Clowning was the "natural" or already long-standing idiom through which the Pueblos could deal with such subject matter, and it also lent itself nicely to the kinds of oppositional commentaries pursued in Hispanic versions.

It seems especially significant that Abuelos carry whips. More than any other tool, the whip represents the brute instrument of domination. Putting it into the hands of a clown symbolizes an act of psychological resistance, as well as adaptation, to the power of its tyranny.[4] Herein lies the deeper import of the dance. Each performance contains what Scott calls a "hidden transcript," whereby the dominated secretly criticizes or even mocks the master. This transcript is embedded within the larger official or "public transcript," which affirms the status quo. The full text of the hidden transcript constitutes the local-level or "track" of meaning, whereas the dance itself makes up the public transcript or "generic" meaning.[5] The dance seen today among the Pueblos represents the myriad ways in which they incorporated and modified this imposed ritual drama about a historic catastrophe. The Hispanic versions commemorate this encounter from the vantage point of those who perpetrated it and then go on to focus inwardly and incorporate concerns subsequent to the colonial period.

Today the Other against which Mexicano ethnic boundaries are defended is as much the Anglo as the Indian, if not more so, even though this new, far more powerful Other is not directly represented in the Matachines—except for an occasional Perejundia. Anglo domination is the context for both contemporary Indian and Mexicano Matachines performances, but it is less a precipitating factor for the Pueblos, whose Matachines persists but does not currently enjoy a resurgence, and which, moreover, is located within a separate ceremonial cycle. This pattern reflects the probability that Americanization constituted a deeper shock for Mexicanos than for Pueblos, who had already experienced the trauma of subjugation and evolved ways of dealing with it. Today the Matachines seems to have become one of the ways Mexicanos deal with *their* subjugation. The dance positively affirms their contemporary identity by referring to a glorious past. Modern resurgence of the Hispanic Matachines appears tied to the pressure of urban development against the resource bases of long-standing communities, as is illustrated by the cases of Arroyo Seco, Bernalillo, and San Antonio. The Hispanic Matachines dance represents the highly individual assertion of a given community's sense of religion, history, kinship, and attachment to its land base. This ritual assertion is by definition a received form, a reflexive encapsulation of Iberian, Mexican, and New Mexican social and interethnic history. Each community arranges the received form a bit differently and embroiders it with the multicolored threads of local meaning.

The appropriate comparative framework for the New Mexico Matachines tradition is Mesoamerican ritual drama. This includes Matachines traditions among Yaqui, Tarahumara, and other groups along or south of the border, as well as ritual drama in the southern highlands. The format and dramatis personae for Matachines traditions outside New Mexico differ from those described in the preceding chapters, although they share important strains of commonality as well, not the least of which is the presence of clowning. Parsons, Beals, and others long ago noted the parallels among ritual clowns throughout the greater Southwest, including northern Mexico, and Bricker has since studied the related role of ritual humor among the highland Maya. Contemporary approaches to Mesoamerican ritual show how ritual performances among Mayan groups provide metaphorical commentary on the historical and present circumstances of those who carry them out. The same holds true for the Matachines dance in New Mexico. There, as in Mexico, the supreme historical drama is the European conquest, a story still told endlessly among countless groups in myriad ritual forms. In New Mexico, the story is told through the Matachines dance. Although its basic ingredients and format remain the same, each version varies, as the reader has seen, according to who tells it and when and where it is told.

The nature of the story is such that it could not be told by those who suffered it without the use of humor, because only humor and other forms of reversal can begin to convey so horrific an event. Much has been written about how and why the language of reversal and paradox is typically and cross-culturally the vehicle for transcendent truth (Suzuki 1956; Freud 1958; 1960; Koestler 1964; Bateson 1972; Babcock 1984). As the ultimate expression of creative flexibility, reversals, like humor itself, afford the symbolic wherewithal for psychic survival under extreme conditions. And because the psychohistorical experience of colonization (involving conquest, revolt, reconquest, miscegenation, and interdependency) was traumatic also for Mexicanos, they too made clowns directors of the dance.

Even at Bernalillo it is the Abuelos, subdued as they are, who keep the dancers in line. Today the dance is not merely an archaic survival but an ongoing way of coping with and commenting on the historical structures of ethnic domination as they continue to unfold for Pueblo and Mexicano communities in the upper Río Grande valley.

NOTES

CHAPTER 1

1. The terms *Hispano* and *Mexicano* will be used more or less interchangeably throughout this book to refer to the genetically mestizo, Spanish-speaking native population of New Mexico. Although these two terms have different connotations, both are generally acceptable to the people in question, particularly when speaking in English and Spanish, respectively. Except for *Mexicano* when speaking in Spanish, perhaps only the term *la raza* or *raza* approaches universal acceptability as an ethnic self-referent among this general population. The genteel term in English has for many decades been *Spanish* or *Spanish American,* which is today considered objectionable by a younger generation of self-identified Chicanos, whereas the term *Chicano* remains unpopular among many who call themselves Spanish or Spanish American. In short, the nomenclature is problematical, and my variable use of terms takes this fact into account.

2. Robb (1961, 1980), Kurath (1970), and Champe (1983) characterize the Río Grande Matachines music only broadly. These authors note both melodic similarities and variation among the villages. Champe (1983:17) reports that she has noted only one melody, in three-four time, which is used by all the groups she has observed. Robb (1980:738–39) has recorded and transcribed Matachines music from San Antonio for three different years, from Bernalillo for two different years, and from Tortugas for two, in addition to melodies from Llano de San Juan, Tierra Amarilla, Taos, and places in Mexico. Brenda Romero, a native of Lyden near Alcalde who teaches at the University of Colorado at Boulder, recently completed her doctoral dissertation (1993) in ethnomusicology at UCLA on the Jémez, San Juan, and Alcalde Matachines music.

3. Social dances involving masquerades of non-Pueblo groups are named after the tribe they caricature, such as Navajo, Comanche, Apache, Sioux, and so forth (Ortiz 1972:147; Sweet 1980, 1985:33–36, 1989). Similar burlesques occur in other Spanish-Mexican-derived dances, such as the Sandaro (or Horse dance) and Santiago pageants done at some pueblos. Ortiz (1972:147–53) notes that such dances,

which often involve sex-role reversals and cross-dressing (usually male to female), tend to occur at times of seasonal-agricultural or other (cyclical) change.

4. The two are not the same, despite Dozier's claim (followed by Ortiz [1979:281]) to the contrary (Dozier 1957:33; also see Champe 1983:3). According to Villagrá (1933:148–49), the epic chronicler of the Oñate expedition, "Moorish and Christian games" were first introduced to New Mexico at San Juan in September 1598. Although Austin (1928:39) described Alcalde's Moros y Cristianos sixty years ago, today that community instead performs Los Comanches as a mock battle played out on horseback (see chapter 5, note 4). In recent years, Moros y Cristianos has been revived in Chimayó. Moro y Cristiano dances are performed in central and southern Mexico (Bricker 1973:198–210), and related forms persist in modern Spain (Espinosa 1985:214–16).

5. Both Champe (1983:89–90) and Kurath (1970:257) note variations in the color of Malinche's dress in different villages, without suspecting a possible pattern or significance. Malinche's color change does not seem to occur in most villages and may vary from one year to another. In some communities, such as Picurís, the change may involve ethnic style, that is, from a more European to a more Indian style costume, or from one Pueblo style to another.

6. My basic methods in the three primary Taos County case studies included systematic, repeated observation of dance performances combined with in-depth, tape-recorded interviews with key and other informants. Extensive still photography was used at Taos and Picurís pueblos, whereas in the case of Arroyo Seco, a videotape made by someone else was studied. Sound recordings of live performances at Picurís were made, whereas in the case of Taos Pueblo I was able to record the music separately. In the secondary case studies, dance observation and photography were carried out, but except in the Santo Niño de Praga parish near Albuquerque, I did not work with key informants. Photography was not conducted at Jémez because it is not allowed. Secondary materials of various kinds were used to support these seven quick studies from Alcalde to Tortugas. Each case merits ethnographic study in its own right, something I did not attempt.

7. Bakhtin uses the term *heteroglossia* to refer to intralanguage differences or "a new sense of the difference between the various discursive strata within a national language," an awareness that first arose out of the polyglot setting of ancient Rome (cited in Clark and Holquist 1984:290). The setting of the Matachines is by definition plural and polyglot, just as the dance itself is about that condition. At the same time, the dance constitutes a kind of symbolic language that has different meanings for different speakers.

CHAPTER 2

1. Taos Pueblo has six active kivas distributed between north and south sides and is said to lack clan organization (Parsons 1936). Parsons states that Taos lacks a north-side/south-side moiety structure. This is contrary to my own observations. Less is known about Taos's social and religious organization and life than about those of many other pueblos. Anthropologists are generally unwelcome at Taos, and only a few have attempted to work there, in comparison to more extensive research done, for example, among the Tewas, Zunis, or Hopis. Parsons's slender monograph (1936) remains the only general ethnological study of Taos, although a number of other scholars have worked on particular topics there, such as tribal government organization (Smith 1969), factionalism (Fenton 1957; Brandt 1980), peyotism (Laswell 1935; Collins 1968), culture change (Siegel 1952; Bodine 1972), land claims (Jenkins 1966; F. Ellis 1974; Bodine 1978; Gordon-McCutchan 1991), and linguistics (Trager 1946).

2. The Pueblo Revolt of 1680 is doubtless the single most dramatic and far-reaching event in New Mexico's colonial history. It represents arguably the most successful native revolt against European occupation in America, in that it managed actually to extirpate the colonizers' presence for about a dozen years. It was preceded by years of secret planning and was fostered by a century of oppression, hardship, upheaval, drought, epidemics, famine, and festering hatred of the colonial system. Popé, a San Juan Pueblo religious leader who had been persecuted by Spanish officials, retreated to the remote pueblo of Taos, where the strategy was plotted and the uprising began on August 10—one day early, because of the accidental interception of some Tesuque messengers. Other important leaders included "El Saca" (Hackett 1942:xxix) or "El Jaca" (Sando 1979:195) of Taos and Luis Tupatú of Picurís. All of the pueblos participated except Isleta, which harbored retreating colonists and itself fled south as a consequence (see chapter 5). The revolt was followed by a decade in which the retreating Spaniards remained in El Paso while the Pueblos struggled to regain balance and unreeled from their momentary unity. Popé died during this period, while Luis Tupatú, as well as his brothers Lorenzo and Antonio from Picurís, remained an important player in the early reconquest period (see Hackett 1942; Dozier 1970:55–63; Sando 1979; Ortiz 1980–81). With the reconquest, led by Vargas between 1692 and 1696, the Pueblos finally reentered, albeit with transformations on both sides, the yoke of the developing Euromexican hegemony.

3. Located in the wilderness above the Taos basin between Taos and Wheeler peaks, Blue Lake is the source of the Río Pueblo watershed. Between 1906 and 1970, Taos Pueblo litigated against the federal government over control of and access to the lake and thousands of surrounding acres. The dispute began when the Taos wilderness was declared national forest, and it was finally resolved by an act of Congress, making Blue Lake the only U.S. Indian land-claims case in which

the original tribal use area was "returned" rather than compensated for with other lands or with a cash settlement (as was the case for Pueblo league land in the town of Taos). The Blue Lake case was won on the basis of a religious-cultural argument which held that without free and exclusive access to the lake—the pueblo's most important sacred use area, or "church in the mountains"—the Taos people and their culture would die out. The case was a cause célèbre for art colony proponents, anthropologists, and other Indianists (non-Indians who advocate, emulate, and extol Indian culture), who over the years contributed significantly to the victory (see Bodine 1978; Gordon-McCutchan 1991).

4. According to Champe (1983:18, 20), the violinist Adolfo Frésquez first began playing for the pueblo in 1919; she also mentions another guitarist, Claudio Montoya. Frésquez was from Cañon. Taos Recordings made a record of Frésquez and Tranquilino Lucero playing the Matachines music in the late 1950s or early 1960s (TRP-4).

5. Robb (1980) recorded and transcribed seven tunes at Taos, probably during the 1950s or 1960s. Champe (1983:20) states that several of the seven tunes are misnamed on the Frésquez-Lucero Taos Recordings record and claims that the true melody for La Malinche is not included. She questions Robb's naming of the tunes he recorded and notes that in general there seems to be no standard system for naming or for linking particular tunes to particular movements, among either scholars or performers. She claims that Taos plays nine tunes, including one for the Maypole. My own 1986 Taos recording contains seven tunes. The absence of the true Malinche melody from the Frésquez-Lucero record is independently corroborated by the Taos Pueblo dance director, who fears the tune is lost, since his own tape recording of it was accidentally erased. I have been told at the pueblo that the current musicians, Sam and Julian Lucero, picked up the music from the Taos Recordings record, and although there are some stylistic differences, their tunes are approximately the same as those on the record. The list of movements given in this chapter came from Mr. Lucero, the violinist.

6. The Abuelos are a long-standing tradition in the Hispanic villages, where they would come out at dusk during Christmas season festivities such as Las Posadas, acting as bogeymen to discipline the children. They howled, scolded, and wore hide or sheepskin masks and carried whips. These figures were said to come out of mountain caves during the winter. Parsons mentions a Christmas bogeyman at Taos Pueblo known as *Pien Tsabaiyuna* or *Pienchapaiuna*, who wore a mask of buffalo hide turned inside out and a spruce collar for "whiskers." This figure entered houses at night to terrorize children and was placated by parents with gifts of sprouted wheat bread wrapped in corn husks (Parsons 1936:110), an interesting combination of native and alien food items. The Tiwa-derived term the 1986 Abuelo used to refer to himself was something like *trabajosusi,* or *trabayo,* which he said meant "old grandfather." The 1992 Abuela told me that some

people called him *chabayuna* and *chabayu*. An older Pueblo man indicated that outsider Abuelos are more effective at scaring the children. Parsons and Beals (1934:500, table 1) suggest a connection between the Yaqui *chapaiyeka* or *fariseo* clowns and the Pueblo clowns known as *chaveyo* to the Hopi, *tsabiyo* in Tewa, and *chapaiuna* at Taos (see also Freese 1991:144). Freese (1991) suggests that such figures became identified with the devil in the eighteenth-century pueblos as a way of perpetuating a hidden transcript of surreptitious resistance to Catholic indoctrination.

7. In 1986 these were represented by a red satin Christmas-tree ornament on the first two days and by an article of fur, allegedly from a deer or elk, on the third day. The 1986 Abuelo recalled that they had also used balloons and baseballs, and a few years back a big, black, bouncing "superball," when he joked about how the Toro's "huevos kept dancing up and down." It seems significant that the bull's balls would be handed to the war chief, who also feasts the Toro and whose official Pueblo duty is to deal with matters outside the village proper yet inside reservation property boundaries, including grazing areas.

8. One dance elder told me he remembered first noticing the birth skit after he came back from the service in the 1950s and saw it performed in front of the governor's house. Because Arroyo Seco revived the dance in 1985 after a lapse of nearly fifty years, whereas Taos Pueblo has performed it more or less continuously, it seems likely that the Pueblo performance is the source or model for this routine, a proposition further supported by the fact that the 1985 Arroyo Seco Abuelo uttered the *engáñalo* line to Malinche. The late Arroyo Seco violinist indicated that the birth routine was part of the 1929 and/or 1934 Arroyo Seco performance and might have been picked up from the pueblo. Whatever its origin, the birth skit has thus been at least a periodic feature of all three Matachines Abuelo routines in the general Taos area, including Picurís (see chapter 4, note 4). Brenda Romero (1993:69) notes a striking parallel to the Perejundia birth burlesque in Westermark's 1926 account of festival masquerades among Moroccan mountain tribes, in which two men dress as an old man and woman: "They sing and play, their talk is most lascivious, and the behavior of the old couple in particular is as indecent as it could be" (Westermarck 1926, II:84). In one episode the old man suspects his wife, dressed as a Jewess, of infidelity, and during the course of the play she "gives birth to a child with shrieks of agony" (1926, II:82).

9. *Danza azteca* is a folkloric Indianist dance form originating in Mexico that has subsequently diffused among Chicano/a cultural nationalists in this country. There are at least two danza groups with slightly different orientations in the Taos area, one of which was founded by the man who played the Taos Pueblo Abuelo in 1992. Most Azteca danzantes in the Taos area are women.

10. Champe (1983:85) notes a similar lack of interpretive concern at San Ildefonso Pueblo: "Today, since the Matachines dance has outlived any original pur-

pose of proselytizing or commemorating a historical event, it may have become a formal routine with very little significance to the individual performer. This possibility is in accord with the response obtained from dancers at San Ildefonso. When asked whether they were aware of any special meaning in the pantomime actions, or whether they feel the dance is a struggle between the powers of good and evil, they shake their heads and say, 'We only know, when you dance it you feel good.'"

11. I am told that the Taos Pueblo Guadalupanas tend the bulto of the Virgin in the San Geronimo church and dress her in white, pale green, pink, blue, and yellow, according to a calendrical or seasonal cycle. At Christmas the bulto is dressed in white, like the normative Malinche. It seems possible that the Malinche-Guadalupe color change could have directional meaning, although the directional colors are not clearly reported for Taos (Parsons 1936:105). People at the pueblo used to conduct a summer procession of the Virgin to a special place up the canyon above the village, and townspeople would come and picnic all day. They would also take the Virgin out for smaller processions made for individual promesas. Certain locales along the way were *descansos,* or designated resting places for the Virgin and saints.

12. The less sympathetic, perhaps more typical Hispano attitude toward Indians, including a reference to the now lapsed Matachines tradition in Valdez (see chapter 3), is illustrated in my field notes from December 30, 1986:

I visited T. (in her late seventies) and L. (her younger brother, probably in his fifties) today and asked her if she remembered the Matachines. She does, but barely, and complains how her memory fails her with age and infirmity. She said they used to do the dance here in Valdez in the *camposanto* in front of the church. There was plenty of room there (unlike the pueblo, which she visited once for the dance, and where it was too crowded between the houses and people were squeezed up against the walls). Her grandfather used to tell people about how these things were done and what it meant. An Indian woman who lived with or worked for them when she was young named Cruz told her what she knew but she has now forgotten about the meaning of the Matachines. Monarca was *el rey de los indios,* who came with gold, meat, and other good things. She described a man who was *muy travieso* (very mischievous) who was el Toro. He chased people and scared children. His mask was made from a bladder or stomach from an animal, which had been dried (as I understood her) with peas inside it (to retain its shape). It had two horns. The effect or personality of this particular Toro was very strong (perhaps Ramoncito or "Torito," from Arroyo Seco [see chapter 3]). They also did the *faja* (Maypole). L. said this was the most interesting of the dances. T. used the words *muy curioso* to describe the custom. When the

Abuela gave birth they had mock padrinos and even a table with mock feast. The Matachines they did here was much finer than the one at the pueblo, she says, where she attended *misa del gallo* (midnight mass on Christmas Eve) once, and would never go again for anything. She recounted how she and R. (her late husband) happened to go, very reluctantly on her part, when he had come home late from work, his clothes still covered with cement. It seems she was pressed into it at the last minute. She described with disgust ("it was a *cochinada* there") how crowded the church was, and the absence of *bancos* to sit on. She had stood against the wall while the Indians and *la gringada* (gringotude) sat on the floor. She did not like going to the pueblo. The dance space there was too narrow and people were pressed against the walls and elbowed by the women. She also went once for San Gerónimo. There was a Ferris wheel in town (Don Fernando), but at the pueblo nothing but someone selling hamburgers and snow cones. And there was no place to go to the bathroom. One of the children with them had to go but all the outhouses were locked and they had to go very far, after wandering all over. Nor was there anything to drink. She finally resorted to drinking out of the river, which she pantomimed with her hand, conveying the indignation she experienced at having to do it. She described the relay race with pairs of runners alternating, and told how she and another (Mexicana) woman had stood near the *jacal de San Gerónimo* at the near end of the race track. The runners are daubed with little feathers, and one fell from a runner's body and the other woman picked it up and said, "*Mira*, a chicken feather," and an irate Indian woman slapped it from her hand and said she shouldn't touch it.

13. The adjudication of water rights involves a suit to determine the priority dates for particular use rights as well as the right to appropriate a fixed quantity of water for a specific purpose (Levine 1990:271). In New Mexico the adjudication process began in 1966 when the Office of the State Engineer filed the so-called Aamodt case to determine the water rights of all non-Indian *parciantes* (water rights owners) and ditches, or *acequias,* in the Pojoaque valley. Adjudications are currently proceeding in areas throughout the state, including the Taos basin. Parties to such litigation include the State Engineer, the U.S. Justice Department, Pueblo Indians and other tribes, ditch and other water-user associations, and individuals. All are engaged in a long, extremely complex and costly process that pits their claims and interests against each other. The result will be final determination of all past, present, and future surface and groundwater use rights as well as a fixed quantification of every drop allocated (see Levine 1990 for a discussion of the nature of the adjudication process). The intent is absolute rationalization of a limiting vital resource for the purpose of market exchange.

14. Miguel Quintana, an elderly native of the Tierra Amarilla area, believes

the *engáñalo* line comes from the verse of a song he remembers hearing in cantinas when he was young. He says it refers to the Monarca's swaggering toward an encounter with La Malinche. Both he and Frances Leon Quintana note that in northern New Mexican slang, "'chile' refers to male genitals, while 'candy' suggests 'biscocho' or 'panocha,' which refer to female genitals or other sexually attractive features of women" (Quintana, personal communication, 1989).

CHAPTER 3

1. The Tenorio tract is a much contested area of approximately 5,696 acres (R. Ellis n.d.:4–6) that lies south of the Río del Arroyo Seco and north and even south of the Río Lucero, near the mountains and north of Taos Pueblo. It acquired the name from its sale in 1818 by Miguel Tenorio (acting as agent for the sons of Sebastian Martín and alleged heirs to the Antonio Martínez grant) to "the sons of the Pueblo," including a corner containing the mouth of the river known as "la Rinconada del Río de Lucero" (Jenkins 1983:24–52). The Tenorio tract lies within the overlapping boundaries of both the Antonio Martínez (1716) and Antoine Leroux, or Los Luceros (1742), land grants, and its Byzantine legal history derives from claims and counterclaims exerted with respect to both of these grants as well as to Río Lucero water. Strips within it were apparently undergoing allotment to Arroyo Seco settlers by at least 1815–16, and within six years their encroachment on the water of the Río Lucero had precipitated joint downstream complaints from the pueblo, Don Fernando de Taos, and Los Estiércoles (now El Prado). All such litigation has recurred periodically ever since (R. Ellis n.d.; Jenkins and Baxter n.d.). The Antoine Leroux grant was approved by the New Mexico surveyor general in 1861 when Taos Pueblo withdrew its initial opposition to the claim because it contained the Tenorio tract. The pueblo thereupon repurchased the tract, this time from an agent for the Leroux grant heirs. The Antonio Martínez grant was confirmed by the Court of Private Land Claims in 1882 and patented in 1902, the same year Arthur Manby sued to confirm his ambitious claim to a large portion of the grant, including the Tenorio tract. In 1916, 43/45 of the entire grant were awarded to Manby and his Taos Valley Land Company (see Waters 1973). As a defendant in the case, the pueblo appealed, and in 1918 the New Mexico Supreme Court ruled that the pueblo's Miguel Tenorio tract deed was valid and, moreover, that the Court of Private Land Claims' confirmation of the Antonio Martínez grant was invalid because of the pueblo's ownership of this and another part (the García de la Mora tract) of the previously confirmed Leroux grant. This position was again argued by the United States in 1929. During the period of the Pueblo Lands Board in the 1920s and 1930s, Hispano "trespassers" were ejected from parcels on the Tenorio tract south of the Arroyo Seco. The pueblo's claim to the midpoint of the Arroyo Seco stream, including the El Salto road and numer-

ous private driveways, was resurrected in 1987 and upheld in 1990, so the county, pueblo, and federal governments set to work on a final settlement for a scheduled payment to the pueblo.

2. A morada is a traditional chapter house belonging to the lay religious confraternity known in New Mexico as Los Hermanos de Nuestro Padre Jesus Nazareño, or sometimes *La Hermandad,* or the Penitentes (see Weigle 1976). Also see note 6, this chapter.

3. A discrepancy exists in the schoolteacher's written documentation of the 1930s performance, which at the time of the 1985 revival he dated as 1938 (as printed on the program). In a more recent article (Torres 1989) and book (Torres 1992), however, he gives the year as 1934 and indicates that the performance was instigated by the retired schoolteacher who is his aunt, the Abuela's mother. I have followed the 1934 date inasmuch as it has been published several times and seemed confirmed in an interview with the late Arroyo Seco violinist.

4. This young man, from Arroyo Hondo and not part of the director's extended family, was the only individual deeply and actively involved in both the 1981–82 Río Hondo and "condo war" protests and the 1986 folk drama revivals, including *El Niño Perdido,* in which he played a major role. His link with the dance director was that he worked as a janitor at the high school and cleaned his classroom. Tragically, he died suddenly in 1987.

5. The term *-tec* is a pun alluding both to the Mexican (Nahuatl) suffix *-tec,* meaning "people," and to "Tex" or Texan, the quintessential colonizing Gringo Other for Nuevomexicanos. The pun was not consciously intended by the director, but he nevertheless later commented (personal communication, 1993) that the current situation of resort encroachment might one day lead to a staging of the folk drama *Los Tejanos* (see chapter 5, note 4).

6. The Arroyo Seco morada, unlike those in Valdez and Arroyo Hondo, is still intact and is actively used by the Hermanos. Although relatively young, the schoolteacher has been a member of the morada for thirty years and thus enjoys a significant degree of seniority within it. The authority of his role in the brotherhood would be evident, but within the larger arena of relations vis-à-vis the clergy, it can also have counterauthoritarian connotations, given the history of church opposition to the Hermanos since the days of Bishop Lamy, a situation mitigated much later under Archbishop Byrne of Santa Fe.

7. On the other hand, the loan of a buffalo robe for the New Year's Day performance suggests that relations between members of the director's family and individuals at the pueblo have a friendly character as well. In sum, the relationship is complex, ambivalent, and ambiguous, and its negative attitudinal aspects not necessarily conscious.

8. As noted in chapter 2, this lapse coincided with the Salto road case as well as with renewed activation of the water rights adjudication process. One rumor had

it that the pueblo decided not to do the dance "because Arroyo Seco was doing it." In fact, the 1986 Taos Pueblo performance took place one year after the last Arroyo Seco dance and *then* dropped off.

9. It should be noted that all nonprivate (including Indian) land in the Arroyo Seco vicinity falls under the jurisdiction of the U.S. Department of the Interior, either the Forest Service or the Bureau of Indian Affairs. Sixty-eight percent of all the land in Taos County is federal and state owned.

CHAPTER 4

1. Picurís actively and successfully sought outside help with its church restoration project and attracted a dedicated and diverse group of supporters from both within and outside New Mexico. Such people contributed money and other goods and services for fundraising, donated expertise of various kinds, and labored physically on adobe making and construction tasks. Out-of-state groups from college students to motorcycle clubs helped make adobes for the church. The roof was completed and the Matachines dance held inside the new church for the first time in 1992.

2. This kind of ethnographically disconcerting irregularity is corroborated in Champe's close, longitudinal study of the San Ildefonso version. There, over a period of twenty-four years, she identified and recorded a total of thirteen tunes but noted that in some years one or two of them were not played (Champe 1983:19–20).

3. These sequences seem groupable into roughly eight segments: (1) the opening sequence with all characters abreast, done to tune A; (2) a stamping dance to B; (3) Malinche's dance, with the alternating slow and fast sequence of ACA-CACA; (4) Monarca's dance over the palmas to tune B; (5) diagonal crossovers between lines to tune D; (6) the Toro, tune C; (7) the Cross, tune E; and (8) either a slightly different repetition of the first one (tune F), or else the Maypole (tune G, slow). In the second performance example mentioned earlier, the Cross was done to tune B. When the Maypole was performed, the preceding sequences seemed somehow compressed into fewer tune changes, although I am not certain exactly how this was done.

4. Frances Leon Quintana reports having seen the birth burlesque at Picurís in the 1960s; its previous occurrence is also corroborated by an elderly Picurís woman who was once the Malinche.

5. The peak crowd at Picurís on Christmas Day is never larger than a small crowd at Taos Pueblo.

6. Weigle (1976:28) notes that Mabel Dodge Luhan quotes her Taos Pueblo husband, Tony Luhan, as saying, "Over in Picurís Pueblo, sometimes Indians walk in parade with Penitentes. I don't know what for they do that, unless they all mixed up with Mexicans now."

7. Interestingly, the Arroyo Seco schoolteacher's brother, who is himself a schoolteacher, is presently teaching the Matachines dance to his students in Peñasco.

8. My interest in the Matachines might well automatically steer me away from the strongest expressions of nativism, whose proponents would be expected to shun Christian displays in favor of aboriginal symbols and to endorse endogamy over miscegenation. As at Taos and other pueblos, the strictest conservatives at Picurís advocate native language use and retention, endogamy, and proper socioreligious conformity. Nor are they likely to suffer anthropologists. Like the cacique, they devote their energies to perpetuating the native system and tend to endorse a stricter set of ethnic boundaries than those crisscrossed by devotees of the Matachines. That ethnocultural conservatism can fluctuate through time is indicated by the fact that in 1947, the adult men of Picurís voted to change the name of the pueblo to San Lorenzo, a decision reversed in 1955 when it officially became Picurís once again (Brown 1979:22).

9. This contradicts Siegel (1959), who claims that Picurís was 90 percent endogamous in 1950 and that all but four out of twenty-one nuclear families were endogamous in 1958. Parsons (1939a:213) reports that in 1925 there were a number of marriages with other tribes, and she was told that "no one had married a Mexican in thirty years." Although I have not conducted a census and my sampling is ethnographic and opportunistic, virtually everyone I know from Picurís belongs to a nuclear and/or extended family that has intermarried or interbred with non-Picurís in one or another generation. I assume this would also have been true thirty or sixty years ago. Siegel (1959:37, 1965) argues that Picurís, and by implication other pueblos, typifies a deme, or endogamous local community, whereas Peñasco "exemplifies the Spanish American peasant type of intermediate society." This discrepancy with my own observation is partly a function of observer bias, in the sense that my focus on the Matachines, rather than on Picurís society and culture as a whole, has in all likelihood served to skew the cross-section of Picurís people I have been in contact with: precisely those involved in the dance and therefore, in keeping with my thesis, belonging to highly miscegenated sectors of the tribal population. But whatever its objective rates of endogamy, exogamy, and miscegenation, Picurís has the contemporary reputation of being very mixed.

10. During the 1960s archaeologist Herbert Dick undertook a series of archaeological recovery projects at Picurís, in cooperation with the tribe. This endeavor provided employment for tribal members and stimulated interest and pride in the pueblo's past, eventually resulting in a small museum located in the new restaurant and store building. They also produced for sale little booklets on Picurís history (Herbert Dick, personal communication, 1990; also see M. Simmons 1979:219).

11. This is not to underestimate the power or persistence of factionalism at Picurís. Factionalism has been manifested, for example, in what amounts almost

to a tradition of tribal governor impeachments since the 1950s, when the male residents voted to replace the cacique with the governor as the official leader of the pueblo (Brown 1979:272). Although the tribal government began to stabilize in the 1970s (Brown 1979:275), factional power struggles in the late 1980s again led to impeachments and to setbacks in the church reconstruction and other development projects. In short, factionalism continues to precipitate major shifts in the internal political ground.

CHAPTER 5

1. The Maypole is evidently done as part of the Danzantes' performance for the San Juan Day fiesta in Tortugas, but not any longer, it seems, for their Día de Guadalupe festivity. Robb (1961:96, 1980:776) observed and photographed the Maypole on Día de Guadalupe in 1953, when the Toro and Abuelo episodes were also still done. A Maypole is part of the Yaqui Matachines dance, which differs from the Río Grande version in numerous respects, including the fact that it is done as part of their Holy Week celebration (Painter 1971). Although some speculate that the Río Grande Matachines Maypole may bear some relationship to the *voladores* of Vera Cruz (Champe 1983:94), its provenience and connection to apparently similar pole dances in Mexico and the U.S. Southwest remain uncertain.

2. Champe (1983:91–93) claims that in all performances she has seen except that at San Ildefonso, the Abuelo-Monarca knee pantomime is done *after* the Malinche's meandering transit. At Taos it is a brief "ceremony" in which the Abuelo and Abuela kneel before the seated Monarca and stroke his knee, after which Monarca rises to dance. In 1992 the Abuela was told to say "We'wha" while making the gesture. Champe (1983:91) describes the following episode at San Juan, corroborated by Kurath (1970:262), although what I saw in 1990 seemed less elaborate: "At San Juan (1964) the Abuelo placed his whip on the ground at the opposite end from Monarca [or as Kurath (1970:262) puts it, in front of the musicians] and pantomimed listening by holding up the big ears of his mask-headdress. Then he went to Monarca and stroked one of Monarca's knees with his hands. The Abuelo returned to his whip but immediately went back to Monarca and stroked the other knee. On returning to his whip, he picked it up and, holding it in a loop, approached Monarca, touching Monarca's left foot with the whip. Again he went to the opposite end, but returned to Monarca and touched his right foot with the whip. Finally, going to the far end, the Abuelo finished with a shout." Romero (1993:302) claims that the foot pantomime is not done at Alcalde, but I took photographs of it there in 1989 (see fig. 10). For more on the significance of the Abuelo-Monarca foot pantomime, see chapter 6, note 2.

3. It is noteworthy that Champe's (1983:96–97) choreographic comparison of the Cruz movement across nine versions indicates that no two are identical.

4. See Espinosa (1985:214–24) for an account of Los Comanches, as well as of Los Moros y Cristianos and yet another folk drama known as Los Tejanos, composed in the nineteenth century about a battle between Nuevomexicanos and Anglo Texans, based on the latter's 1841 expedition to Santa Fe. According to Espinosa, Los Comanches was probably composed after 1779 to commemorate a series of ultimately successful expeditions against Comanches who were led by Cuerno Verde. The scripted version of the play Espinosa published in 1907 consists of 515 octosyllabic verses (also see Espinosa 1931:133–46, 1985:217). The play has long been a popular tradition in New Mexico and has also undergone a resurgence of interest in recent years, although to a lesser degree than the Matachines.

5. Several communities have organized the Matachines dancers as troupes who practice and perform on a more or less regular basis, not only for the traditional feast day but also for other special religious or secular events, at home and elsewhere. Alcalde and El Rancho are perhaps best known for this, although other communities have also performed away from home, such as the Arroyo Seco group at the Museum of International Folk Art in Santa Fe, the Bernalillo group at the National Association of Chicano Scholars (1990), and even the Jémez Turquoise Matachines at a folkloric event in California (1990). Romero (1993:372) states that in Alcalde, the occasional performances throughout the year reduce the need for an extensive practice period prior to the December 27 performance. There is also a tradition in some villages of performing the dance for velorios, or all-night rosary prayer sessions in honor of or in supplication to a particular saint. This may be done in their own and neighboring communities, within and across ethnic lines. For velorios the Abuelos and Toro do not appear and the full dramatic sequence is not carried out; rather, a somewhat processionlike dance formation is executed (see the Bernalillo, Tijeras Canyon, and Tortugas sections of chapter 5).

6. A noteworthy dispute erupted in late 1990 or early 1991 when people in El Rancho sued to block operation of a large power substation that had been constructed by Jémez Mountain Electrical Cooperative directly south from the cantina parking-lot dance ground, on land leased from San Ildefonso Pueblo. The power company had apparently proceeded without proper compliance with federal regulations or consultation with El Rancho villagers. El Rancho sued on these grounds, and its lawyer hired an archaeologist-ethnohistorian to argue in favor of having the parking-lot dance ground declared worthy of preservation — and therefore protection — as an (official) historic site listed on the National Register of Historic Places. The power company then hired another archaeologist to prepare a report arguing that the revived Matachines done next to the cantina is somehow more secular and less authentic than the old version and that the present dance site is not truly "traditional." In the meantime, San Ildefonso exerted claim to part of the parking lot because the area overlapped onto its league. The pueblo's likely motivation for doing this is that declaration of the site on the National

Register might imperil its lease agreement with the power company. Even though the previous Pueblo governor opposed the lease, some non-Indian locals speculate that the pueblo is also spurred by the pervasive climate of interethnic mistrust fostered in the Pojoaque valley by the Aamodt water adjudication case (see Levine 1990; chapter 2, note 13). In any case, the issue may serve to intensify such feelings.

7. Champe studied the San Ildefonso Matachines over a period of twenty-three years, between 1947 and 1970, and sporadically observed other versions as well, through the 1970s. She believed the dance became less frequent at San Ildefonso during the 1970s but noted that there was still enthusiasm for its persistence among some participants in 1981 (Champe 1983:87–88). Her analysis divided the San Ildefonso performance into seven major component parts that include the Entrada, Prologue, Acts One, Two, and Three, La Despedida, and *La Salida,* or exit. Each act in turn consists of three scenes that broadly correspond to the usual dance sets: El Monarca, La Malinche, La Brincada, La Cambiada, El Toro, La Cruz, El Zapateado, and La Cortesía, fast and slow (Champe 1983:21).

8. The woman from Lyden is Brenda Romero, who since 1989 has served as a violinist for the Jémez Turquoise version. Women Matachines musicians are rare but not unheard of; as noted in chapter 3, there used to be one, a San Juan woman, at Picurís.

9. Chililí is said to be one of the oldest place names in New Mexico and the site of a Tompiro pueblo abandoned in the seventeenth century because of Apache depredations (Pearce 1965:33). The Hispanic settlers of Chililí acquired their town grant in 1841. Both the community and its Matachines tradition are said to be old, but it only recently joined the Holy Child parish and presumably belonged to another one prior to that.

10. The *brinda,* I was told, is like the symbolic distribution of meat after slaughtering the bull. Sometimes the Perejundia (out of costume) helps serve the dessert, as if "handing out food to all her children."

11. Robb (1961:92–93) reproduces a poem (song) to San Antonio Matachines dancer José Apodaca:

Señores, voy a cantar	Gentlemen, I am going to sing to you
Lo que traigo en mi memoria	That which I carry in my memory
De un hombre que fué notable	Of a man who was notable
Voy a cantarles la historia.	I am going to sing the history.
Del pueblo de San Antonio	In the village of San Antonio
Nació un hombre muy brillante,	Was born a very brilliant man,
Y con el tiempo llegó	And with the passage of time
A ser el mejor danzante.	He came to be the best dancer.
Esta dichosa carrera	This distinguished career
Circunstancia mucho abarca,	Was favored by circumstances,

Y con el tiempo llegó	And with the passage of time
A ser el mejor Monarca.	He came to be the best Monarca.
José Apodaca era el hombre	José Apodaca was a man
De tan grande corazón.	With a very great heart.
Siempre lleva en su mente	Always he carried in his mind
De servirle a su patrón.	The thought of service to his Lord.
Con su guajito y su palma	With his guajito and his palma
Y aquel cupil de diamantes	And his headdress of diamonds
Se enfrentava de San Antonio	He presented himself before San Antonio
Con un grupo de danzantes.	With a group of dancers.
Con aquel cupril dorado	With his gilded headdress
Le nació del corazón	He touched his heart
Y la Malinche a su lado	And with the Malinche at his side
Bailandole a su patrón.	He danced before his patron.
Vestido de mil colores	In vestments of a thousand colores
En nuestra iglesia se alegrabe,	In our church he danced,
Y el pueblo llenó de gusto	And the entire village rejoiced
Cuando Apodaca bailaba.	When Apodaca danced.
Quedó triste San Antonio,	San Antonio was left sad
Con grande luto se vía;	And appeared in deep mourning;
Tan palido y tan sereno	Pale and so serene
Como un surora [*sic*] del día.	Like the dawn of the day.
En su tumba está grabado	On his tomb is engraved
Con letras interesantes	In interesting letters
Con un letrero que dice:	An inscription which says:
Viva el rey de los danzantes.	"Long live the king of the dancers."
Nos despedimos, señores,	Now farewell, gentlemen.
Aquí termina la historia.	This is the end of the story.
Y Apodaca está en el cielo	And Apodaca is in heaven
Gozando de Dios y gloria.	Rejoicing with God in his glory.

12. Dierdre Sklar (personal communication, 1992) claims it is likely that the celebration, as a true novena, would have lasted nine days.

13. Unpublished sources on the Tortugas Guadalupe fiesta include a manuscript that later became a doctoral dissertation by Diedre Sklar (1991) and the basis of a book forthcoming from the University of California Press, and part of a manuscript by Jacqueline Dunnington (n.d.) available at the New Mexico State Records Center and Archives in Santa Fe.

14. Knowlton (1973), Van Ness (1976, 1987), and other revisionist land grant scholars have contested the claim that the subdivision of land among heirs is a principal cause of land reduction and economic impoverishment among

Nuevomexicanos. They point instead to the massive incorporation of *ejidos* (community-owned grazing and other wilderness lands) into the public domain as a major cause of the population's economic duress since Americanization. Although the situation in Tortugas is no doubt somewhat different from that in the north, the reader should keep this issue in mind when evaluating Oppenheimer's casual reference to the consequences of the Mexicano subdivision of land among heirs.

CHAPTER 6

1. Parmentier (1979) provides probably the best overall discussion of the Montezuma legends among the Pueblos. He argues that the mythological triangle of Poseyemu, Montezuma, and Jesus symbolizes the European intrusion into the Pueblo world. He concludes that "the name of Montezuma acts as a buffer or shield between the native religion (Poseyemu) and the alien religion (Jesus)" (1979:622). Parmentier (1979:619) reasons that "if, according to the compartmentalization model (Spicer 1962:508), two religious systems coexist in the pueblos, then one of the few points of contact between the two traditions is the existence of these legends of competition between the gods." The Matachines dance is the living ritual expression par excellence of this confrontation, which assumes more compartmentalized form in some pueblos (Jémez) and a greater degree of fusion or amalgamation in others (Picurís).

2. Juliette Cunico (personal communication, 1993), a Shakespearean and Renaissance scholar, has called my attention to the fact that the Abuelo's gestures of kneeling before the Monarca and placing his hand under his foot, or stroking his knees or calves, "are strikingly similar to Medieval ritual gestures which were associated with paying homage, profession of loyalty, submission to a conqueror, allegiance of vassal to lord, payment of tribute, swearing of fealty, and reciprocal obligations of lords to vassals."

3. Abuelos unaccompanied by a Perejundia also sometimes carry dolls, as at Tortugas (Azteca dance), or, as Griffith notes (1979:771), they may simply have rag dolls attached to their costumes.

4. The whip as symbol occurs in a variety of contexts in New Mexico. It represents the quintessential instrument of subordination and torture for Hispanics, Indians, and blacks alike, but carries additional meanings in different cultural contexts as well. For example, among the Pueblos, the whip is used by "scare" or "whipper" kachinas and kachina dancers who discipline the young or initiate them into a higher status and thereby impart power (see, for example, Parsons 1936:467–76; L. Simmons 1942:82–87). Thus a strong didactic aspect attends the inherent inequality conveyed by the whip. The braided yucca whip, or *disciplina*, used by the Penitentes is not a tool of domination but of self-discipline and puri-

fication through suffering. All such meanings plus others may be collapsed and playfully reversed in the Abuelo's *chicote*.

5. Scott (1990:200) argues that the infrapolitics of subject classes constitute the hidden, undeclared "realm of informal leadership and nonelites, of conversation and oral discourse, and of surreptitious resistance" which typically escapes official notice but which social analysts would do well to recognize. His notion of public and hidden transcripts and the role of the latter "as a condition of practical resistance [in subordinates] rather than a substitute for it" (1990:191) easily applies to the colonial Indo-Hispano interface as well as to contemporary interethnic relations in New Mexico. Drawing on Scott, Freese (1991) contends that the historical role of the Pueblo clowns through time has been to enact a hidden transcript of ethnocultural resistance and boundary maintenance against Euroamerican encroachment and assimilation. Although Scott focuses on the strategies of the subaltern, he points out that dominant as well as subordinate sectors each have their own hidden transcripts. My argument here is that the generic Río Grande Matachines constitutes the official or public transcript regarding Spanish Christianization of the Pueblos, as agreed upon and shared by both Indian and Hispano/Mexicano groups. At the same time, each particular Pueblo version enacts a hidden transcript which tells how that community has managed to defend its boundaries and negotiate an adjustment to the specific conditions of its incorporation within successive hegemonic systems. Hispanic versions contain and build upon the substratum of a hidden transcript evolved from a previous position of domination, but today they also enact new hidden transcripts of resistance and accommodation to a larger, dominant system which is ethnically "Other" but crisscrossed nonetheless by class.

REFERENCES CITED

Austin, Mary. "A Drama Played on Horseback." *The Mentor* 16 (1928): 38–39.

Babcock, Barbara. "Ritual Undress and the Comedy of Self and Other: Bandelier's *The Delight Maker.*" In *A Crack in the Mirror,* edited by Jay Ruby, 187–203. Philadelphia: University of Pennsylvania Press, 1982.

———. "Arrange Me into Disorder: Fragments and Recollections on Ritual Clowning." In *Rite, Drama, Festival, Spectacle: Rehearsals Toward a Theory of Cultural Performance,* edited by John MacAloon, 102–28. Philadelphia: Institute for the Study of Human Issues, 1984.

———. "Pueblo Clowning and Pueblo Clay: From Icon to Caricature in Cochiti Figurative Ceramics, 1875–1900." *Visible Religion* 4 (1986): 280–300.

Babcock, Barbara, ed. *The Reversible World.* Ithaca: Cornell University Press, 1978.

Bakhtin, Mikhail. *The Dialogic Imagination: Four Essays by M. M. Bakhtin,* edited by Michael Holquist, translated by Caryl Emerson and Michael Holquist. Austin: University of Texas Press, 1981.

———. *Rabelais and His World,* translated by Helen Iswolsky. Bloomington: Indiana University Press, 1984.

Barker, George C. "Some Functions of Catholic Processions in Pueblo and Yaqui Culture Change." *American Anthropologist* 60 (1958): 449–55.

Barth, Fredrik. *Ethnic Groups and Boundaries: The Social Organization of Cultural Difference.* Boston: Little Brown and Co., 1969.

Bateson, Gregory. *Steps to an Ecology of Mind.* New York: Ballantine Books, 1972.

Bauman, Richard, with supplementary essays by Barbara A. Babcock et al. *Verbal Art as Performance.* Prospect Heights, Illinois: Waveland Press, 1984.

Beckett, Patrick H., and Terry L. Corbett. *Tortugas.* Las Cruces, New Mexico: COAS Monograph 8 (1990).

Bennett, Wendell Clark, and Robert Zingg. *The Tarahumara: An Indian Tribe of Northern Mexico.* Chicago: University of Chicago Press, 1935.

Bloom, Lansing B., ed. "Bourke on the Southwest." *New Mexico Historical Review* 11, no. 3 (1936).

Bodine, John J. "A Tri-Ethnic Trap: The Spanish Americans in Taos." In *Spanish-*

Speaking People in the United States, edited by June Helm, 145–54. Proceedings of the American Ethnological Society. Seattle: University of Washington Press, 1968.

———. "Acculturation Processes and Population Dynamics." In *New Perspectives on the Pueblos,* edited by Alfonso Ortiz, 257–85. Albuquerque: University of New Mexico Press, 1972.

———. "Taos Blue Lake Controversy." *Journal of Ethnic Studies* 6, no. 1 (1978): 42–48.

———. "Taos Pueblo." In *Handbook of North American Indians,* vol. 9, edited by Alfonso Ortiz, 255–67. Washington, D.C.: Smithsonian Institution Press, 1979.

Bowden, J. J. "Private Land Claims in the Southwest." Master's thesis, Southern Methodist University, 1969.

Brandt, Elizabeth. "On Secrecy and the Control of Knowledge." In *Secrecy: A Cross-Cultural Perspective,* edited by Stanton K. Tefft, 123–46. New York: Human Sciences Press, 1980.

Bricker, Victoria. *Ritual Humor in Highland Chiapas.* Austin: University of Texas Press, 1973.

———. *The Indian Christ, the Indian King: The Historical Substrate of Maya Myth and Ritual.* Austin: University of Texas Press, 1981.

Briggs, Charles. *Competence in Performance.* Philadelphia: University of Pennsylvania Press, 1988.

Brown, Donald N. "Picurís Pueblo." In *Handbook of North American Indians,* vol. 9, edited by Alfonso Ortiz, 268–77. Washington, D.C.: Smithsonian Institution Press, 1979.

Bustamante, Adrian. "The Matter Was Never Resolved: The Casta System in Colonial New Mexico, 1693–1823." *New Mexico Historical Review* 66, no. 2 (1991): 143–63.

Champe, Flavia W. "Origins of the Magical Matachines Dance." *El Palacio* 86, no. 4 (1980–81): 38.

———. *The Matachines Dance of the Upper Rio Grande.* Lincoln: University of Nebraska Press, 1983.

Clark, Katerina, and Michael Holquist. *Mikhail Bakhtin.* Cambridge: Belknap Press of Harvard University Press, 1984.

Cobos, Rubén. *A Dictionary of New Mexico and Southern Colorado Spanish.* Santa Fe: Museum of New Mexico Press, 1983.

Collins, John J. "A Descriptive Introduction to the Taos Peyote Ceremony." *Ethnology* 7, no. 4 (1968): 427–49.

Crumrine, N. Ross. "Capakoba, the Mayo Easter Ceremonial Impersonator: Explanations of Ritual Clowning." *Journal for the Scientific Study of Religion* 8, no. 1 (1969): 1–22.

deBuys, William. "Fractions of Justice: A Legal and Social History of the Las Trampas Land Grant." *New Mexico Historical Review* 56, no. 1 (1981): 71–97.

Dozier, Edward P. "Spanish-Indian Acculturation in the Southwest: Comments on Spicer." *American Anthropologist* 56 (1954): 680–83.

———. "Rio Grande Pueblo Ceremonial Patterns." *New Mexico Quarterly* 27, no. 1–2 (1957): 27–34.

———. "Spanish Catholic Influences on Rio Grande Pueblo Religion." *American Anthropologist* 60 (1958): 441–48.

———. *The Pueblo Indians of North America.* New York: Holt, Rinehart, and Winston, 1970.

Dumarest, Father Noel. *Notes on Cochiti, New Mexico,* translated and edited by Elsie Clews Parsons. Memoirs of the American Anthropological Association 6, no. 3 (1919): 137–236.

Dunnington, Jacqueline. Unpublished manuscript. Dunnington Collection, New Mexico State Archives, Santa Fe, n.d.

Ebright, Malcolm. "The Embudo Grant: A Case Study of Justice and the Court of Private Land Claims." *Journal of the West* 3 (1980): 74–85.

Ellis, Florence Hawley. "Comments on Spanish-Indian Acculturation in the Southwest." *American Anthropologist* 56 (1954): 678–80.

———. "Anthropological Data Pertaining to the Taos Land Grant." In *Pueblo Indians,* edited by David A. Horr, 29–150. New York: Garland Publishing, 1974.

Ellis, Richard. "Taos Pueblo." Unpublished manuscript, n.d.

Espinosa, Aurelio. "Los Comanches." Albuquerque: University of New Mexico Bulletin, 1907.

———. "Los Comanches," translated by Gilberto Espinosa. *New Mexico Quarterly* 1 (1931): 133–46.

———. *The Folklore of Spain in the American Southwest.* Norman: University of Oklahoma Press, 1985.

Fenton, William. "Factionalism at Taos Pueblo, New Mexico." Anthropological Papers 56, Bureau of American Ethnology 164:297–344. Washington, D.C., 1957.

Forrest, John. *Morris and Matachin: A Study in Comparative Choreography.* Sheffield, England: CECTAL Publications, 1984.

Foster, George. Culture and Conquest: America's Spanish Heritage. New York: Viking Fund Publications in Anthropology 27 (1960).

Freese, Alison. "Send in the Clowns: An Ethnohistorical Analysis of the Sacred Clowns' Role in Cultural Boundary Maintenance among the Pueblo Indians." Ph.D. diss., University of New Mexico, 1991.

Freud, Sigmund. "On Creativity and the Unconscious." In *Papers on the Psychol-*

ogy of Art, Literature, Love, and Religion, edited by Benjamin Nelson. New York: Harper and Brothers, 1958.

———. *Jokes and Their Relation to the Unconscious,* edited and translated by James Strachey. New York: W. W. Norton, 1960.

Geertz, Clifford. *The Interpretation of Cultures.* New York: Basic Books, 1973.

Goffman, Erving. *Frame Analysis: An Essay on the Organization of Experience.* New York: Harper Colophon Books, 1974.

Gordon-McCutchan, Robert. *The Taos Indians and the Battle for Blue Lake.* Santa Fe: Red Crane Books, 1991.

Gossen, Gary. "The Chamula Festival of Games: Native Microanalysis and Social Commentary in a Maya Carnival." In *Symbol and Meaning beyond the Closed Community: Essays in Mesoamerican Ideas,* edited by Gary Gossen, 227–54. Albany, New York: Institute for Mesoamerican Studies, 1986.

Griffith, James Seavey. "Kachinas and Masking." In *Handbook of North American Indians,* vol. 10, edited by Alfonso Ortiz, 764–77. Washington, D.C.: Smithsonian Institution Press, 1983.

Gutiérrez, Ramón. "The Politics of Theater in Colonial New Mexico." Unpublished manuscript, 1989.

———. *When Jesus Came, the Corn Mothers Went Away.* Stanford, California: Stanford University Press, 1991.

Hackett, Charles Wilson, ed. *Revolt of the Pueblo Indians of New Mexico and Otermín's Attempted Reconquest, 1680–1682.* 2 vols. Translated by Charmion C. Shelby. Albuquerque: University of New Mexico Press, 1942.

Hall, G. Emlen. "The Pueblo Land Grant Labyrinth." In *Land, Water, and Culture,* edited by Charles Briggs and John R. Van Ness, 67–138. Albuquerque: University of New Mexico Press, 1987.

Handelman, Don, and Bruce Kapferer. "Symbolic Types, Mediation, and the Transformation of Ritual Context: Sinhalese Demons and Tewa Clowns." *Semiotica* 30, no. 1–2 (1980): 41–71.

Hawley [Ellis], Florence. "The Role of Pueblo Social Organization in the Dissemination of Catholicism." *American Anthropologist* 48 (1946): 407–15.

———. "An Examination of Problems Basic to Acculturation in the Rio Grande Pueblos." *American Anthropologist* 50, no. 4 (1948): 612–24.

Hieb, Louis. "Meaning and Mismeaning: Toward an Understanding of the Ritual Clown." In *New Perspectives on the Pueblos,* edited by Alfonso Ortiz, 163–95. Albuquerque: University of New Mexico Press, 1972.

Houser, Nicholas P. "Tigua Pueblo." In *Handbook of North American Indians,* vol. 9, edited by Alfonso Ortiz, 336–42. Washington, D.C.: Smithsonian Institution Press, 1979.

Jaramillo, Cleofas. *Shadows of the Past.* 1941. Reprint. Santa Fe: Ancient City Press, 1974.

————. *Romance of a Little Village Girl.* San Antonio, Texas: Naylor Co., 1955.

Jenkins, Myra Ellen. "Taos Pueblo and Its Neighbors, 1540–1847." *New Mexico Historical Review* 41, no. 2 (1966): 85–114.

————. "Development Potential of the Taos Pueblo Area in 1906." Unpublished manuscript, 1983.

Jenkins, Myra Ellen, and John Baxter. "Land History of the Pueblo of Taos." Unpublished manuscript, n.d.

Kessell, John. *The Missions of New Mexico since 1776.* Albuquerque: University of New Mexico Press, 1980.

Kloeppel, Richard J. "Los Matachines—A Dance Drama for San Lorenzo." Unpublished manuscript, 1970.

Knowlton, Clark. "Causes of Land Loss among the Spanish Americans of Northern New Mexico." In *The Chicanos: Life and Struggles of the Mexican Minority,* edited by Gilberto López y Rivas. New York: Monthly Review Press, 1973.

Koestler, Arthur. *The Art of Creation.* New York: Macmillan, 1964.

Kurath, Gertrude. "Mexican Moriscas: A Problem in Dance Acculturation." *Journal of American Folklore* 62, no. 244 (1949): 87–106.

————. "The Origin of the Pueblo Indian Matachines." *El Palacio* 64, no. 9–10 (1957): 259–64.

Kurath, Gertrude, with the aid of Antonio García. *Music and Dance of the Tewa Pueblos.* Santa Fe: Museum of New Mexico Press, 1970.

Lange, Charles H. "The Role of Economics in Cochiti Pueblo Culture Change." *American Anthropologist* 55 (1953): 674–94.

Laswell, Harold. "Collective Autism as a Consequence of Culture Contact: Notes on Religious Training and the Peyote Cult at Taos." *Zeitschrift fur Sozialforschung* 4, no. 2 (1935): 232–46.

Lawrence, Aleta. "Transcripto de Entrevista." Unpublished manuscript, n.d.

Lea, Aurora W. "More about the Matachines." *New Mexico Folklore Record* 20 (1963–64): 7–10.

Leatham, Miguel. "Indigenista Hermeneutics and the Historical Meaning of Our Lady of Guadalupe of Mexico." *Folklore Forum* 22, no. 1–2 (1989): 27–39.

Levine, Frances. "Dividing the Water: The Impact of Water Rights Adjudication on New Mexican Communities." *Journal of the Southwest* 32, no. 3 (1990): 268–77.

————. "An Evaluation of a Traditional Cultural Property in El Rancho, New Mexico." Unpublished report, 1991.

Lynn, Janice. "The Dance in Your Heart." *Santa Fe New Mexican,* 7 December 1988.

Moss, Larry. "Amenity Migration." Unpublished paper, 1991.

Oppenheimer, Alan James. *An Ethnological Study of Tortugas, New Mexico.* New York: Garland Publishing, 1974.

Ortiz, Alfonso. *The Tewa World: Space, Time, Being and Becoming in a Pueblo Society.* Chicago: University of Chicago Press, 1969.

———. "Ritual Drama and the Pueblo World View." In *New Perspectives on the Pueblos,* edited by Alfonso Ortiz, 135–61. Albuquerque: University of New Mexico Press, 1972.

———. "San Juan Pueblo." In *Handbook of North American Indians,* vol. 9, edited by Alfonso Ortiz, 278–95. Washington, D.C.: Smithsonian Institution Press, 1979.

———. "Popay's Leadership: A Pueblo Perspective." *El Palacio* 86, no. 4 (1980–81): 18–22.

Painter, Muriel Thayer. *A Yaqui Easter.* Tucson: University of Arizona Press, 1971.

Parmentier, Richard J. "The Pueblo Mythological Triangle: Poseyemu, Montezuma, and Jesus in the Pueblos." In *Handbook of North American Indians,* vol. 9, edited by Alfonso Ortiz, 609–22. Washington, D.C.: Smithsonian Institution Press, 1979.

Parsons, Elsie C. *The Social Organization of the Tewa of New Mexico.* Memoirs of the American Anthropological Association, 36. Menasha, Wisconsin: American Anthropological Association, 1929.

———. *Taos Pueblo.* 1936. Reprint. New York: Johnson Reprint Co., 1970.

———. "Picurís, New Mexico." *American Anthropologist* n.s. 41 (1939a): 206–22.

———. *Pueblo Indian Religion,* vol. 2. Chicago: University of Chicago Press, 1939b.

Parsons, Elsie C., and Ralph Beals. "The Sacred Clowns of the Pueblo and Mayo Yaqui Indians." *American Anthropologist* 36, no. 4 (1934): 491–514.

Peacock, James. *Rites of Modernization: Symbolic and Social Aspects of Indonesian Proletarian Drama.* Chicago: University of Chicago Press, 1968.

Pearce, T. M. "Chilili." In *New Mexico Place Names,* edited by T. M. Pearce, 33. Albuquerque: University of New Mexico Press, 1965.

Phillips, John. "The Bernalillo Matachines Dance: The Presentation of a Cultural Tradition within a Hispano Community." Unpublished paper, 1987.

Quintana, Frances Leon. "Land, Water, and Pueblo Hispanic Relations in Northern New Mexico." *Journal of the Southwest* 32, no. 3 (1990): 288–99.

Robb, John D. "The Matachines Dance—A Ritual Folk Dance." *Western Folklore* 20 (1961): 87–101.

———. *Hispanic Folk Music of New Mexico and the Southwest: A Self-Portrait of a People.* Norman: University of Oklahoma Press, 1980.

Robinson, Natalie V. "Bernalillo's Fiesta de San Lorenzo." Unpublished manuscript, n.d.

Rodríguez, Sylvia. "Land, Water, and Ethnic Identity in Taos." In *Land, Water, and Culture,* edited by Charles Briggs and John R. Van Ness, 313–403. Albuquerque: University of New Mexico Press, 1987.

———. "Art, Tourism, and Race Relations in Taos: Toward a Sociology of the Art Colony." *Journal of Anthropological Research* 45, no. 1 (1989): 77–99.

———. "Ethnic Reconstruction in Contemporary Taos." *Journal of the Southwest* 32, no. 4 (1990): 541–55.

———. "The Tourist Gaze, Gentrification, and the Commodification of Subjectivity in Taos." In *Essays on the Changing Images of the Southwest,* edited by R. Francaviglia and D. Narrett, 105–26. Arlington, Texas: Texas A&M University Press, 1994.

Romero, Brenda. "The Matachines Music and Dance in San Juan Pueblo and Alcalde, New Mexico: Context and Meanings." Ph.D. diss., University of California at Los Angeles, 1993.

Sando, Joe S. "Jemez Pueblo." In *Handbook of North American Indians,* vol. 9, edited by Alfonso Ortiz, 418–29. Washington, D.C.: Smithsonian Institution Press, 1979.

Schroeder, Albert H. "Pueblos Abandoned in Historic Times." In *Handbook of North American Indians,* vol. 9, edited by Alfonso Ortiz, 236–54. Washington, D.C.: Smithsonian Institution Press, 1979.

Scott, James C. *Domination and the Arts of Resistance.* New Haven, Connecticut: Yale University Press, 1990.

Sharp, D. D. "The San Antonio Fiesta." Unpublished manuscript, New Mexico State Records Center and Archives, Santa Fe, S-240, Folkways File 5, D-5, fo. 2., 1936.

Siegel, Bernard. "Suggested Factors of Cultural Change at Taos Pueblo." In *Proceedings and Selected Papers of the 29th Annual Congress of Americanists,* edited by Sol Tax, 133–40. Chicago: University of Chicago Press, 1952.

———. "Some Structure Implications for Change in Pueblo and Spanish New Mexico." In *Intermediate Societies, Social Mobility, and Communication,* edited by Ray Verne, 37–44. Proceedings of the American Ethnological Society, 1959.

———. "Social Disorganization in Picurís Pueblo." *International Journal of Comparative Sociology* 6, no. 2 (1965): 199–206.

Simmons, Leo, ed. *Sun Chief: The Autobiography of a Hopi Indian.* New Haven, Connecticut: Yale University Press, 1942.

Simmons, Marc. "History of the Pueblos since 1821." In *Handbook of North American Indians,* vol. 9, edited by Alfonso Ortiz, 206–23. Washington, D.C.: Smithsonian Institution Press, 1979.

———. *Albuquerque: A Narrative History.* Albuquerque: University of New Mexico Press, 1982.

Sklar, Deidre. "Enacting Religious Belief: A Movement Ethnography of the Annual Fiesta of Tortugas, New Mexico." Ph.D. diss., New York University, 1991.

Smith, M. Estellie. *Governing at Taos Pueblo.* Eastern New Mexico University Contributions in Anthropology, vol. 2, no. 1, 1969.

Snow, David. "Review of Socio-Ritual Performances and Land-Use with Reference to Matachines in El Rancho, New Mexico." Unpublished report, 1991.

Spicer, Edward H. *Pascua: A Yaqui Village in Arizona.* Chicago: University of Chicago Press, 1940.

———. "Spanish-Indian Acculturation in the Southwest." *American Anthropologist* 56 (1954): 663–78.

———. "Social Structure and the Acculturation Process." *American Anthropologist* 60 (1958): 433–41.

———. *Cycles of Conquest: The Impact of Spain, Mexico, and the United States on the Indians of the Southwest, 1533–1960.* Tucson: University of Arizona Press, 1962.

Suzuki, D. T. *Zen Buddhism,* edited by William Barrett. Garden City, New Jersey: Doubleday Anchor, 1956.

Sweet, Jill D. "Play, Role Reversal and Humor: Symbolic Elements of a Tewa Pueblo Navajo Dance." *Dance Research Journal* 12, no. 1 (1980): 3–12.

———. *Dances of the Tewa Pueblo Indians: Expressions of New Life.* Santa Fe, New Mexico: School of American Research Press, 1985.

———. "Burlesquing 'The Other' in Pueblo Performance." *Annals of Tourism Research* 16 (1989): 62–75.

Tedlock, Dennis. *The Spoken Word and the Work of Interpretation.* Philadelphia: University of Pennsylvania Press, 1983.

Torres, Larry. "Qué bueno qué todavía tenemos a los matachines." *Taos News,* 28 December 1989.

———. "Antigua tradición tenemos de San Gerónimo." *Taos News,* 27 September 1990.

———. *Yo siego de Taosi.* Taos, New Mexico: El Crepúsculo, 1992.

Trager, George. "An Outline of Taos Grammar." In *Linguistic Structures of Native America,* edited by Harry Hoijer et al., 184–221. New York: Viking Fund Publications in Anthropology, 1946.

Trujillo, Velinda. "San Lorenzo Inspires Year-Round Devotion." *Albuquerque Journal,* 10 August 1989.

Turner, Victor. *The Forest of Symbols: Aspects of Ndembu Ritual.* Ithaca, New York: Cornell University Press, 1967.

———. "Comments and Conclusions." In *The Reversible World,* edited by Barbara Babcock, 276–96. Ithaca, New York: Cornell University Press, 1978.

Turner, Victor, and Edith Turner. *Image and Pilgrimage in Christian Culture.* New York: Columbia University Press, 1978.

Van Ness, John R. "Spanish American versus Anglo American Land Tenure and the Study of Economic Change in New Mexico." *Social Science Journal* 13 (1976): 45–52.

———. "Hispanic Village Organization in Northern New Mexico: Corporate Community Structure in Historical and Comparative Perspective." In *The Survival of Spanish American Villages,* edited by Paul Kutsche. Colorado Springs: Research Committee, Colorado College, 1979.

———. "Hispanic Land Grants: Ecology and Subsistence in the Uplands of Northern New Mexico and Southern Colorado." In *Land, Water, and Culture,* edited by Charles Briggs and John R. Van Ness, 141–214. Albuquerque: University of New Mexico Press, 1987.

Villagrá, Gaspar Pérez de. *History of New Mexico,* translated by Gilberto Espinosa. Los Angeles: Quivira Society, 1933.

Waters, Frank. *To Possess the Land: A Biography of Arthur Rochford Manby.* Chicago: Sage Books, 1973.

Weigle, Marta. *Brothers of Light, Brothers of Blood: The Penitentes of the Southwest.* Albuquerque: University of New Mexico Press, 1976.

Weigle, Marta, and Peter White. *The Lore of New Mexico.* Albuquerque: University of New Mexico Press, 1988.

Westermarck, Edward. *Ritual Belief in Morocco.* 2 vols. London: Macmillan and Co., 1926.

White, Leslie. *The Pueblo of Santo Domingo.* Memoirs of the American Anthropological Association, no. 43, 1935.

———. *The Pueblo of Zia, New Mexico.* Bureau of American Ethnology Bulletin, no. 184. Washington, D.C.: Smithsonian Institution Press, 1962.

Wolf, Eric. "The Virgin of Guadalupe: A Mexican National Symbol." *Journal of American Folklore* 71 (1958): 34–39.

INDEX

Note: Citations preceded by the letter "P" (P1, P2, P3 . . .) indicate plates.